KING ARTHUR
AND HIS KNIGHTS

KING ARTHUR

and his

KNIGHTS

A Noble and Joyous History

Edited and arranged by
PHILIP SCHUYLER ALLEN

With line illustrations by
MEAD SCHAEFFER and JOHN R. NEILL

BARNES
& NOBLE
BOOKS
NEW YORK

The Contents

THE CONTENTS

The Introduction

Fifteen hundred years ago (or ever the Roman Empire fell, while yet barbarian Hun and Vandal laid waste the broad fertile plain of western Europe) there walked the earth in England the Celtic chieftain Arthur Pendragon.

But, if you love the likely truth of history, you should think of our hero as an Arthur very different from the king of medieval romance or the ideal monarch of Tennyson's *Idylls*. A reigning Welsh prince he doubtless was, and of the blood royal — so much we are told by the ancient chronicler Nennius. And besides this he was widely famed in the world of men as a brave leader and a general of much military genius. But long after the death of Arthur the Britons were still a half-savage folk, as we may learn from the codes of law set down by Howell Dha; and even in the late Middle Ages Welshmen limped far behind their English brethren both in civilization and in knowledge.

So, as with the eye of your dreaming mind you see him crouched on a lonely hilltop and with his Britons joyfully viewing the departure of the last Roman legion on its long southward journey for the defense of Italy, you should not picture Arthur clad in the court dress of a young Norman noble, or French prince, or English gentleman, but rather as Gerald of Barry describes the son of Rhys: "A young man of fair complexion, with curled hair, tall and handsome: clothed only, as is the custom of his country, with a thin cloak and inner garment; his legs and feet bare, regardless of thorns and thistles."

The real son of Uther Pendragon, you may be sure, was never the magnificent lord of Christendom whom romancers like Crétien de Troies have imagined, outshining a Hugh Capet and a Richard Lion-Heart. No—he rode into battle on no caparisoned charger; rather like skulking Highland chieftains of blissful memory, Arthur ranged the forest primeval with dog Caval at his heels. And not once in all his stormy life did he wear such a panoply of mail and bronze as covers his statue in the Swiss cathedral where he stands unwearying guard by the tomb of Emperor Maximilian; rather did he haunt the dark glens amidst gaunt English hills, protected from hostile spears by no other armor than rough buckler and shield and sword.

Likewise, when one reads in Crétien or Wolfram or Malory of the great feasts held in Arthur's palaces of Westminster and Cardigan, Carlisle and Camelot, one should not believe them celebrated in an elegant banqueting hall amid the pomp and circumstance of cloth of gold and bejeweled plate—unless for the moment carouse was made in some old Roman villa that the chance of war had brought into Celtic hands. No— rather was such royal entertainment given in rude but hospitable fashion (as again described by Gerald):

The kitchen does not supply many dishes, the house is not furnished with tables, cloths, or napkins. When the guests are seated upon the ground in companies of three, the hosts place the dishes before them all at once upon rushes or fresh grass, in large wooden platters or trenchers.

Beds made of rushes or new heath pulled up by the roots, and covered with a coarse kind of cloth, are then placed along the side of the hall, and all people in common lie down to sleep. Nor is their dress at night different from what is worn by day, for in all weathers alike the Welsh protect themselves from cold only by a thin cloak and tunic.

The fire continues to burn throughout the night, and besides every person receives much comfort from the natural heat of the one lying next him.

And yet it is a great epoch to which modern youth is looking back. For in the year of grace 410 the Roman garrisons had left Britain, and that tight little island which was to cradle the noblest ideals of our twentieth-century America was again free from the insolent foot of the foreign intruder. And, what is more, this very Britain was the only part of all the Celtic realm, once so universal in its sway, to retain its independence or even its native tongue. For in the remotest corners of Gaul every vestige of Celtic speech had disappeared during the fourth century before the tidal wave of Germanic invasion. Along the river Danube the Celts of central Europe had been ground to death between the upper and nether millstones of Teutonic-Roman cruelty. And even in the Near East those Galatians to whom St. Paul once wrote a kindly letter had through "benevolent assimilation" by neighboring peoples lost all traces of their beloved Celtic nationality. Thus in Britain alone was the Celtic race dominant and distinct — that folk that went ever forth to the fray and always fell. And Arthur, son of Uther Pendragon, was its chosen overlord.

Sir Thomas Malory, the author of this book of ours, was born about 1400. In his youth he served in the French wars with Richard, Earl of Warwick, an Englishman whom all Europe recognized as embodying the knightly ideal of the age. No better schooling for the future composer of the *Morte D'Arthur* can be imagined, for an excellent authority (the Emperor Sigismund) said to Henry V "that no prince Cristen for wisdom, norture, and mannode, hadde such another knyght as he had of therle Warewyk; addyng therto that if al curtesye were lost yet myght hit be founde ageyn in hym; and so ever after by the emperours auctorite he was called the Fadre of Curteisy."

Malory was just the man to write our book. His birth, education, and training fitted him to do so. Excluded from the pardon granted political offenders by King Edward IV, he was obliged to keep out of public life, even in his native Warwickshire. Under such conditions an elderly gentleman with the literary taste which Malory possessed had to seek occupation for his idle hands in composition.

Fortunately for English literature, Malory, so well equipped to produce the *Morte D'Arthur*, lived at a time which demanded it. It was about the middle of the fifteenth century that the Arthurian stories were very popular in England. And yet, outside of the chronicles, which omitted many of the most romantic adventures in the Round Table stories, there was in English nothing like a full history of Arthur and his knights. So Malory set to work to acquaint himself with the French *Merlin*, *Tristram*, and *Lancelot*, where he learned of the Grail, of Elaine of Astolat, and of Arthur's death. And thereafter he took the son of Uther to be the central figure of his tale and wrote the greatest of all English prose romances.

In fine, Malory lives today because he is a peerless epic writer — he has the three traits of style which are Homer's:

swiftness, simplicity, nobility. Like Homer, he has swiftness only in detail; he does not hurry us to the final catastrophe. Often he takes us aside for the moment, rather than ahead, but always he leads us steadily onward to the end in view. And as to simplicity and nobleness in thought — it is just these qualities that make Malory the earliest prose writer in English of whom we can read many pages at a time with pleasure. Except for the Book of Common Prayer, the *Morte D'Arthur* is the best known English prose before the King James Bible, whose diction it often suggests. And when you have added to these three the *Pilgrim's Progress* of John Bunyan, you have practically all the English prose before Queen Anne's day which is still widely read.

"So always for us, when we will, the horns of Elfland shall blow again. Then rude British Arthur shall change into the great king of romance. At Christmas, Easter, or Whitsuntide, he and Guinever shall hold high feast. They shall speed Perceval to seek again the Castle of the Grail, where he may ask the healing question; and welcome Iseult, fled from loveless state at Tintagel by the Cornish sea; and gay pied heralds shall call the knights to tourneys at Caerleon and Camelot."[1]

PHILIP SCHUYLER ALLEN

UNIVERSITY OF CHICAGO

[1] For the full story of King Arthur in English literature, see Howard Maynadier's excellent book, *The Arthur of the English Poets*, published by Houghton Mifflin Company (Boston and New York), from which the above final paragraph is quoted and from which I have gleaned other facts in this Introduction.

Book the First

KING ARTHUR AND HIS KNIGHTS

A NOBLE AND JOYOUS HISTORY

MERLIN AND UTHER PENDRAGON

I

NOW UTHER PENDRAGON, king of England, had long loved the fair Igraine, wife of the Duke of Cornwall and the most beautiful woman in all Britain, and would have no other lady as his queen. So when the Duke of Cornwall was slain in fair battle with his enemies, the knights of Uther Pendragon and all the barons of England prayed the king to wed Cornwall's widowed duchess.

"Our king is a great knight and wifeless," they said, "and the lady Igraine is a noble lady. It would give us great joy if the king would make her his queen."

Gladly King Uther assented to their wish, and the king and the duchess were married with great mirth and joy. . . . .

Now the wizard Merlin knew through his magic arts that the first child of Uther would be the long-wished-for prince, King

3

Arthur. So, when the queen had borne a son, the wizard came to King Uther and said, "Sir, you must provide for the care and training of this child. Now I know a lord of yours in this land, a true and faithful man, who should have the bringing up of your son. His name is Sir Ector, and he is the lord of fair estates in many parts of England and of Wales. Now send for Sir Ector and ask him to have his wife take care of your son. Let the babe be brought to me unchristened at the postern gate."

King Uther did as Merlin suggested. And when Sir Ector came, he agreed to care for the child, and was granted great rewards. Then the king commanded two knights and two ladies to take the babe, wrapped in rich cloth of gold, and to deliver him at the postern gate of the castle to the first poor man they met there. So they delivered the child to a beggar, the wizard Merlin in disguise, who brought the babe to Sir Ector and found a holy man to christen him "Arthur." And Sir Ector's wife nourished the young child.

Within two years after this time King Uther became very ill. Then his enemies laid waste his lands and slew many of his people.

"Sir," said Merlin, "you may not lie sick in your chamber, but you must go to the field of battle, even though you ride in a horse litter. You shall never conquer your enemies until you appear before them in person. Then you shall have the victory."

So the king followed Merlin's suggestion, and Uther's knights carried him forth in a horse litter toward his

enemies, with a great army. And at St. Albans the
king met a great host from the North. That day Sir
Ulfius and Sir Brastias did great feats of arms. King
Uther's men won the battle, slew many people, and put
the rest to flight. The king returned to London and
rejoiced over his victory, but soon afterward became
ill, so that for three days and three nights he was speech-
less. All the barons were sorrowful and asked Merlin
for counsel.

"God will have His will," said Merlin. "See to it
that all his barons are with him tomorrow, and God
and I shall make him speak."

On the morrow, when all the barons were with the
king, Merlin said to Uther in a loud voice, "Sir, shall
your son Arthur be king after you in this realm?"

Then Uther Pendragon turned on his bed and said
in the hearing of them all, "I give the child God's blessing and mine. I bid him pray for my soul and rightly
to claim the crown."

After speaking these words the sovereign died, and
was buried with the splendor befitting a king. Then
Igraine, the queen, and all the barons mourned for
him.

Thereafter, for a long while, the realm of England
was in great danger, for every lord that had many men
strove to win the vacant throne. Many there were who
longed to be king.

So Merlin went to the Archbishop of Canterbury and
advised him to bid all the lords of the realm and all the
gentlemen of arms come to London before Christmas.

"For," said Merlin, "as Jesus was born on that holy night to show that He was come to be the King of all mankind, so might the Archbishop of Canterbury at that time show by miracle who was to be rightful king of the realm of Uther Pendragon."

Therefore, by the advice of Merlin, the archbishop ordered all the lords and gentlemen to appear in London by Christmas Eve, unless they would be cursed. Many of them confessed their sins and made clean their lives so that their prayers might be more acceptable to God. Long before it was dawn, in the greatest church in London all the lords were seen kneeling in prayer.

Now, when matins had been sung and the first mass was over, a great stone was seen in the churchyard against the high altar, four-square like a block of marble. And in the midst of the stone was a steel anvil, a foot high, in which was stuck the point of a fair, naked sword. In letters of gold around the point of the sword these words were inscribed:

"He who shall pull the sword out of this stone and anvil is the rightfully born king of England."

Then the people wondered, and told the archbishop of this marvel.

"I command you," said the archbishop, "to remain within the church and quietly pray to God. Let no man touch the sword until the high mass is done."

Thereafter the lords and knights went forth to behold the stone and the sword. And after they had read what was written in the letters of gold, many a man who wished to be king wrenched at the sword with

all his might. But no one could move the weapon even
the least part of an inch.

"The one that shall move the sword is not yet here,"
said the archbishop. "But doubt not that in His own
time God will make him known to us. Meanwhile, let
us choose ten knights, men of good fame, to guard
this sword."

So a proclamation was made throughout the land
that every man who so desired should try to win the
sword. The archbishop ordered the barons to hold a
joust and tournament on New Year's Day, that the
lords and common people might come together, because
the archbishop trusted that God would then make known
to them the one who should win the sword.

II

On New Year's Day, therefore, the barons and their
followers rode to the field, some to joust and some to
tourney. And it happened that Sir Ector rode to the
games, and with him came Sir Kaye his son, and young
Arthur, the foster brother. Sir Kaye had been made
knight at Allhallowmas, and as they rode to the tournament, he found that he had left his sword behind him
at his father's lodging and prayed young Arthur to ride
back and get it.

"With a right good will!" said Arthur, and rode at
full speed after the forgotten sword. But when he
reached home he discovered that Sir Ector's lady
and all her household had gone forth to see the
jousting.

Then was Arthur angry and said to himself, "I will hasten to the churchyard and there draw out the sword that sticketh in the stone, for my brother Kaye must not be without a sword this day."

When he reached the great block of stone he alighted from his horse and tied him to the stile. He then walked to the tent that covered the huge stone, but found no knights there, for they had all gone to the jousting. So he seized the sword by the handle. Lightly and fiercely he drew it from the stone, mounted his horse, and rode until he came to his brother Sir Kaye, and delivered him the sword. But as soon as this young knight saw the shining blade he knew full well that it was the sword of the stone. So he rode up to his father and said, "Look, sir! Here is the sword of the stone. Therefore I must be king of this land."

When Sir Ector saw the sword in Sir Kaye's hand, he rode with his son and young Arthur to the church. There all three alighted and went inside. And straightway the father made his son swear upon a book how he got the weapon.

"Sir," said Sir Kaye, "my brother Arthur brought it to me."

"And how did you come by this sword?" said Sir Ector to the other.

"Sir," said Arthur, "when I came home for my brother's sword, I found no one there to give it to me. And, since I thought he should not be without a weapon, I came here eagerly and drew it out of the stone without trouble."

"Did any knight see you do this thing?"

"No," said Arthur.

"Well," said Sir Ector to Arthur, "I understand you must be king of this land. No man could draw forth this sword except him who should be rightful king of England. Now let me see if you can put the sword back as it was, and then pull it out again."

"Why, that I can do easily!" said Arthur.

So Arthur put the weapon back into the stone. Then Sir Ector tried to pull it out, but failed.

"And now you try," said Sir Ector to Sir Kaye.

The young man pulled at the sword with all his might, but he could not stir nor move it.

"Now it is your turn," said Sir Ector to Arthur.

"With a good will," said the youth, and he pulled it out easily. Then Sir Ector knelt down on the earth, and Sir Kaye also.

"My own dear father and brother," said Arthur, "why do you kneel to me?"

"My lord Arthur, I was never your father nor even of your kin. But now I know well enough that you are more nobly born than I thought."

Then Sir Ector told young Arthur the whole story; how he had been commanded to care for the unchristened babe, and how Merlin by King Uther's order had put the child in his care.

When Arthur understood that Sir Ector was not his father, he was very sorrowful.

"Sir," said Sir Ector to Arthur, "will you be good and gracious to me and mine when you are my lord king?"

"I should be much to blame if I were not kind to you," said Arthur, "for I owe more to you than to any other man in the world. And my good lady and mother, your wife, has fostered me as her son. If ever it be God's will that I shall be king, then she and you shall ask what you will of me and I shall not fail you."

"Sir," said Sir Ector, "I will ask no more than that you make my son Kaye, your foster brother, seneschal of all your lands."

"That shall be done, sir," said Arthur. "By the faith of my body, no man but my foster brother Kaye shall be seneschal so long as he and I live."

After this they went to the archbishop and told him who had drawn the sword from the stone. And upon the twelfth day there came together all the barons who wished to try to take the sword. But, of all there, none could take the sword from the stone but Arthur, and this made many great lords exceedingly angry.

"It is a great shame to us all," they said, "and to the realm, that we should be governed by a boy who is not of noble blood."

And so angry were they at Arthur's deed that the test of the sword was put off again until Candlemas, when they were all to meet in the same spot. Ten knights were ordered to keep watch of the stone both day and night and so they built a pavilion over the place, and five were always on guard.

Now at Candlemas many more great lords went thither to try to win the sword, but none of them succeeded. And as Arthur had done at Christmas, so he did again at Candlemas; he pulled the sword from the stone easily. The barons were so vexed that once more they delayed, this time until the high Feast of Easter.

When that time came, Arthur again prevailed, but the great lords demanded that the final test be put off until the Feast of Pentecost. Then the Archbishop of Canterbury, by Merlin's advice, summoned the knights whom King Uther Pendragon had in his lifetime most loved and trusted, and made them Arthur's guard. Sir Boudwin of Britain, Sir Kaye, Sir Ulfius, Sir Brastias— all these and many more were with Arthur always, day and night, until the high Feast of Pentecost.

At the Feast of Pentecost every man who wished to try pulled at the sword, but none could prevail but Arthur. He drew it forth before all the lords and the common people that were there. Then all the common people cried with one voice, "We will have Arthur for our king. We will delay no longer, for now we see that it is God's will that he should be our king. And we will slay all who stand against him."

Then they all knelt down together and begged Arthur to forgive them for not choosing him sooner to be their king. Arthur forgave them, took the sword between his hands, and held it up to the altar where the archbishop was standing. Then was Arthur made knight by the best man that was present there, and soon thereafter was crowned king. And Arthur took an oath to deal justly with the lords and common people from that moment on through all the days of his life.

Within a few years King Arthur had won all the North—Scotland and all the peoples under her sovereignty. A part of Wales held out against King Arthur, but he overcame them through the prowess of himself and his knights of the Round Table.

III

Then King Arthur went into Wales and proclaimed a great feast to be held at Pentecost after his coronation in the city of Carlion. To this feast came King Lot, of Lothian and Orkney, with five hundred knights in his train, and King Urience of Gore, with four hundred knights. With King Nentres of Garlot rode seven hundred knights. The King of Scotland, who was but a young man, came with six hundred knights to serve him. And there came, too, a king that was called "the King with the Hundred Knights," and also the King of Carados with five hundred knights to serve him.

Arthur was glad of their coming, for he thought that all the kings and knights had come to honor him. So he rejoiced and sent splendid gifts to the kings and to all their men.

But the kings would receive none of Arthur's gifts, and told the messengers that they did not wish to receive the gifts of a beardless boy who was come of low blood. They sent back word, also, that they were come to give him gifts with hard swords between the neck and shoulders.

When the messengers brought the news to King Arthur, his barons advised him to go to a strong tower with a company of five hundred good men of arms. And all the kings besieged him there, but King Arthur was well victualed.

About fifteen days later Merlin came among these kings in the city of Carlion. All the kings there were glad of Merlin's coming and asked him, "Why has that beardless boy Arthur been made your king?"

"Sirs," said Merlin, "because he is King Uther Pendragon's son."

"Then," said they all, "he must be basely born, and not in the line of honest descent."

"No," said Merlin, "he is not basely born, but is the son of Uther's wedded wife, the fair Queen Igraine. Arthur shall, in spite of all, be king and overcome his enemies. Before he dies he shall long have been king of England, and he shall have under his dominion Wales, Ireland, and Scotland."

Some of the kings marveled at Merlin's words, but others laughed him to scorn, while some of them, among them King Lot, called Merlin a witch. But before Merlin left they agreed that Arthur should come out and speak with them and go back safely.

So Merlin went to King Arthur and told him what had happened, and bade him come out boldly and speak with them as their king and chieftain.

"For you shall overcome them all," said Merlin, "whether they will or will not."

Then King Arthur came out of his tower, and he wore underneath his gown a strong jesseraunt, or coat, of double mail. With him went the Archbishop of

Canterbury, Sir Boudwin of Britain, Sir Kaye the seneschal, and Sir Brastias.

And when the kings were met together, there was little meekness, but brave words on both sides. Always King Arthur answered his enemies, "If I live, I shall make you bow."

Therefore they parted in great wrath, and the king returned to the tower and armed himself and all his knights.

"What will you do?" said Merlin to the angry kings. "Take care, for here you could not prevail, although you were ten times your number."

But King Lot turned to the kings and asked, "Are you afraid of a witch and a dream reader?"

Then Merlin vanished from them and, coming to King Arthur, bade him attack his enemies fiercely. When three hundred of the best men that were with the kings went straight over to King Arthur's side, Arthur was glad.

Then Merlin counseled King Arthur, "Fight not with the sword that you procured by miracle unless you see that you are losing. Then draw it forth and do your best."

Thereupon King Arthur attacked his enemies and, with Sir Boudwin, Sir Kaye, and Sir Brastias, slew men to the right and to the left. King Arthur on horseback did such marvelous deeds of arms that even the enemy kings admired his hardiness.

Then King Lot came from the rear and, with the King with the Hundred Knights and King Carados,

attacked King Arthur.   King Arthur immediately turned
with his knights and in the foremost press fought until
his horse was slain under him.   King Lot bore down on
King Arthur, but Arthur's four knights set him again
on horseback.

Then Arthur drew his sword, Excalibur, which shone
so bright in his enemies' eyes that it gave light like thirty
torches.   With Excalibur he drove them back and slew
great numbers.   Thereafter all the common people of
Carlion with clubs and staves attacked the enemy until
all the knights that were left alive fled.   Merlin then
came to King Arthur and advised him to follow them
no farther.

IV

After the feast and tourney were held, at Merlin's
suggestion King Arthur went to London and called all
his barons into council.   For Merlin had told the king
that the six kings who had made war upon him would
quickly seek to be revenged.   The king's barons said
only, "We are big enough to help you."

And King Arthur answered, "I thank you for your
good courage.   But will all that love me ask Merlin for
his advice?   He has done much for me, and he knows
many secret things."

And the barons said that they would ask Merlin's
counsel.

Merlin warned them all that their enemies were
strong and as good men of arms as any alive.

"By this time," he said, "they have the aid of four

more kings and of a mighty duke, also. Unless our king has more knights than he can find within the bounds of his own realm, if he fight with them he shall be overcome and slain."

"What is it best to do in this case?" asked all the barons.

Then Merlin told them of two kings, brothers they were, who lived beyond the sea. "One is King Ban of Benwicke, and the other King Bors of Gaul. A mighty man, King Claudas, is now warring with them for the possession of a castle. This Claudas is so rich that he has many good knights and so is putting these two kings to the worse. Therefore I counsel that our king send two trusty knights to the two kings Ban and Bors, with letters to promise that, if they will come to help King Arthur with his wars, he will be sworn to help them in their wars against King Claudas."

"This is excellent counsel," said the king and barons.

So letters were written which the two knights Ulfius and Brastias were to carry quickly to the two kings. They rode forth well horsed and well armed and, passing over the sea, rode toward the city of Benwicke.

But eight knights espied them, and at a narrow passage these eight tried to take Sir Ulfius and Sir Brastias prisoners. But the two faring knights prayed that they might pass, for they were messengers unto King Ban and King Bors, sent from King Arthur.

"Then," said the eight knights, "you shall certainly die or be our prisoners, for we are knights of King Claudas."

Therewith two of them dressed their spears, as did Sir Ulfius and Sir Brastias, and the four ran together with great strength. But the knights of Claudas broke their spears, and the other two held and bore the two knights out of their saddles on to the earth. So Arthur's messengers left their enemies lying, and rode on their way.

The other six knights of Claudas rode on ahead to another passage to challenge the messengers again. But Ulfius and Brastias smote two of them down and so passed on.

At the third passage they smote down two more, and likewise at the fourth, so that all of the eight knights were either hurt or bruised. When the faring knights came to Benwicke, it happened that both King Ban and King Bors were there.

When the kings heard that messengers had come, two knights of worship, the one called Lionses, lord of the country of Payarne, and the other Sir Phariaunce, a worshipful knight, were sent to them. When the messengers said that they came from King Arthur of England, the two knights of worship took them in their arms and welcomed them joyfully.

The two kings received the messengers of King Arthur with great joy. The couriers kissed the letters and delivered them straightway. When King Ban and King Bors understood the letters, they gave this answer:

"We will fulfill the desire of King Arthur's writing."

And Ulfius and Brastias were entertained royally there. When they told the kings of the adventure of their passage against the eight knights, King Ban and King Bors said that they wished they had known of the combats, for they would surely not have allowed the eight knights to escape.

The messengers were given great gifts—as many as they could bear away. And, moreover, they had their answer by word of mouth and by writing that those two kings would come to King Arthur as quickly as they could.

So the two knights rode back, passed the sea, and, coming to their lord, told him how they had sped. When he heard the good tidings, King Arthur was passing glad.

"By what time will the two kings arrive?" Arthur asked.

"Sir," said they, "before Allhallowmas."

Then the king proclaimed a great feast and joust. And by Allhallowmas the two kings had come over the sea with three hundred knights well arrayed both for peace and for war. King Arthur met them ten miles out of London and welcomed them with great joy. And at Allhallowmas, at the great feast in the hall, the three kings sat together. Sir Kaye the seneschal served in the hall, and with him were Sir Lucas the butler, who was Duke Corneus' son, and Sir Griflet, who was the son of Cardol.

As soon as they had washed and had risen, all the knights that would joust made ready, and there were seven hundred knights ready on horseback. And King Arthur, King Ban, King Bors, with the Archbishop of

Canterbury and Sir Ector, Kay's father, were in a place like a hall which was covered with cloth of gold, with ladies and gentlewomen to judge who jousted best.

V

King Arthur and the two kings divided the seven hundred knights into two parties. In one party were King Arthur's knights, while three hundred knights of the realm of Benwicke and those of Gaul turned on the other side. Then they dressed their shields, and many good knights couched their spears. Sir Griflet was the first to meet a knight, one called Ladinas, and they came together so fiercely that all wondered. They fought until their shields fell in pieces and both horses and men fell to the earth. Both the English and the French knight lay so long that all thought they must be dead.

But when Lucas the butler saw Griflet lie there so, he quickly horsed him again, and both knights performed many marvelous deeds of arms with many squires. Sir Kaye came with five good knights as companions, and they smote down six others, both men and horses. Then came Sir Placidas, a goodly knight, who met with Sir Kaye and smote him down. Thereat Sir Griflet was angry, and met Sir Placidas so hard that both man and horse fell to the earth. But when the five knights knew that Sir Kaye had fallen, they were filled with wrath and therewith each of them bore down a knight.

As soon as King Arthur and the two other kings saw that the fight was beginning to be fierce on both

sides, they proclaimed that all men should depart to their
lodgings.   Then they all went home and unarmed, and
went so to evensong and supper.   Thereafter the three
kings went into a garden and gave the prizes to Sir
Kaye and to Sir Lucas the butler, and to Sir Griflet.
Later the kings and Gwenbaus, a brother of King Ban
and King Bors, a wise clerk indeed, and Ulfius, Brastias,
and Merlin met in council.

On the morrow after mass and dinner they met again
in council and argued what it were best to do.   At last
they concluded that Merlin should go, with a ring of
King Ban's as his token to get Ban's men and the men
of King Bors.   They agreed also that Gracian and
Placidas should go back with Merlin, so that they could
guard the castles of their sovereigns, Ban of Benwicke
and Bors of Gaul.

So the three passed over the sea to France and came
to Benwicke.   When the people saw King Ban's ring
and Gracian and Placidas, they were very glad and made
great rejoicing.   And, at their sovereign lord's desire,
the men of war made ready in all possible haste.   Fifteen
thousand on horseback and on foot were assembled, with
plenty of victuals, by Merlin's provision.   Gracian and
Placidas were left to guard the castles of the kings against
King Claudas.

When Merlin came to the sea he sent the footmen
home, and took with him only ten thousand men on
horseback, mostly men of arms.   And Merlin and the
men passed over the sea and landed at Dover.   Then
Merlin led the host by the most secret way he knew

into the forest of Bedegraine, where he lodged them safely.

Then Merlin rode to King Arthur and the two kings and told them how he had fared, and they marveled greatly that any man could go and come so soon. Merlin told them that ten thousand men were in the forest of Bedegraine, well armed at all points. To horseback went all the host of King Arthur. With twenty thousand men he passed by night and day.

VI

After a short while the three kings came into the castle of Bedegraine and found there a fair fellowship and all the victuals they wanted.

The six kings of the North were gathering great armies because of the rebuke they had suffered at Carlion. Those kings had secured the aid of five other kings who had begun to gather their forces. And they swore an oath that they should not desert one another until they had destroyed King Arthur.

The Duke of Cambenet swore that he would bring with him five thousand men of arms on horseback. Then King Brandegoris vowed that he would bring his five thousand men of arms also. King Clarence of Northumberland promised three thousand men of arms; the King with the Hundred Knights, who was a young man, four thousand men on horseback; King Lot, Sir Gawaine's father, five thousand men on horseback. King Urience, Sir Uwaine's father, of the land of Gore, swore that he would bring six thousand men. And five other kings swore each to bring five thousand men of arms on horseback: King Lares of Cornwall, King Cradelmont, King Nentres, King Carados, and King Agwisaunce of Ireland.

So their whole host of men of arms on horseback was fifty thousand, and on foot, ten thousand men. As soon as all were ready and mounted they sent forth their advance riders. And these eleven kings laid siege to the castle of Bedegraine, but soon left and advanced toward Arthur, leaving a few men to continue the siege, for the castle of Bedegraine was held by King Arthur, some of whose men were within.

By Merlin's advice advance riders were sent to scour the country, and when these met with the advance riders of the North they forced the latter to tell them which way the host was coming. This information they speedily brought to King Arthur, and according to the counsel of King Ban and King Bors they burned and destroyed all the country before them as they rode.

The King with the Hundred Knights had a wonderful dream two nights before the battle. It seemed to him in his vision that a great wind arose and blew down the castles and their towns. And after that came water and bore them all away. All that heard of this dream said that it was a token of a great battle.

When Arthur's army knew which way the eleven kings and their armies would ride and where they would lodge that night, by the counsel of Merlin they set upon the northern host at midnight when they were in their pavilions. But the scout watch of the northern host cried, "Lords, to arms! For here are your enemies at your hand."

Then King Arthur, King Ban, King Bors, and their good trusty knights attacked their foes so fiercely that they overthrew their pavilions on their heads. The armies of the eleven kings fought valiantly. But of the fifty thousand hardy men, there were slain ten thousand.

When it was almost dawn Merlin said unto the three kings, "Now shall you follow my advice. King Ban and King Bors with their ten thousand men should be put in ambush in the wood here before the daylight comes. They must not stir until you and your knights, King Arthur, have fought with the foe for a long time. At daylight arrange your men so that the enemy may see all your host. They will be more hasty when they see you have but twenty thousand men and will be more willing to allow you and your host to come over the passage."

All the three kings and the barons agreed that Merlin's advice should be followed.

On the morrow were three thousand men of arms delivered to Ulfius and Brastius, and they fought the enemy fiercely in the passage.

When the eleven kings saw that so few men were performing such marvelous feats of arms, they were ashamed and set on them fiercely again. And when Sir Ulfius' horse was slain under him, he did great fighting on foot. But when Sir Brastias saw the Duke of Cambenet and King Clarence of Northumberland attacking Sir Ulfius, he smote the duke with a spear so that both horse and man fell down. Then King Clarence returned to Brastias, and they smote each other so that both fell to the earth, and there they lay for a long time.

Then came Sir Kaye the seneschal and six fellows with him and fought stoutly. After that the eleven kings came, and Sir Griflet was put to the earth, horse and man, and Lucas the butler by King Brandegoris and King Idres and King Agwisaunce.

Then the battle became more fierce on both sides. When Sir Kaye saw Sir Griflet on foot, he rode to King Nentres and smote him down and, leading the horse to Sir Griflet, horsed his friend again. Sir Kaye with the same spear smote down King Lot. When the King with the Hundred Knights saw that, he ran to Sir Kaye, smote him down, took his horse, and gave it to King Lot.

When Sir Griflet saw Sir Kaye and Lucas the butler on foot, he took a sharp spear, great and square, rode to Pynell, smote him down, and gave Pynell's horse to Sir Kaye. Then King Lot unhorsed Melot de la Roche and horsed King Nentres again; so also did the King with the Hundred Knights for King Idres. And King Lot smote down Clariance de al Forest Savage, and gave the horse to Duke Eustace.

Then the eleven kings came together and said that they would be revenged for the damage they had taken that day.

Now when Sir Ector came he found Ulfius and Brastias in great peril of death under the horses' feet. Then King Arthur ran like a lion unto King Cradelmont of North Wales and smote him through the left side. Then taking his horse by the reins Arthur led him to Ulfius, saying, "Have this horse, my old friend, for great is your need."

In revenge, when the King with the Hundred Knights

saw King Cradelmont on foot, he smote down Sir Ector and gave his horse to Cradelmont. But when King Arthur saw this he was wroth, and with his sword he smote the rebel king on the helm so that a quarter of the helm and shield fell down, and, as the sword curved down into the horse's neck, both the rebel king and the horse fell to the ground.

Then Sir Kaye smote Sir Morganore and took the horse for his father, Sir Ector. Immediately Sir Ector ran into a knight called Kardens and took his horse for Sir Brastias, who was badly hurt. Sir Lucas the butler was lying under the horses' feet, and Sir Griflet tried to rescue him, but there were fourteen knights attacking Lucas. Then Brastias smote one of them on the helm. On he rode to another and smote him so fiercely that he could fight no longer. A third he smote on the shoulder. Then Sir Griflet smote a knight on the temples so that head and helm went to the earth together, and Griflet took that knight's horse, led him to Sir Lucas, and bade him revenge his hurts.

And when Lucas saw King Agwisaunce, who had slain Moris de la Roche, he ran to him with a short spear and gave him such a fall that his horse sank down to the earth. When he saw Blyas de la Flaundres and Sir Gwinas on foot, he slew in his anger two young knights that he might horse these friends again.

King Arthur performed such marvelous feats of arms that all there wondered. The noise of the armies fighting together rang through the wood, and at the sound King Ban and King Bors made ready and dressed their shields and harness for the encounter.   Many of the knights trembled in their eagerness.

All this while Lucas, Gwinas, Briaunt, and Belias of Flanders held valiantly against six kings—King Lot, King Nentres, King Brandegoris, King Idres, King Urience, and King Agwisaunce. With the help of Sir Kaye and Sir Griflet the knights held these six kings as long as they had any power to defend themselves.

But when King Arthur saw the battle could not be ended, he rode about like a mad lion and did not stop until he had slain twenty knights. He wounded King Lot on the shoulder and made him leave the fighting ground. Sir Ulfius, Sir Brastias, and Sir Ector fought with the Duke Eustace, King Cradelmont, King Candelmas, King Clarence of Northumberland, King Carados, and the King with the Hundred Knights.

Then King Lot said unto the other ten kings, "If you will not do as I say, we shall all be slain. Let me have the King with the Hundred Knights, King Agwisaunce, King Idres, and the Duke of Cambenet. We five kings will have fifteen thousand men of arms with us. We will go apart, while you six kings combat with your twelve thousand. And when you have fought with the enemy a long time, we will come back into the combat fiercely."

So the five kings departed as they had arranged, and the six kings strove against King Arthur for a long time.

In the meantime King Ban and King Bors came out of ambush with Lionses and Phariaunce in the vanguard. The two kings met King Idres and his men, and there was a great breaking of spears and smiting of swords. Agwisaunce put Lionses and Phariaunce in great danger of their lives. When King Bors saw those knights in such peril, he came on so fast that his men seemed as black as the men of Ind.

When King Lot caught sight of King Bors, he recognized him, and said, "O Jesus! defend us from death and horrible injuries! For I see yonder a king, one of the best knights in the world, who is joined to Arthur's men."

"Who is he?" asked the King with the Hundred Knights.

"He is King Bors of Gaul," said Lot. "I marvel how he and his men came into this country without our knowing of it."

"It was by the help of Merlin," said a knight.

"As for King Bors, I will combat him," said King Carados. Rescue me if need be."

Then all bade him go on and said that they would do what they could. So King Carados and his host rode until they came within bowshot of King Bors, then rushed at him, letting their horses run as fast as they could. Sir Bleoberis, the godson of King Bors, and a fine young knight, was bearing his chief's standard.

"Now we shall see," said King Bors, "how these northern Britons can bear their arms."

King Bors fought with a knight and struck him with a spear so that he fell down dead. Then Bors drew his sword and performed marvelous deeds of arms, and his knights, too, failed not. When King Carados was unhorsed, the King with the Hundred Knights came and rescued him mightily with force of arms.

Then came King Ban into the field, as fierce as a lion, with his bands of green and gold gleaming in the sun.

"Now," said King Lot, "we shall indeed be defeated, for yonder I see the most valiant knight of the world and the man of most renown. No more valorous men than those two brothers, Ban and Bors, live in the world. Unless we retreat wisely, there is but death."

When King Ban came into the battle the sound of his strokes resounded through the wood, and king Lot wept for sorrow that so many good knights should die. Then both divisions of the men from the North came together in their fear. And the three kings slew so many that it was a pity to behold the great multitude of dead. Many knights fled from the field.

But King Lot and the King with the Hundred Knights and King Morganore gathered the scattered men and held the battle all that day. And the King with the Hundred Knights advanced toward King Ban and smote him upon the helm. Then was King Ban astonished and angry. When the other saw him about to set upon him, he cast up his shield and spurred his horse forward. But the stroke of King Ban fell and carved into the shield, and the sword, sliding down by the hauberk behind the back of the rebel king, cut in twain the trapping of steel, cut the horse in two pieces, and then fell to the ground. Then the King with the Hundred Knights leaped lightly from his dying horse and with his sword broached King Ban's horse through and through. Then King Ban smote the other so fiercely that he fell to the earth. And King Ban killed King Morganore.

When King Arthur in the press found King Ban standing among dead men and horses, fighting on foot like a mad lion, he allowed no one to come within reach of his sword without being slain. And King Arthur's shield was so bloody that no man could know him by it.

As King Arthur saw a knight passing that was well horsed he ran to that knight and smote him so that his sword cut the fellow into two pieces. Then Arthur gave the riderless horse to King Ban, saying, "Fair brother, have this horse, for you have dire need of it. I am sore grieved for your great hurt."

"It shall soon be revenged," said King Ban. "Some of them may soon sore repent this."

Finally King Arthur and the two kings made their knights withdraw a little, but the eleven kings and their horsemen never turned back; however, they withdrew to a little wood, over a small river, where they rested. And the eleven kings and their knights crowded together as men who were afraid. But no man could pass them, for they held together very firmly. King Arthur marveled at their valor and was very angry.

"Sir Arthur," said King Ban and King Bors, "blame them not. They do as good men ought to do. They are knights of great prowess. If they were yours, no king under heaven would have such valiant knights."

"I may not love them," said King Arthur, "for they would destroy me."

"We know that well," said King Ban and King Bors. "That they are your mortal enemies has been proven. It is a great pity that they are so obstinate."

Meanwhile the eleven kings met in council, and King Lot said, "Lords, you see what people we have lost, because we always wait upon our footmen. This is my advice: Let us leave the footmen, for it is almost night. They may save themselves in this wood which is close at hand."

"And what shall we do then?" asked the King with the Hundred Knights.

"We horsemen shall make an ordinance that none may break upon pain of death. If any man tries to run away, let him be slain quickly, for it is better that we slay a coward than that through a coward all shall be slain. What say you to this plan?"

"It is a good plan," said King Nentres, and all the kings swore that they would never fail one another, either in life or in death, and that whoever fled should be slain. Then they mended their harness, righted their shields, set new spears on their thighs, and stood firm as a clump of trees.

VII

When King Arthur, King Ban, and King Bors beheld them with their knights, they praised them greatly for their chivalry as the hardiest fighters that they had ever seen. Then forty noble knights told the three kings that they would break their battle. Among these knights were Lionses, Phariaunce, Ulfius, Brastias, Ector, Kaye, Lucas the butler, Griflet le Fise de Dieu, Gwinas de la Bloy, and Briant de la Forest Savage; also Ladinas de la Rouse, Bellaus, and Morians of the Castle of Maidens, and many others.

Now these forty knights rode toward the enemy with great spears on their thighs and spurred on their horses as fast as they could run. And the eleven kings with some of their good knights rushed toward them as fast as their horses could carry them, and both parties fought valorously.

Into the thickest of the press came King Arthur, King Ban, and King Bors, and slew until their horses were wet with blood up to their fetlocks. And at last the northern host were driven back over a little river.

Then Merlin came upon a great black horse and said to King Arthur, "Have you not done enough? Of threescore thousand, you have left alive only fifteen thousand. God is angry at you, because you will never have done. Yonder eleven kings will not be overthrown at this time. If you fight any longer, all your fortune will turn."

"What shall be done?" asked Arthur.

"Withdraw at once to your lodging and there rest. Reward your knights well with gold and silver, for they richly deserve it. No riches are too great for them, for never have men shown more prowess than they have shown this day. You have today matched with the best fighters in the world."

"That is true," said King Ban and King Bors.

"Withdraw wherever you wish," said Merlin. "For these three years they will not hurt you nor grieve you, and by that time you shall have new tidings."

Then Merlin said privily to King Arthur, "These eleven kings have more in hand than they now know.

More than forty thousand Saracens have landed in their countries. They have burned, slain, and laid siege to the castle Vandesborough. You need not dread these men for three years."

"That is strange news indeed," said Arthur.

"Gather all the goods that you have gained from this battle," Merlin continued. "Let it be given freely to these two kings, Ban and Bors, that they may reward their knights with it."

King Arthur said that he would do as Merlin suggested, and to King Ban and King Bors he gave the plunder, which these kings gave as freely to their knights.

Then Merlin took his leave of King Arthur and of the two kings to visit his master, Bleise, who dwelt in Northumberland.

And Merlin's master was glad of his coming. Merlin told him how King Arthur and the two kings had fared in the battle, and gave him the names of every king and knight of worship who had fought there.

Bleise wrote an account of the battle, just as Merlin told it to him; how it began and how it ended, and who was the victor. And after this Merlin had Bleise, his master, write about every battle that took place during King Arthur's reign, and about the combats of every knight of King Arthur's court.

VIII

Then Merlin left his master and came to King Arthur, who was in the castle of Bedegraine that stood in the Sherwood forest. And King Arthur did not know

Merlin in his disguise, for he was all in sheepskins, and a russet gown, with a great pair of boots and a bow and arrows. It was on the morrow after Candlemas Day, and Merlin brought wild geese in his hand.

"Sir," said Merlin to King Arthur, "will you give me a gift?"

"Churl," said the king, "why should I give you a gift?"

"Sir," said Merlin, "you had better give me a gift which is not in your hands than to lose great riches, for here, in the same place where the great battle was, is great treasure hid in the earth."

"Who told you so, churl?" asked King Arthur.

"Merlin told me so," said the man in black sheepskins.

Then Ulfius and Brastias knew him well enough, and smiled. "Sir," said the knights, "it is Merlin."

King Arthur was greatly abashed, and King Ban and King Bors marveled at Merlin, disguised in his cheap russet gown.

Then word came that King Rience of North Wales was making war upon King Leodegraunce of Cameliard. King Arthur was angry at this news, because he loved Leodegraunce well and hated Rience, who was always against him.

So King Arthur and King Ban and King Bors left with their men, who numbered about twenty thousand, and in six days came into the country of Cameliard. There they rescued King Leodegraunce and slew ten thousand of the people of King Rience, and put him to

flight. Then King Leodegraunce thanked the three
kings for their kindness in revenging him on his enemies.

And there King Arthur saw Guenever, daughter of
Leodegraunce, for the first time, and ever after loved
her. They were afterward wedded, as shall be shown
hereafter.

Then King Ban and King Bors took their leave to
go to their own country, for King Claudas was destroying
their lands.

"Then," said King Arthur, "I will go with you."

"No," said the two kings, "you must not go at this
time, for you have yet much to do here. We will leave,
and with the great goods which have been gifts to us
we shall hire many good knights to fight against King
Claudas. By the grace of God, if we need your help,
we will send for you. And if you need us, send for us,
and, by the faith of our bodies, we will not delay."

Then Merlin said, "You two kings will not be needed
again for war here, but I know well that it will not be
long before you will again see the noble King Arthur.
Ere twelve months be past, you shall have great need of
him, and then he shall revenge you on your enemies,
just as you have revenged him on his. For these eleven
kings shall die all in one day because of the great might
of two knights as valiant as any now living—Balin le
Savage and Balan, his brother."

IX

Now turn we to the eleven kings who returned to
the city of Sorhaute, in King Urience's land. There

they rested as well as they could, and had leeches examine their wounds. And they sorrowed greatly for the death of so many of their men.

Then a messenger came with sad news.

"Lawless people are coming into your lands," he said, "and forty thousand Saracens. They have burned and slain without mercy all the people they have met, and now are besieging the castle of Vandesborough."

"Alas!" said the eleven kings. "Here is one sorrow after another. If we had not made war upon King Arthur, he would help revenge us. As for King Leodegraunce, he loves King Arthur better than us; and as for King Rience, he is busy with King Leodegraunce, for he has besieged him."

They agreed to keep the marches of Cornwall, Wales, and of the North. They put King Idres in the city of Nauntes in Britain, with four thousand men, to watch both water and land. They put in the city of Windesan, King Nentres of Garlot, with four thousand knights.

They had more than eight thousand men to fortify all the fortresses in the marches of Cornwall. And they put more knights in all the marches of Wales and Scotland, with many good men of arms.

For the space of three years they held together and made allies of kings, dukes, lords, and gentlemen. And to them fell King Rience of North Wales, who was a mighty man, and also Nero, who had many brave knights. All this while they trained good men of arms and gathered together victuals and all manner of war equipment to revenge the battle of Bedegraine.

X

After King Ban and King Bors had left, King Arthur rode to Carlion. And Lot's wife, Belisent, came there from Orkney as a messenger, but in truth she had been, sent as a spy to the court of King Arthur. She came richly clothed, and with her came her four sons, Gawaine, Gaheris, Agravaine, Gareth, and many knights and ladies.

Now she was a very fair lady, and the king, who did not know that she was queen to his hated enemy King Lot, loved her and desired her to be his wife. Though King Arthur did not know it, she was his sister, on his mother Igraine's side. From this unhappy mating the child Mordred later was born. The false queen stayed at Carlion a month and then departed secretly.

Then the king dreamed a wonderful dream, which made him greatly afraid. This was King Arthur's dream:

It seemed to him that many griffins and serpents came into the land and that they burned and slew all the people there. And then it seemed that he fought with them and that they wounded him grievously, but that at last he seemed to slay them all.

Now when the king awoke from sleep he was unhappy and thoughtful about his dream. To put away these thoughts, he went hunting, with many knights accompanying him.

As soon as he reached the forest, the king saw a great hart before him.

"This hart will I chase," said King Arthur.

So he spurred his horse and rode after it. The king chased the hart so long that his horse fell down dead.

When the king saw the hart in ambush and his horse dead, he sat down by the fountain and fell into deep thought. And as he sat there alone he thought he heard a noise of about thirty hounds. Then the king saw a strange beast coming toward him—the strangest beast that he had ever heard of, or seen.

The beast went to the fountain and drank. Although the noise inside the beast was like the questing of thirty couple of hounds, while the beast drank there was no noise inside him. But the beast departed with great noise, which made the king wonder. While he was thinking about this, he fell asleep.

As he awakened a knight on foot came to him.

"Sleepy and thoughtful knight," said the stranger, "tell me if you saw a strange beast pass this way."

"I saw such a one," said King Arthur to the knight. "What do you want with that beast?"

"Sir, I have followed that beast a long time and, thereby, have killed my horse. Would God I had another to follow my quest."

Then some one came with another horse for the king. And when the knight saw this, he asked the king to give him the horse.

"For I have followed the quest these twelve months," said he, "and I shall either take the beast or bleed of the best blood of my body."

It was King Pellinore who followed the questing beast at that time, and after his death Sir Palamides followed it.

"Sir knight," said King Arthur, "leave that quest and let me have it. I will follow it another twelve months."

"Fool," said the knight to King Arthur, "your desire is vain, for it shall never be achieved but by me, or by my next of kin."

Therewith he went to the king's horse and mounted, saying, "Gramercy, this horse is mine."

"Well," said King Arthur, "you may take my horse by force, but if I might prove which is better on horseback, you or I, I should be content."

"Then," said the knight, "seek me here whenever you wish, and near this well you will find me."

Thus the strange knight passed on his way.

Then King Arthur sat in deep thought, and bade his men bring another horse as quickly as they could.

Then Merlin came, transformed into a child about fourteen years of age. He saluted the king and asked him why he was so thoughtful and sad.

"I may well be thoughtful and sad," said the king, "for here just now I saw the most marvelous sight in all my life."

"That I know," said Merlin, "as well as yourself. And I know all your thoughts. You are a fool to be thoughtful and sad, since it will not help you. I know also, who you are, and who were your father and your mother. They were, King Uther and Igraine."

"That is false," said King Arthur. "For how should you know? You are not old enough to have known my father."

"Yet," said Merlin, "I know better than you or any man living."

"I will not believe you," said King Arthur, and he was angry at the child.

So Merlin left and came back again in the likeness of an old man of fourscore years. The king was glad, for the old man seemed to be very wise.

"Why are you so sad?" the old man asked.

"Well may I be sad," said King Arthur, "for many things. A child who was here just now told me many things that he should not know."

"Yes," said the old man, "the child told you the truth, and would have told you more had you allowed it. You have done something lately for which God is displeased with you. You have had Belisent as your wife, and the child Mordred has been born who will destroy you and all the knights of your realm."

"Who are you," asked King Arthur, "that tell me this news?"

"I am Merlin, and it was I in the child's likeness also."

"You are a marvelous man," said King Arthur. "But I wonder much at your words that I must die in battle."

"Do not wonder," said Merlin, "for it is God's will that your body should be punished for your misdeeds. But well may I be sad, too, for I shall die a shameful death and be put into the earth alive, while you shall die an honorable death."

As they talked thus, one came with the king's horses.

So the king mounted his horse and Merlin another, and they rode to Carlion.

Shortly thereafter the king asked Ector and Ulfius who his father had been. And they told him that Uther Pendragon was his father and Queen Igraine his mother.

Then King Arthur said to Merlin, "I wish that my mother be sent for, so that I may speak to her. If she says this is true, then I will believe it."

The queen was sent for in all haste. She came and brought with her Morgan le Fay, her daughter, who was as fair a lady as any might be. And the king welcomed Igraine heartily.

Then Ulfius came and said openly, so that the king and all there might hear, "You are the most false woman in the world and the most traitorous to the king's person."

"Take care what you say, Ulfius," said King Arthur.

"I am well aware of what I say," said Sir Ulfius. "And here is my glove to prove it to any man who says the contrary, that this Queen Igraine is the cause of all your trouble and of the great war that you have fought. For if she had told, during Uther Pendragon's life, of your birth and the fact that he was your father, you would never have had as many mortal battles as you have had. For most of your great lords, the barons and the gentlemen of your realm, never knew whose son you were. Queen Igraine should have made your birth known openly, for her own sake and for yours, as well as for the honor of the realm. Therefore I prove her false to God and to you. Who will say the contrary I will prove it upon his body."

Then Queen Igraine spoke: "I am a woman and may not fight. But rather than that I should be dishonored, I wish some knight would take my quarrel. Merlin knows that after the child was born Uther gave it to Merlin, who had some one bringin₈ up the child. So I never saw the child after, nor even knew his name."

Then Sir Ulfius said to the queen, "Merlin is more to blame than you."

"I know that I gave a son to my lord King Uther," said Queen Igraine, "but I know not what he has become."

Then Merlin took the king by the hand, saying, "This is your mother."

Therewith Sir Ector told how he had taken care of the infant Arthur by the command of King Uther. King Arthur took his mother Queen Igraine in his arms and kissed her, and they wept from joy. Then the king proclaimed a feast which lasted eight days.

XI

One day a squire on horseback came into the court, leading before him a knight, mortally wounded. The man spoke to the king and said:

"A knight in the forest has put up a pavilion by the side of the well and he has slain my master, a good knight, whose name was Miles. I therefore beseech you that my master may be buried and that some good knight may revenge his death."

There was much talk then in the court about the knight's death, and every man gave his advice.

Then came Griflet, who was but a squire and as young as King Arthur. And Griflet asked the king that for all the service he had done he should be given the order of knighthood.

"You are very young," said King Arthur, "to take so high an order."

"Sir," said Griflet, "I beseech you to make me a knight."

"Sir," said Merlin, "it would be a pity to lose Griflet, for he will be a great knight when he comes of age, staying with you all of his life. If he should adventure his body against that of the knight of the fountain, he may never come back again, for that knight is one of the best in the world and the strongest in arms."

"Well, so be it," said King Arthur. Then the king made Griflet a knight.

"Now," said King Arthur to Griflet, "since I have given you your desire and made you a knight, you must grant me a favor."

"What you will, my lord," said Sir Griflet.

"You must promise me, by the faith of your body, that when you have jousted with the Knight of the Fountain, whether you are on foot or on horseback, you will come again to me without any question."

"I will promise you that," said Sir Griflet.

Then the young man in great haste mounted his horse, dressed his shield, and took a great spear in his hand. He rode at a fast gallop until he came to the fountain. There he saw a rich pavilion, near which, under a canopy stood a fair horse well saddled and bridled. On a tree near by was a shield of divers colors, and a great spear near it. Sir Griflet smote upon the shield with the point of the spear so that the shield fell to the ground.

Then the knight came from the pavilion and said, "Fair knight, why did you strike down my shield?"

"Because I will joust with you," said Sir Griflet.

"It would be better if you did not," said the knight, "for you are young and but lately made a knight, and your strength is as nothing compared with mine."

"Sir," said Griflet, "I will joust with you."

"For that I am loath," said the knight, "but since I must, I will dress my shield. But from whence do you come?"

"Sir," said Griflet, "I am of Arthur's court."

Then they ran together so that Sir Griflet's spear broke in pieces, and the knight struck Sir Griflet through the shield and the left side. He broke his spear so that the truncheon stuck in the knight's body. Both horse and knight fell down, and when the knight of the Fountain saw Griflet lying on the ground he alighted and was very sorrowful, for he thought he had killed the youth. He unlaced the helmet to give him air. Then with the truncheon as it was, he set him upon his horse and commended the youth to God, saying, "You have a mighty heart, young sir, and if you live you will prove a passing good knight."

So Sir Griflet rode to the court, where they grieved for him. But by the aid of good leeches he was healed and his life saved.

XII

Shortly thereafter twelve knights who were aged men came to the court. And they said that they came from the Emperor of Rome to ask King Arthur tribute for his kingdom. Unless he paid it, the emperor vowed that he would destroy Arthur and his land.

"Well," said King Arthur, "as you are messengers, you may say what you wish, or you would die for the insult you have given. This is my answer: I owe the emperor no tribute, nor shall I send him any. But upon a fair field I shall give him my tribute, with a sharp spear or a sharp sword. And that shall be within a short time, by my father's soul!"

Thereupon the messengers departed angrily.

But King Arthur was as angry as they were, for they came in an evil time when he was wrathful because of the hurt that Sir Griflet had suffered. That day Arthur commanded one of his men to see that before daybreak, on the morrow, his best horse and armor should be outside the city walls.

So in the morning, before daybreak, Arthur met his man and his horse. He mounted, dressed his shield, took his spear, and bade his chamberlain wait there till he came again.

King Arthur rode but slowly until it was day, when he saw three churls pursuing Merlin to slay him. King Arthur rode up to them, crying, "Flee, churls!"

They were afraid when they saw a knight, and fled immediately.

"O, Merlin," said King Arthur, "here, for all your

craft, you would have been killed had I not been near."

"No," said Merlin, "I could save myself if I wished. But you are nearer death than I was, for you are going toward it, and God is not your friend now."

As they went along the road talking they came to the rich pavilion by the fountain. There King Arthur saw a knight, fully armed, sitting in a chair.

"Sir knight," said King Arthur, "why do you stay here? Is it so that no knight may ride this way unless he joust with you? I advise you to give up that custom."

"That is my custom," said the knight, "and I will continue it in spite of who says nay. Let him who is not pleased with my custom try to change it!"

"I will change it," said King Arthur.

"And I will defend it," said the knight.

Then the Knight of the Fountain mounted his horse, dressed his shield, and took his spear. And the two champions charged and met so hard they shivered their spears into pieces. Then King Arthur drew his sword.

"No," said the knight, "it is fairer that we use sharp spears."

"I am willing," said King Arthur, "but I have no more spears."

"I have spears enough," said the knight.

So a squire came and brought two good spears, one for King Arthur and the other for the Knight of the Fountain. Then they spurred their horses and came together with all their might, so that their spears broke in their hands. Then King Arthur put his hand to his sword again.

"No," said the knight, "you shall do better. You are as good a jouster as ever I met. For the love of the high order of knighthood, let us joust once again."

"I am willing," said King Arthur.

Two good spears were brought then, and this time they ran together so that Arthur's spear was shivered into pieces, and the knight hit Arthur so hard in the middle of his shield that horse and man fell to the earth.

Then, indeed, was King Arthur angry, and drew his sword, saying, "I will try you, sir knight, on foot, since I have lost the honor on horseback."

"I will be on horseback," said the knight.

Then King Arthur angrily advanced toward the knight with his sword drawn. But the knight alighted for him, because he thought it was no honor to fight a knight at such a disadvantage, he on horseback and the other on foot. A great combat began then, and they cut so with their swords that pieces of their armor fell in the field and they both bled so much that all the place where they fought was bloody.

They fought long and rested, and then went to battle again like two wild boars, so fiercely that both of them fell to the earth. At last the knight's weapon struck Arthur's sword into two pieces. Arthur was very sorrowful. And the stranger knight said to the king, "You are in my power. I can either save you or slay you. Unless you confess me victor, you shall die."

"As for death," said King Arthur, "it will be welcome when it comes. But to yield to you—to confess myself conquered—I should rather die than be so shamed."

Then the king leaped toward the knight, took him by the waist and threw him down, and pulled off his helmet. But the knight soon brought King Arthur under him, tore off his helmet, and would have cut off his head but that Merlin came, and said, "Knight, hold your hand. If you kill that champion, you will put this kingdom in the greatest danger that ever a country was in. For this knight is a man of more honor than you know."

"Why, who may he be?" asked the knight.

"He is King Arthur."

Then the knight wished to slay the king for fear of his wrath afterward, and so lifted up his sword, but Merlin cast an enchantment on the knight so that he fell to the earth in a deep sleep. Merlin then took King Arthur up and rode forth with him upon the knight's horse.

"Alas!" said King Arthur. "What have you done, Merlin? Have you slain this good knight by your craft? Never lived a more worshipful knight than he. I should rather lose my land for a year than have him slain."

"Fear not," said Merlin, "for he is better off than you are, for he is only asleep and will awake in three hours. I told you what manner of knight he is. Here you would have been slain if I had not been near. No better knight lives than he. His name is Pellinore, and he shall do you right good service hereafter. His two sons will be great knights, and, save one, they shall have no equal in prowess and good living. One son shall be named Percivale of Wales and the other Lamorak of Wales. And one day they will tell you the name of your own son who shall be the destruction of this land."

Then the king and Merlin went to a hermitage where the hermit examined all of Arthur's wounds and gave him good salves. The king remained there three days until his wounds were healed and he might ride.

So Merlin and the king left, and as they rode King Arthur said, "I have no sword."

"No matter," said Merlin. "Near here is a sword that shall be yours."

So they rode until they came to a broad, fair lake. And in the midst of it Arthur saw an arm clothed in white samite, and the hand held a fair sword.

"Look," said Merlin to the king, "yonder is the sword of which I spoke."

Then they saw a damsel on the lake.

"What damsel is that?" asked the king.

"That is the Lady of the Lake," said Merlin. "In the lake there is a rock, and thereon as fair a place as any on earth. And this damsel will come to you soon. Speak pleasantly to her so that she will give you the sword."

Then the damsel came to King Arthur.

"Damsel," said the king, "what sword is that which the arm holds yonder above the water? I would it were mine, for I have no sword."

"King," said the Lady of the Lake, "that sword is mine, and if you will give me a gift when I ask it of you, you shall have the sword."

"By my faith," said King Arthur, "I will give you any gift that you will ask or desire."

"Then," said the damsel, "get into yonder barge and row toward the sword. Take the sword and the scabbard with you. I will ask you for my gift when the time comes."

So King Arthur and Merlin alighted, tied their horses to two trees, and stepped into the barge. When they came to the sword held by the hand, King Arthur seized it by the handle and took it with him. Then the arm and the hand went under the water and the two men came to the land and rode away.

Soon King Arthur saw a rich pavilion.

"Whose pavilion is that yonder?" he asked Merlin.

"That is the pavilion of the knight with whom you fought last," said Merlin. "But Sir Pellinore is not there, since he fought with a knight of yours called Eglame. They fought together a long while, but at last Eglame fled or he would have been killed. Sir Pellinore followed him even to Carlion, and we shall soon meet him on the highway."

"I am glad," said King Arthur. "Now that I have a sword I will wage battle with him and be revenged."

"Sir, do not so," said Merlin, "for the knight is weary from fighting and chasing, so that it would be no honor to fight with him. Also he will not lightly be matched with any knight living. Therefore my counsel is that you let him pass, for he will do you good service in a short time, and after, his days, his sons will be loyal to you. You will soon see the day when you will be right glad to give him your sister as wife."

"I will do as you advise me," said King Arthur.

Then Arthur examined the sword, and liked it passing well.

"Which do you like better," asked Merlin, "the sword or the scabbard?"

"I like the sword better," said King Arthur.

"You are not wise, then," said Merlin, "for the scabbard is worth ten of the sword. For as long as you have the scabbard upon you, you shall lose no blood, no matter how grievously you are wounded. Therefore keep the scabbard always with you."

So they rode to Carlion, and on the way they met Sir Pellinore. But Merlin arranged that Pellinore should not see Arthur, and so he passed by without any words.

"I marvel that the knight would not speak," said the king.

"Sir, he did not see you," said Merlin. "For if he had seen you he would not have passed you quietly."

When they came to Carlion the knights were very glad to see Arthur. And when they heard of his adventures, they marveled that their king would put himself in such jeopardy. Yet all the knights agreed that it was pleasant to serve a chieftain who would risk his life in adventure just as poor knights did.

XIII

Soon after this, a messenger came hastily from King Rience, who was king of North Wales and of all Ireland.

This was his message, his greeting to King Arthur:

"I, King Rience, have overcome eleven kings. Each of them does me this homage: he gives me his beard clean cut off, as much as there is.   Therefore my messenger is come for your beard, King Arthur."

Now King Rience had hemmed a mantle with the beards of the eleven kings, but, needing more material, had sent for the beard of King Arthur.

"And if you do not send it," said the messenger, "King Rience will invade your lands, and burn and slay, and never leave until he has your beard and your head also."

"You have given your message," said King Arthur, "the most villainous and insolent message that ever a man sent to a king.   You may see that my beard is yet too young to use for a hem, but tell your king this: I owe him no homage, nor do any of my elders.   But before long he shall do homage to me on both of his knees or lose his head, by the faith of my body!   For this is the most shameful message that ever I heard.   It is plain that King Rience has never known honorable knights. Tell him I will have his head unless he do me homage."

Then the messenger departed.

"Now is there one here who knows this King Rience?" asked King Arthur.

Then a knight called Naram answered, "Sir, I know the king well.   He is a strong man and proud.   Doubt not, sir, that he will make war on you with a great following."

"Then," said King Arthur to the knight, "I shall prepare for him."

When the messenger returned to King Rience, that king's anger was terrible and he made ready a great host, as is shown in the Book of Balin le Savage that follows here, which tells also how, by adventure, Balin got the sword.

Then King Arthur proclaimed that all the children of gentle birth born on May Day should be brought to him on pain of death, for Merlin had told King Arthur that he who should destroy him should be born on May Day. Many lords' sons were found who had been born on May Day, and all were sent to the king. And Mordred was sent by King Lot's wife. Some of these children were four weeks old and some were older, but all were put to sea in a ship.

Now is so happened that the ship drove against a castle and was destroyed, but Mordred was cast up on the shore. A good man found him and took care of him until he was fourteen years old, and then brought him to the court. The lords and barons were angry because their children had been lost. Many put the blame on Merlin more than on King Arthur, but all of them, some from dread, and from some love, held their peace.

Book the Second

SIR BALIN LE SAVAGE

When King Arthur was in London there came a knight with tidings that King Rience of North Wales had gathered a great number of people and had entered Arthur's land, burning and slaying the people.

"If this be true," said King Arthur, "great dishonor would be mine unless I resist Rience mightily."

"It is the truth," said the knight, "for I saw the host myself."

Then King Arthur proclaimed that all the lords, knights, and gentlemen of arms should come to the castle that was called Camelot, for there he would have a general council and a great joust.

So when the king had come there with all his barons, and had lodged them there, a damsel came who was a messenger from the great lady Lily of Avelion. And when she came before King Arthur she let her richly furred mantle fall, and they saw that she was girded with a noble sword.

"Damsel," he asked, "why are you girded with that sword? It is not fitting."

"I will tell you," said the damsel, "This sword with which I am girded causes me great sorrow, for none but a good knight can relieve me from it. And he must be a valorous knight, without villainy or treachery."

"Surely such a knight you can find here," said the king.

"If I can find a knight that has all these virtues, he

55

can draw this sword out of the scabbard. I have been at the court of King Rience, for I was told that there were many good knights there, but, although he and all his knights tried, none could succeed."

"That is a great marvel," said Arthur. "And if it be true, I will myself try to draw out the sword, not because I consider that I am the best knight, but so that all the other barons will try one after the other."

Then King Arthur took the sword by the scabbard and the girdle. But, although he pulled at it eagerly, the weapon would not come out.

"Sir," said the damsel, "you need not pull half so hard. For he who shall pull it out will do it with little might."

"You say truly," said the king. "And now, my barons, try, each of you. But beware if you are defiled with shame, treachery, or guile."

"It will not avail," said the damsel, "unless the knight is clean, without villainy, and of gentle blood on both father's and mother's side."

Most of the barons of the Round Table who were there at the time tried, in turn, but none could succeed. Therefore the damsel was very sorrowful and said, "Alas, I thought that in this court the best knights of the world were to be found!"

"By my faith," said King Arthur, "here are as good knights as any in the world. I am greatly displeased that they cannot help you."

Now it so happened that at that time there was a poor knight at Arthur's court who had been prisoner half a year or more because he had slain a knight who was a cousin to King Arthur. The name of this poor gentleman was Balin le Savage, and he was born in Northumberland. By the help of the barons he had been freed from prison.

When Balin went secretly into the court and saw this adventure of drawing the damsel's sword from its scabbard, he wished to try with the other knights, but because he was poor and not richly clothed he did not push forward with the other knights who were trying. However, when the damsel took her leave of King Arthur and the barons, Balin le Savage called after her and said, "Damsel, I pray you of your courtesy to allow me to try as these lords have done. Though I am poorly clothed, I think I may succeed."

The damsel looked at the poor knight and saw that he was a likely man, although of poor appearance.

"Sir," she said then to Balin, "there is no need to put me to any more pain or distress, for you could hardly succeed where others have failed."

"Ah, fair lady," said Balin, "worthiness and good graces are not shown in raiment only. Manhood and honor are within the man's heart. Besides, many a worshipful knight is not well known."

"God knows you speak the truth," said the damsel. "Therefore you may try to do what you can."

Then Balin took the sword by the girdle and scabbard, and drew it out easily. And when he looked upon the blade it pleased him well. Then the king and all the barons marveled that Balin had succeeded in the adventure. And many of the knights were angry at

Balin and said that he had been successful in this adventure, not by might, but by witchcraft.

"Truly," said the lady, "this is a good knight, and the best man that ever I have found, without treason, treachery, or villainy. He should be greatly honored and should achieve many marvels. And now, gentle and courteous knight, give me the sword again."

"No," said Sir Balin, "for I will keep this sword unless it is taken from me by force."

"Well," said the damsel, "you are not wise to keep the sword. You will slay with its blade the best friend you have, and the man you most love in the world. That sword, likewise, will be your own destruction."

"I will take the adventure," said Balin, "that God ordains for me. But the sword you shall not have now, by the faith of my body!"

"You will repent within a short time," said the damsel. "I asked for the return of the sword more for your sake than mine. It is great pity that you will not believe that the sword will be your destruction."

With those words the damsel left in great sorrow. Then Balin sent for his horse and armor and desired to take leave of the court and of King Arthur.

But the king said, "I hope you will not leave this court so soon. I believe you are displeased because I have been unkind to you. Blame me less, for I was misinformed about you. I had not thought you were a knight of such worship and prowess. If you will stay in this court with my good knights, I will so advance you that you will be well pleased."

"God thank your highness," said Balin, "but I must needs leave, beseeching your kindness always. No man may praise your grace half enough."

"Truly," said King Arthur, "I am grieved that you are leaving. I beseech you, fair knight, that you will not tarry long. You shall be right welcome to me and to all my barons when you return, and I shall make amends for all that is amiss and for all I have done against you."

"God thank your lordship," said Balin, and made ready for his travels.

While Balin was getting ready to leave, the Lady of the Lake came, richly clothed, on horseback, into the court. She saluted King Arthur and asked for the gift that he had promised her when she gave him the sword.

"That is true," said King Arthur, "a gift I promised you. But I have forgotten the name of the sword which you gave me."

"The name of it is 'Excalibur,'" said the lady, "which means 'Cut-Steel.'"

"You say truly," said King Arthur. "Ask what you will and, if it is in my power to give it, you shall have it."

"Well," said the Lady of the Lake, "I ask the head of the knight that has won the sword from the damsel, or the head of the maiden that brought it. For he slew my brother, a full good and true knight, and the gentle-woman caused my father's death."

"Truly," said King Arthur, "I may not grant you either of their heads with honor. Therefore ask what else you will, and I shall fulfill your desire."

"I will ask nothing else of you," said the lady.

Then Balin, who was ready to leave, saw the Lady of the Lake there, through whose means his own mother had been slain. He had sought this woman for three years, and when it was told him that she asked his head of King Arthur he went straight to her and said, "Evil you are! You would have my head, and therefore you shall lose yours." Then with his sword he struck off her head in the presence of King Arthur.

"Alas! for shame!" cried the king. "Why have you done this? You have shamed me and all the court, for this is a lady to whom I am much indebted, and she came hither under my safe conduct. I shall never forgive this deed."

"My lord," said Balin, "this lady was the most untrue lady living. By her enchantment and witchcraft she has destroyed many good knights, and through her falsehood and treachery she caused my mother to be burnt."

"Whatsoever cause you had," said King Arthur, "you should not have done this in my presence. Therefore you will repent it. Withdraw from my sight in all haste."

Then Balin picked up the lady's head and took it with him to his lodging place. And there he met his squire, who was sorry his master had displeased King Arthur, and together they rode out of town.

"Now," said Balin, "we must part. Take you this head and bear it to my friends and tell them how I have fared. Tell my friends in Northumberland that my greatest foe is dead, also that I am out of prison, and relate the adventure that resulted in my getting this sword."

"Alas!" said the squire, "you are greatly to blame for so displeasing King Arthur."

"As for that," said Balin, "I will go with all haste to meet Rience and destroy him or else die. And if it happen that I defeat him, then perhaps King Arthur will be my good and gracious lord."

"Where shall I meet you?" asked the squire.

"In King Arthur's court," said Balin.

So his squire and he parted.

And King Arthur and all the court mourned and were ashamed of the death of the Lady of the Lake, for whom the king made a rich burial.

II

At that time there was in King Arthur's court a knight called Lanceor who was the son of the King of Ireland. He was a proud knight, and was very angry at Balin for winning the sword, as he counted himself one of the best knights of the court.

"Will you not give me leave to ride after Balin," he asked King Arthur, "to revenge what he has done to you?"

"Do your best," said the king, "for I am angry with Balin. He should be punished for the shame he has done here."

So Lanceor went to his lodging place to make ready to leave.

In the meantime Merlin came to the court, and was told of the adventure of the sword and of the slaying of the Lady of the Lake.

"I will tell you," said Merlin, "why this damsel brought the sword into your court. She is the falsest maiden alive."

"Do not say so," they said.

And Merlin said: "She has a brother, a good knight and a true man. Now this damsel loved another most unwisely, and the good knight, her brother, met the false knight who loved her to her dishonor, and killed him. When this wicked damsel learned of it, she went to the lady Lily of Avelion and besought her help to revenge this deed on her brother. And this lady Lily of Avelion gave her that sword which she brought with her here, and told her that no man should draw it out of the scabbard unless he were of the best knights of the realm and that with that sword he would slay her brother. This was the reason she came into this court."

"I know it as well as you," said Merlin. "Would to God she had never come hither. For she never comes to do good, but always great harm. And that knight who has won the sword shall be destroyed by it. There shall be great trouble, because there is no knight living of more prowess than he, and he will do for King Arthur great kindness. It is a great pity that he will live only a little while, for, in strength and bravery, I do not know his equal."

But Lanceor, the knight of Ireland, rode after Balin as fast as his horse could run. And when he saw Balin he cried with a loud voice, "Stay, knight! For you shall stay whether you will or will not. And the shield that is before you shall not help you."

When Balin heard him, he turned his horse fiercely.

"Fair knight," he cried, "what would you do with me? Would you joust with me?"

"Yes," said the Irish knight. "To do so I have come after you."

"Perhaps," said Balin, "it had been better for you to have stayed at home. For many a man thinks he can bring defeat to his enemy, and brings it to himself instead. Of what court are you?"

"I am from the court of King Arthur," said Lanceor, "and have come hither to revenge the shame you have done this day to King Arthur and his court."

"Well," said Balin, "I see well that I must joust with you. But the lady that is dead had done great harm, or else I should have been as loath as any knight that lives to slay a lady."

"Make you ready," said the knight Lanceor, "for one of us shall stay forever on this field."

Then they took their spears and came together as fast as their horse could drive. And the son of the King of Ireland struck Balin upon his shield so that his spear broke into pieces. And Balin smote him with such force that his spear went through Lanceor's shield and pierced through his body and the horse's croup. Then Balin turned his horse fiercely and drew out his sword. He knew not that he had slain Lanceor until he saw him lying on the ground.

Then Balin saw a damsel come riding as fast as her horse could gallop. And when she saw that Sir Lanceor was slain, she sorrowed greatly and said, "O Balin, you have slain two bodies and one heart! And two hearts in one body and two souls you have lost!"

And then she took the sword from her love that lay dead, and, as she took it, she fell to the ground in a swoon. And when she arose she wept bitterly, and her sorrow made Balin grieve. He went to her to take the sword out of her hands, but suddenly she put the pommel of the sword on the ground and ran the sword through her body.

Now when Balin saw her dead he was very sorrowful that so fair a damsel had destroyed herself for the love she had for Lanceor.

"Alas!" said Balin. "I repent the death of this knight because of the love of this damsel, since there was much true love between them."

And for sorrow he could no longer look at them, but turned his horse and looked toward the forest. And there he saw the arms of his brother Balan. And when they were met they put off their helmets and kissed each other and wept for joy.

Then said Balan, "I little expected to meet you. I am very glad of your deliverance from your prison. A man in the Castle of Fourstones told me that you were delivered and that he had seen you in King Arthur's court. And therefore I came hither into this country, for here I hoped to find you."

Then Balin told his brother of all his adventures of

the sword, and of the death of the Lady of the Lake, and that King Arthur was displeased with him.

"Wherefore," he said, "it seems that he sent this knight after me that lies here dead, and the death of this damsel grieves me greatly."

"It grieves me also," said Balan, "but you must take whatever adventure God orders for you."

"Truly I am very sad," said Balin, "because my lord King Arthur is displeased with me, for he is the most worshipful knight that now reigns on earth. And his love I will get, or else I will put my life in adventure. For King Rience of North Wales is besieging the Castle Terabil, and to that place we will go in all haste to prove our worship and prowess upon him."

"I am willing," said Balan, "that we do so, and we will help each other as brothers ought to do."

While they talked, a dwarf came from the city of Camelot on horseback as fast as he could, and found the dead bodies. He showed great sorrow and plucked his hair in his grief.

"Which of you knights did this deed?" he said.

"Why do you ask?" said Balin.

"Because I wish to know," said the dwarf.

"It was I," said Balin. "I slew this knight in my own defense, for hither he came to fight with me, and either I must slay him or he me. And this damsel slew herself for his love. This makes me repent, and for her sake I shall owe all women the better love and favor."

"Alas!" said the dwarf. "You have caused great trouble for yourself. For this knight who is dead here was one of the most valiant men that ever lived. And trust well, Balin, that his kin will follow you through the world until they have slain you."

"As for that," said Balin, "I do not fear it greatly. But I am sad because I have displeased my sovereign lord King Arthur, by the death of this knight."

As they talked, there came riding by them King Mark of Cornwall. And when he saw the two dead bodies, and understood how they came to this end, King Mark showed great sorrow for the true love that they had had for each other.

"I will not leave," he said, "until I have made a tomb here for them."

And he pitched his pavilions there, and sought through all that country to find a tomb. And when he found one that was rich and fair in a church, King Mark put them in the earth, and placed the tomb over them, with their names on the stone.

This was the inscription:

"Here lieth Lanceor, son of the King of Ireland, who at his own request was slain by Balin in combat, and here lieth also his lady Colombe who slew herself with her love's sword, for grief and sorrow."

Then Merlin came to King Mark and, seeing what had occurred, said, "Here in this place shall be the greatest battle between two knights that ever was or ever will be, and the truest lovers they will be. Yet neither of them shall slay the other."

And Merlin wrote their names there upon the tomb with letters of gold. And the names of those who should fight there were Launcelot du Lake and Tristram de Lyones.

"You are a marvelous man," said King Mark to Merlin, "who can do such wonders. But you seem a boisterous fellow and an unlikely one to tell such deeds. What is your name?"

"I will not tell you at this time," said Merlin. "But when Sir Tristram shall be taken with his sovereign lady, then you will know my name. And at that time you will hear tidings which will not please you."

"You have done yourself great harm, young sir," Merlin said further, as he turned to Balin, "because you did not save this lady who slew herself. You might have saved her if you had wished to do so."

"By the faith of my body," said Balin, "I could not save her, for she slew herself suddenly."

Then said Merlin, "Because of the death of that lady, you shall strike the most unhappy stroke that ever a man struck, for you shall hurt the truest knight and the most worshipful man who now lives. And through that stroke three kingdoms will be in great poverty, misery, and wretchedness for twelve years. And the knight will not be healed of that wound in many years."

"If I knew that what you say is true," said Balin, "if I knew that I should do as dreadful a deed as that, then would I slay myself to prove you a liar."

Then Merlin suddenly vanished, and Balin and his brother took their leave of King Mark.

"But first," said the king, "tell me your name."

"Sir," said Balin, "you see he bears two swords. Therefore you may call him the Knight of the Two Swords."

So King Mark departed and rode to Camelot to King Arthur, and Balin and his brother took the way toward King Rience. As they rode they met Merlin disguised, but they did not know him.

"Where are you riding?" asked Merlin.

"We have little to do to tell you," said the two knights.

"But what is your name?" asked Balin.

"At this time," said Merlin, "I will not tell you."

"Are you a true man when you will not tell your name?" answered the two knights.

"As for that, be it as it may," said Merlin. "But I can tell you why you ride this way. It is to meet King Rience; but it will not avail you unless you have my counsel."

"Ah," said Balin, "you are Merlin. We will be ruled by your counsel."

"You will have great honor," said Merlin. "See that you be valorous, for you will have great need of bravery."

"As for that," said Balin, "do not fear. We will do what we can."

III

Then Merlin hid them in a leafy wood near the highway. He took the bridles off their horses and put them to grass; and the knights rested until it was nearly midnight.

At that time Merlin bade them arise and make ready, for King Rience was near them. Rience had stolen away from his army, with threescore of his best knights. And twenty of his men rode before him to warn the Lady de Vance that the king was coming.

"Which is the king?" asked Balin.

"Wait," said Merlin.

Thereupon he showed Balin and his brother where Rience rode. Then the two knights met the king and smote him down and wounded him grievously, so that he lay on the ground. And they killed there more than forty of the royal escort, and the rest fled. Then they went toward King Rience again and would have killed him if he had not yielded to them.

Then King Rience said, "Knights full of prowess, do not slay me. For by my life you may win something, but by my death you will win nothing."

"You speak truly," said the two knights, and so they laid him on a horse litter.

Merlin vanished then, and came to King Arthur to tell him how his greatest enemy had been defeated.

"By whom?" asked King Arthur.

"By two knights that would please your lordship," said Merlin, "and tomorrow you shall know who they are."

Soon thereafter came the Knight of the Two Swords and Balan, his brother, bringing King Rience with them They delivered their captive to the porters and went away.

King Arthur then came to King Rience and said,

"Sir king, you are welcome.   By what adventure came
you here?"

"Sir," said Rience, "I came hither by a hard adventure."

"Who won you?" asked King Arthur.

"The Knight of the Two Swords and his brother,
who are marvelous knights of prowess," said Rience.

"I do not know them," said King Arthur, "but I
am much indebted to them."

"I shall tell you," said Merlin.   "It is Balin who won
the sword, and his brother Balan, a good knight.   There
lives no better knight than Balan and there will be great
sorrow for him, for he will not live long."

"Alas!" said King Arthur.   "That is a great pity,
for I am very grateful to him, and I have never deserved
his kindness."

"No," said Merlin, "but he will do much more for
you yet, as you will know before long.   But, sir, are
you prepared?   For tomorrow Nero, brother to King
Rience, will set upon you before noon with a great host.
Make you ready, for I must leave you."

IV

Then King Arthur made ready his host, and arranged
them in ten divisions.

Now Nero was ready in the field before the Castle
Terabil, and he also had ten divisions, but many more
men than King Arthur had.   Nero himself had the vanguard with the greater part of his men.

Then Merlin came to King Lot of the Isle of Orkney

and held his attention with a tale of prophecy until Nero and his people were almost destroyed.

In that combat Sir Kaye the seneschal did great deeds so that he was honored all the days of his life. Sir Hervis de Revel did marvelous feats with King Arthur, and the king himself that day slew twenty knights and maimed forty.

When the Knight of the Two Swords came in with his brother Balan, these knights were so powerful in arms that the king and all the knights marveled. All that saw the brothers said that they were angels sent from heaven or devils from hell. King Arthur himself said they were the best knights that ever he had seen.

In the meantime some one came to King Lot and told him that while he delayed, Nero and all his people had been slain.

"Alas!" said King Lot. "I am ashamed, for through my fault many a worshipful man has been slain. If we had been together, no host under heaven would have been able to match us. This flatterer with his prophecy has tricked me."

Merlin had done this because he knew that if King Lot had been there with his army at the first battle, King Arthur and all his people would have been destroyed. Merlin knew that one of the kings would die that day, and he preferred that Lot should die rather than King Arthur.

"Now what is best to do?" said Lot. "Shall we make terms with Arthur or fight, since most of our people are slain?"

"Sir," said a knight, "set upon King Arthur, for he and his men are weary from fighting and we are fresh."

"I wish," said King Lot, "that every knight would do his part as I will do mine."

Then Lot and his men advanced their banners, but King Arthur's knights, with the aid of the Knight of the Two Swords and his brother Balan, worsted King Lot and his host. But always King Lot fought bravely in front of his men and did great deeds of arms, and all his host were cheered and strengthened while Lot stayed and withstood all combat. But he could not last forever!

It was a great pity that this knight should die. He had been one of King Arthur's knights and had wedded King Arthur's sister. But for the wrong King Arthur did him, therefore King Lot became his enemy and fought against him.

And the noble that was called the "Knight with the Strange Beast," whose real name was Pellinore, struck King Lot as he fought with his enemies. But Pellinore's stroke failed and he smote the horse's neck so that the horse fell to the ground with King Lot. Then Sir Pellinore struck Lot through the helmet and cut him to the brows. And all the host of Orkney fled when they saw that King Lot was slain.

But Pellinore bore the blame for King Lot's death, and Sir Gawaine revenged this, the death of his father, ten years after he was made a knight, and slew Pellinore with his own hands.

Twelve kings were slain at this battle—the twelve who fought on Nero's side—and all were buried in the

Church of St. Steven in Camelot. The bodies of the knights were buried in a great rock.

To the burial came King Lot's wife, with her four sons, Gawaine, Agravaine, Gaheris, and Gareth. And King Urience came also, and Morgan le Fay his wife, who was King Arthur's sister.

Arthur made the tomb of King Lot the most rich and most beautiful of all the tombs of the twelve kings that were slain on Nero's side. King Arthur had twelve images of copper made, overlaid with fine gold, in token of the twelve kings, and every image held a taper of wax which burned night and day. And King Arthur's figure was standing above them all, with a drawn sword in his hand. And the twelve figures were real likenesses of the twelve that had been overcome—all this Merlin did by his subtle craft.

Then Merlin said to King Arthur, "When I am dead the twelve tapers will burn no longer. Soon after that will come the adventure of the Holy Grail." Merlin told King Arthur also how Balin would give a sad stroke after which great vengeance would come.

"And where are Balan, Balin, and Pellinore?" asked King Arthur.

"As for Pellinore," said Merlin, "he will meet you soon, and Balin will not be long away from you. But the other brother, Balan, will leave, and you will see him no more."

"Now, by my faith," said King Arthur, "they are two marvelous knights, and Balin surpasses in valor any knight that I have ever found. I am much indebted to him. Would to God that he would stay with me!"

"Sir," said Merlin, "take good care of the scabbard of Excalibur. For, as I told you, you will lose no blood as long as you have that scabbard on you, though you should have many wounds on your body."

After this Merlin told Arthur of the prophecy that there should be a great battle near Salisbury and that Mordred, his sister's son, would fight against him, and he told him that Bagdemagus was his cousin.

Soon after, for greater safety, King Arthur took the scabbard to Morgan le Fay, his sister. But Morgan loved another knight better than her husband, King Urience, or King Arthur. Therefore she had another scabbard, very like Arthur's, made by enchantment, and she gave the true scabbard of Excalibur to her lover, a knight names Sir Accolon, who later almost killed Arthur.

V

Not very long after this battle King Arthur was ill. He pitched his pavilion in a meadow, and lay down to sleep. But he could not rest, for he heard the noise of a great horse's hoofs. When he looked out through the door of the pavilion, he saw a knight riding by, weeping sorrowfully.

"Wait, fair sir," said King Arthur, "and tell me why you grieve."

"You cannot help me," said the knight, and passed on.

Soon Balin came, and when he saw King Arthur he alighted from his horse and came to the king on foot and saluted him.

"By my head," said the sovereign, "you are welcome. Just now a knight came riding this way, crying bitterly, and I cannot tell why. Therefore I would desire you of your courtesy and gentleness to bring that knight again, either by force or by his good will."

"I would do more for your lordship than that," said Balin.

And so he rode on and found the knight with a damsel in the forest, and he said to him, "Sir knight, you must come with me to my lord King Arthur to tell him the cause of your sorrow."

"That will I not," said the doleful knight, "for it would harm me greatly and would avail him nothing."

"Sir," said Balin, "I pray you make ready, for you must needs go with me, or else I will fight with you and bring you by force. And that am I loath do to."

"Will you be my warrant," said the knight to Balin. "if I go with you quietly?"

"Yes," said Balin, "or else I will die therefor."

And so the knight made ready to go with Balin, and left the damsel there. And when they were near King Arthur's pavilion there came an invisible person and smote the knight that went with Balin through the body with a spear.

"Alas!" said the knight. "I am slain under your guidance and guard by a traitorous knight called Garlon. Therefore take my horse, which is better than yours, ride to the damsel, and follow the quest that I was in wherever she may lead you. And revenge my death when you may best do so."

"That will I do," said Balan. "And so I vow to you by my knighthood."

And so Balin, sorrowing, left the knight.

King Arthur had this knight buried richly, and upon the tomb inscribed how Herleus le Berbeus (for so was he called) was slain by the treachery of the knight Garlon.

VI

So Balin joined the damsel in the forest and together they rode forth and she carried with her the truncheon of the spear by which Sir Herleus was slain.

Presently they met a knight who had been out hunting. And that knight asked Balin why his face was so sad.

"I do not wish to tell you," said Balin.

"Now," said the knight, "if I were armed as you are, I would fight with you."

"That is not necessary," said Balin, "for I am not afraid to tell you about it."

And he told him what had happened.

"Ah," said the knight, "is that the reason for your sadness? Here I promise you by the faith of my body that I will never leave you as long as my life lasts."

And so the knight armed himself and rode forth with Balin and the damsel. And as they passed a hermitage near the churchyard the invisible knight Garlon came up and smote this good knight Perin de Mountbelgard with a spear through the body.

"Alas!" said the fallen knight. "I am slain by this traitor knight that rides invisible."

"Woe be it!" said Balin. "It is not the first shame that he has done to me."

And there the hermit and Balin buried the knight under a rich stone in a royal tomb. And on the next day they found a gold inscription there telling how Sir Gawaine should revenge the death of King Lot, his father, upon King Pellinore.

After this adventure Balin and the damsel rode until they came to a castle. There Balin alighted, and he and the damsel were going to enter the castle, but as Balin entered within the gate the portcullis fell down at his back, leaving the damsel outside. And many men came toward her, as if to slay her.

When Balin saw that he went upon the walls, leaped over into the ditch, and, unharmed, rushed toward the attacking men. He pulled out his sword and would have fought with them. But they all said that they would not, for they were only following the old custom of the castle. Then they told him how their lady had been ill for many years, and that she might not be made well unless she had a silver dish full of the blood of a maid, and a king's daughter. And therefore the custom of the castle was that none should pass that way unless she gave a silver dish full of her blood.

"Well," said Balin, "she shall bleed as much as she pleases. But I will not let her die while my life lasts."

Then the maiden gave some of her blood, but it did not help the lady. But as you will hear later, in the Holy Grail, it was Sir Percivale's sister who helped that lady with her blood.

So Balin and his charge rested there all night and had excellent entertainment. And on the morrow they passed on their way.

VII

They rode on for three or four days without meeting with any adventures. Then it happened that they were lodged at the house of a rich gentleman. Aud while they were sitting at supper Balin heard some one near by him in a chair, complaining grievously.

"What noise is that?" asked Balin.

"Forsooth," said his host, "I will tell you. At a jousting some time ago I jousted with a knight who is King Pellam's brother, and twice I smote him down. He promised then to be revenged on me through the suffering of my best friend, and so he wounded my son, who cannot be well until I have that knight's blood. This traitor knight always rides invisible, and I do not know his name."

"Ah," said Balin, "I know that knight, and his name is Garlon. He has slain two knights of mine in the same manner. I should, therefore, rather meet him than find all the gold in this realm."

"Well," said his host, "I shall tell you. King Pellam of Listenise has proclaimed through all this country a great feast that shall be held within twenty days, and no knight may come there unless he brings his wife with him, or his lady love. And that knight, your enemy and mine, you would doubtless see on that day."

"Then I promise you," said Balin, "part of his blood with which to heal your son."

"We will start tomorrow," said his host.

So on the morrow all three rode toward Listenise and traveled fifteen days before they came there. And on that same day the great feast began; so they alighted and stabled their horses and went into the castle. But Balin's host could not be admitted because he had no lady with him.

Balin, however, was well received and brought into a room, and unarmed. Robes were brought him there, and they wished him to leave his sword behind him.

"No," said Balin, "that I will not do, for it is the custom of my country for a knight to keep his weapon always with him. And I will keep that custom or depart as I came."

Then they gave him leave to wear his sword. And so he went to the castle, and was set among knights of worship, and his lady near him. Soon Balin asked a knight, "Is there not a knight in this court whose name is Garlon?"

"Yonder he goes," said Balin's companion, "he with the black face. He is the greatest knight now living, since he goes invisible and destroys many good knights."

"Ah, well," said Balin, "so that is he!"

Then Balin thought for a long time about what he should do.

"If I slay Garlon here," he thought, "I shall not escape. But if I leave him now, perhaps I shall never

meet with him again at such a good time. In that case
he will do much harm if he lives."

When this scowling Garlon saw that Balin was looking at him, he came over and smote Balin on the face
with the back of his hand. And he said, "Knight, why
do you look at me so? For shame! Eat your meat, and
do what you came for."

"You say truly," said Balin. "This is not the first
time that you have wronged me. Therefore I will do
what I came for."

And he rose up fiercely and cleaved Garlon's head
to his shoulders. Then Balin said to his lady, "Give
me the truncheon wherewith he slew your knight."

Then she gave it to him, for she carried that truncheon
with her always. And therewith Balin smote Garlon
through the body and said openly, "With that truncheon,
traitor, you killed a good knight, and now it sticks in
your own body."

Then Balin called his host of the journey and said,
"Now may you fetch blood enough to heal your son."

VIII

Then all the knights rose up from the table to attack
Balin. And King Pellam himself rose up fiercely, and
said, "Knight, why have you slain my brother? You
shall die for this."

"Then," said Balin, "slay me yourself."

"Yes," said King Pellam, "there shall no man have
to do with you but myself, for the love of my brother."

Then King Pellam caught in his hand a grim weapon

and smote at Balin eagerly. But Balin put his sword
between his head and the stroke, and the stroke burst
the sword in sunder.

And when Balin was thus made weaponless he ran into
a chamber to seek some other sword, and so from one
room to another he went, and no weapon could he find.
And always King Pellam followed him closely, but at
last Balin reached a room that was richly decorated.
There was a bed draped with the richest cloth of gold,
and some one lying there. Near by stood a table of
clear gold, with four pillars of silver to bear up the top;
and on the table stood a marvelous spear, strangely
wrought.

And when Balin saw the spear he took it in his hand,
turned to King Pellam, and smote him with that spear,
so that King Pellam fell down in a swoon. Then suddenly,
the castle walls broke and fell down to the earth. And
Balin fell down, caught so that he might not stir hand or
foot. The part of the castle that was fallen down through
that awful stroke lay upon King Pellam and Balin
three days.

IX

Then Merlin came there and took Balin up, and got
a good horse for him, for his horse was dead. And he
bade him ride out of that country.

"I would take my damsel," said Balin.

"Lo, see where she lies dead," said Merlin.

"For in that place was part of the blood of our Lord
Jesus Christ that Joseph of Arimathea brought into this

land, and he it was who lay there in that rich bed. It was with that same spear that you used, that Longius smote our Lord to the heart."

And King Pellam was nigh of Joseph's kin, and the most worshipful man that lived in those days. Great pity it was that he was hurt, for the stroke caused him pain and grief. And King Pellam lay wounded for many years, and could never be whole until Galahad the exalted prince, healed him in the quest of the Holy Grail.

Then Balin left Merlin, saying, "In this world we shall never meet more."

So he rode forth through the fair countries and cities, and found the people dead on every side. And all that were alive cried, "O Balin! You have caused great trouble in these countries. Because of the unfortunate stroke that you gave to King Pellam, three countries have been destroyed. And do not doubt but that vengeance will fall on you at last."

When Balin was beyond the boundaries of these three countries, he was passing faint. So he rode eight days before he met with any adventure. But at last he came into a fair forest in a valley, where he saw a tower. Near it was a great horse of war tied to a tree, and a fair knight sat on the ground there and mourned. He was a likely man and well made.

"God save you," said Balin. "Why are you so sad? Tell me, and I will help you if it be in my power."

"Sir knight," said the other, "you make me unhappy. For I was in merry thoughts, and now you put me in pain."

Balin walked away from the stranger and looked at his horse. Then Balin heard the man say, "Ah, fair lady, why have you broken your promise? For you promised to meet me here by noon, and I may curse you that you ever gave me this sword, for with this blade I will slay myself."

But as he pulled the weapon out, Balin went to him and took him by the hand.

"Let go my hand," said the knight, "or I will slay thee."

"There is no need," said Balin, "for I will promise you my help to get you your lady if you will tell me where she is."

"What is your name?" asked the knight.

"My name is Balin le Savage."

"And I," said the other, "am Garnish of the Mount, a poor man's son. But for my prowess and valor a duke has made me a knight and given me lands. His name is Duke Hermel, and it is his daughter that I love, and she me, as I thought."

"How far is she from here?" Balin asked.

"Only five miles," said the lover.

"Now ride we hence," said Balin.

So they rode until they came to a fair castle, well walled and ditched.

"I will go into the castle," said Balin, "and see if she be there."

So in he went and searched from one room to another. He found her chamber, but she was not there. Then Balin looked into a fair little garden. And under a laurel tree he saw her seated upon a quilt of green samite, with a knight beside her! When Balin saw the fair lady with this knight, he returned and told his companion how he had found her, and brought him to the place where the lady sat with the foul knight.

X

And when Garnish saw her there, from sorrow and anger his mouth and nose bled, and with his sword he smote off both their heads. Then he grieved much.

"O Balin," he said, "much sorrow have you brought to me. For had you not shown me that sight, I should never have known."

"Forsooth," said Balin, "I did it so that you might see and know their falsehood, and leave that lady's love. God knows I did just as I would have you do for me."

"Alas!" said Garnish. "Now must I endure double sorrow, for I have slain what I loved most in all my life."

And therewith suddenly he threw himself on his sword unto the hilt. When Balin saw that, he left quickly for fear people would say he had slain all three.

And so Balin rode forth again, and within three days he came up to a cross, with this inscription in letters of gold:

"It is not for a knight alone to ride toward this castle."

Then Balin saw a hoary old gentleman coming toward him. "Balin le Savage," he said, "you pass your bounds this way. Therefore turn back."

And the hoary man vanished. Then Balin heard a horn blow, as at the death of a beast.

"That blast," said Balin, "is blown for me. For I am the prize, and yet I am not dead, though the horn is blown over me."

And then he saw a hundred ladies and many knights, and they welcomed him, and made him good cheer, and led him into the castle. And there was dancing and minstrelsy and all manner of joy.

Then said the chief lady of the castle, "Knight of the Two Swords, you must joust with a knight that keeps an island near by. For no man may pass this way without jousting before he passes."

"That is a strange custom," said Balin, "that a knight may not pass this way unless he joust."

"You shall have to joust with but one knight," said the lady.

"Well," said Balin, "since I must, I am ready. But men who travel are often weary, and their horses also. But, though my horse is weary, my heart is not weary and I would fain be where my death is to occur."

"Sir," said a knight to Balin, "I think your shield is not good. I will lend you a bigger; give me that, I pray you."

So Balin took the shield offered him, and left his own. He rode unto the island and went with his horse into a great boat. And when he came to the other side he met a damsel.

"O knight Balin," she said, "why have you left your own shield? Alas, you have put yourself in great danger, for by your shield you should have been known. It is great pity, since as a knight of prowess and hardiness you have no equal living."

"I am sorry," said Balin, "that I ever came into this country. But I may not turn back now for shame. I will take the adventure that shall come to me, be it life or death."

And then he examined his armor and saw that he was well armed. Then he blessed himself and mounted his horse.

XI

Then before him he saw a knight in red come riding out of a castle on a horse with red trappings.

And when this knight in red beheld the stranger knight he thought it should be Balin because of the two swords. But because the shield was not like Balin's, the red knight decided that it could not be Balin.

Then both knights couched their spears and came together so marvelously fast that, after they struck each other, they both lay on the ground in a swoon. But Balin was badly bruised by the fall from his horse, because he was weary when he began.

Then the knight in red rose on foot, drew his sword, and advanced toward Balin. Balin arose, also, and went against the other. But the red knight struck the Knight of the Two Swords first, smote through his shield, and broke his helm. Then Balin smote the red knight with his fatal sword, and almost killed him, and they fought there together until breath failed them.

Then Balin looked up to the castle and saw the towers full of ladies. So they began fighting again and wounded each other grievously. They rested often, but returned to the fight so that all the place there where they fought was red with blood. Each of them had at least seven great wounds, the least of which might have caused the death of a great warrior.

At last the red knight withdrew a little and lay down.

Then said Balin le Savage, "Who are you, knight? For until now I have never found a knight that could match me."

"My name is Balan," said the red knight faintly, "brother of the noble Balin."

"Alas!" said the other. "That I should ever see this day!" And he fell backward in a swoon.

Then Balan crawled on his feet and hands to the other, and took off his helm, but he could not recognize the face because it was so cut and torn.

Soon the fainting one awoke.

"O Balan, my brother," he said, "you have slain me and I you!"

"Alas!" said Balan. "That I should ever see this day! That by accident I should not know you! For I noticed your two swords, but because you carried another shield I thought I did not know you."

Then Balin said, "An evil knight in the castle is to blame, for he made me leave my own shield there, to the destruction of both of us. If I could but live, I would destroy the castle for its evil customs."

"It would be right," said Balan, "for they have not

allowed me to leave since I came. I slew the knight that kept this island, and since then they have not let me depart. Nor would they allow you to leave, brother, even if you had escaped with your life after combat with me."

Then the lady of the tower came to them with four knights and six ladies and six yeomen. And there she heard them mourning, "We were both born of one mother, and so shall we both lie in one pit of darkness."

For his true service then Balan asked the lady, of her gentleness, that she would bury them both in that place where the battle had been fought. She granted the request and, weeping, promised that their burial should be magnificent and with great honors.

"Now will you send for a priest," said they, "that we may receive the sacrament and blessed body of our Lord Jesus?"

"Yes," said the lady, "it shall be done."

And so she sent straight for a priest, who gave them the rites.

"Now," said Balin, "when we are buried in one tomb, and the inscription over us tells how two brothers unknowingly killed each other, every good knight and good man who sees our tomb will pray for our souls."

And all the ladies and gentlewomen there wept in sympathy for them.

Balan died very soon, but Balin lived until midnight. Then both were buried, and the lady had an inscription made, telling how Balan was slain there by the hands of his own brother. But she did not know Balin's

name, and hence, on the next day, Merlin came and
wrote Balin's name also upon the tomb with letters
of gold:

"Here lies Balin le Savage, the Knight of the Two
Swords, who smote the dolorous stroke."

Merlin had a bed made there, also, which made a
man lose his wits if he should lie in it. But Launcelot
du Lake afterward changed the curse of this bed by his
noble deeds.

And Merlin took Balin's doomed sword and put
another pommel on it. Then Merlin asked a knight who
stood near him to take the sword. The knight tried,
but could not handle it. Then Merlin laughed.

"Why do you laugh?" asked the knight.

"Because," said Merlin, "no man shall ever handle
this blade unless he is the best knight in the world. And
that man shall be either Launcelot or Galahad, his son.
Launcelot with this sword will kill the man whom he
loves best in this world, Sir Gawaine."

And all this he had them write on the pommel of
the sword.

Then Merlin had a bridge of iron and steel only half
a foot broad made to that island.

"No man shall ever pass that bridge," he said, "or
have the courage to go over, unless he is a brave and
good knight without treachery or villainy."

The scabbard of Balin's sword Merlin left on one
side of the island so that Galahad should find it, but the
sword, Merlin, by his subtlety and craft, fixed in a
marble stone as large as a millstone. There the blade

stood upright, and the stone floated above the water for many years. And so, by chance, it floated down the stream to the city of Camelot one day.

On that same day Galahad, the haughty prince, came with King Arthur. And Galahad brought with him the scabbard, and took the sword that was in the marble stone floating upon the water. On Whitsunday he won the sword, as is told in the book of the Holy Grail.

Very soon after all this was done at Balin's tomb Merlin came to King Arthur and told him of the sad stroke that Balin had given to King Pellam, how Balin and Balan had fought together the most wonderful combat that ever was heard of, and how they were buried in one tomb.

"Alas," said King Arthur, "this is the greatest pity that ever I heard of! In the whole world I do not know two such knights as they were."

Thus ends the tale of Balin and Balan, the two brother knights born in Northumberland.

Book the Third

THE ROUND TABLE AND THE
THREE QUESTS

I

For many years after King Arthur had been chosen king, most of the barons did not know that he was Uther Pendragon's son, except as Merlin made it known.

Arthur, during most of his reign, was greatly influenced by Merlin's counsel.

It happened one day that King Arthur said to Merlin, "My barons will let me have no rest, but insist that I take a wife. I will choose none except by your advice."

"It is well," said Merlin, "that you take a wife, since a man of your bounty and nobleness should not be without one. Now is there any fair lady that you love better than another?"

"Yes," said King Arthur, "I love Guenever, daughter of King Leodegraunce, of the land of Cameliard. This Leodegraunce has in his house the Round Table that you told me he had received from my father, Uther. The damsel is the most gentle and the fairest lady that I have ever known, or that I could ever find."

"Sir," said Merlin, "she is surely one of the fairest alive. But if you did not love her so well, I would find you a damsel of beauty and of goodness who would love you and who should please you. But when a man's heart is turned toward a woman, he is loath to change."

"That is true," asid King Arthur.

But Merlin warned the king secretly that Guenever was not the best wife for him; that she would love some one else later.

But since Arthur was determined to wed Guenever, Merlin asked the king for a number of men to go with him to inquire about her; and the king gave him men. And Merlin went to King Leodegraunce of Cameliard and told him of the desire of King Arthur to marry Guenever, his daughter.

Said King Leodegraunce, "That is the best news I have ever heard, that so worthy and noble a king would wed my daughter. If he wished my lands, I would give him them to please him. But he has lands enough, and needs none. I will send him a gift, however, that shall please him much more. For I will give him the Round Table, which Uther Pendragon gave me. And when it is filled completely there are one hundred and fifty knights. I have a hundred good knights myself, but I lack fifty, since so many have been killed in my time."

And so Leodegraunce gave his daughter Guenever to Merlin to take to King Arthur, and also the Round Table with the hundred knights. Then they rode with great magnificence, by water and by land, until they came nigh unto London.

When King Arthur heard of the coming of Guenever and the hundred knights of the Round Table, he was very joyful.

"This fair lady is welcome to me," he said to all, "for I have loved her a long time and there is nothing so pleasing to me. And the gift of these knights, with the Round Table, pleases me more than great riches."

Then in all haste the king arranged for the marriage and coronation to be performed with the most luxurious and richest ceremonies.

"Now, Merlin," said King Arthur, "go and find for me in all this land fifty knights that are of the greatest valor and honor."

Merlin did the best he could do within a short time, and found twenty-eight good knights, but no more could he find. Then the Archbishop of Caterbury was sent for, and he blessed the new knights of Arthur's Round Table.

And when this was done Merlin said, "Fair sirs, you must all arise and come unto King Arthur to do him homage."

Then they arose and did their homage.

Afterward young Gawaine came and asked a boon from the king.

"Ask," said Arthur, "and I will grant you."

"Sir, I ask that you will make me knight on the day that you shall wed the fair Guenever."

"I will do it with a good will," said King Arthur, "and give you all the honor that I can. For you are my nephew and my sister's son."

II

Thereafter a poor man came into the court, bringing with him a fair young man, eighteen years of age, who

rode upon a lean mare.   This poor man asked all the
men that he met where he might find King Arthur.

"Yonder he is," said the knights.   "Do you wish
to ask anything of him?"

"Yes," said the poor man, "for that I came here."

Then, as he came before the king, he saluted him and
said, "O King Arthur, flower of all knights and kings, I
beseech Jesus save thee.   Sir, it was told me that at this
time of your marriage you would give any man the gift
he would ask, unless it were unreasonable."

"That is the truth," said the king.   "I made such a
proclamation and I will keep that promise unless it
injure my realm."

"You are gracious," said the poor man.   "Sir, I ask
nothing else save that you will make my son here a
knight."

"It is a great thing that you ask of me," said the
king.   "What is your name?"

"Sir," said the poor man, "my name is Aries, the
cowherd."

"Is this wish yours or your son's?" the king asked.

"This is my son's desire and not mine," said Aries.
"I will tell you, I have thirteen sons, and all of them are
right glad to do whatever labor I ask of them.   But
this child will not work for me.   No matter what either
my wife or I may do, he will always be shooting or casting
darts and anxious to see battles and to behold knights.
And always he asks day and night that he be made a
knight."

"What is your name?" said the king to the young man.

"Sir, my name is Tor."

The king looked at him, and saw he was well made for his years.

"Well," said King Arthur to Aries the cowherd, "bring all thy sons before me that I may see them."

And so the poor man did, and all were very much like their father. But Tor did not resemble them either in shape or in countenance.

"Now," said King Arthur unto Aries the cowherd, "where is the sword with which he shall be made a knight?"

"It is here," said Tor.

"Take it out of the sheath," said the king, "and request me to make you a knight."

Then Tor alighted from the mare, and, pulling out his sword, kneeled and asked the king that he would make him a knight of the Round Table.

"A knight I will make you," and therewith Arthur smote him on the shoulder with the sword, saying, "Be you a good knight; and so I pray to God you may be. And if you be of valor and of worth, you shall be a knight of the Round Table."

"Now, Merlin," said King Arthur, "say whether this Tor shall be a good knight or no."

"Yes, my lord," said Merlin, "he ought to be a good knight, for he is come of as good lineage as any man alive, and of king's blood."

"How so, sir?" asked the king.

"I shall tell you," said Merlin. "This poor man, Aries the cowherd, is not the boy's father. You saw that he is not at all like him. King Pellinore is his father."

"No," said the cowherd.

"Bring your wife before me," said Merlin, "and she will not say no."

Soon the wife was brought. She was a fair housewife, and she answered Merlin directly. She told the king and Merlin that when she was a maid and went to milking, "A stern knight met me, and he would fain have me to be his wife though not his lady. The child Tor was born to us. This stern knight took from me my greyhound that I had at that time, and said that he would keep the greyhound for the love that I had given him."

"Ah," said the cowherd, "I did not know this. But I may believe it easily, for the boy never showed any likeness to me."

"Sir," said Tor to Merlin, "speak not dishonor of my mother."

"Sir," said Merlin, "it is more for your worship than hurt, for your real father is a good man and a king. He may right well advance you and your mother, for you were born before your mother was married to Aries."

"That is true," said the wife.

"It is the less grief to me," said the cowherd to his stepson.

So on the morrow King Pellinore came to the court of King Arthur, who told him of Tor; how the boy was his son, and how he had made the lad a knight at the request of the cowherd. When Pellinore looked at Tor, he was much pleased.

Then the king made Gawaine knight, but Tor was the first knight that he had made at the feast.

"Why," King Arthur asked, "are two places vacant at the Round Table?"

"Sir," said Merlin, "no man shall sit in those places unless he is of the greatest worship. But in the Seat Perilous no man shall sit save one. And if any man be so rash as to do so he shall be destroyed. He that shall sit there shall have no equal."

Then Merlin took King Pellinore by the hand and led him to the seat of honor.

"This is your place," said he, "and you are the most worthy to sit here of any knight present."

This made Sir Gawaine very envious, and he said to Gaheris, his brother, "Yonder knight is greatly honored, and the fact grieves me greatly, because he killed our father, King Lot. Therefore I will slay him with a sword that was sent me, which is passing keen."

"Do not so now," said Gaheris. "For now I am but a squire, but when I am made knight I, too, will be revenged on Pellinore. Therefore, brother, it is best that you wait until another time, when we have him out of the court. For if we killed him now, this high feast would be spoiled."

"I will do," said Sir Gawaine, "as you wish."

III

Then was the great feast prepared, and the king was wedded with great solemnity to Guenever in the Church of Saint Stevens at Camelot. And when every man was

seated according to his degree, Merlin went unto all the
knights of the Round Table, and bade them sit still,
saying that none should leave.

"For you shall see a marvelous adventure," said he.

Then, as they sat there, a white hart ran into the hall,
and a white brachet or hound after him, with thirty
couple of black running hounds. And the hart ran about
the Round Table. As he went by the other tables the
white brachet caught him by the flank and pulled out a
piece of his flesh. Immediately the hart leaped and
overthrew a knight that sat by the table. Then the
knight arose, took up the brachet, and left the hall, and
rode away on his horse.

Right afterward a lady came in on a white palfrey,
and cried aloud to King Arthur, "Sir, do not allow this
outrage to me, for the brachet that the knight took away
was mine."

"I will have nothing to do with the matter," said
the king.

Then a knight came riding all armed, on a great
horse, and took the lady with him by force. And she
cried and moaned. When she was gone the king was
glad, because she had made such a disturbance.

"No," said Merlin, "you cannot allow these adventures to pass at your feast unrevenged."

"I am willing," said the king, "to follow your advice."

"Then," said Merlin, "call Sir Gawaine, for he must
bring the white hart again. Also, sir, you must call
Sir Tor, for he must bring again the brachet and the
knight, or else slay him. King Pellinore must bring the

lady again, and the stranger knight that carried her away. These three knights shall do marvelous adventures before they return."

Then all three were called, and each of them took his charge.

IV

Sir Gawaine rode at a fast pace, and Gaheris his brother rode with him as a squire.

As they rode they saw two knights fighting desperately on horseback. Sir Gawaine and his brother rode between them and asked them why they fought.

One knight answered, "We fight for a simple matter, for we are two brothers."

"Alas!" said Sir Gawaine. "Why do you fight then?"

"Sir," said the elder, "a white hart came this way today, with many hounds chasing him. A white brachet was always near him, and we understood that it was an adventure made for the high feast of King Arthur. I wanted to go after it to win honor, but my younger brother said he would go after the hart, for he was a better knight than I. For this cause we quarreled, and fought to prove which of us was the better knight."

"This is a simple case," said Sir Gawaine. "Strangers you should contest with, and not brother with brother. If, therefore, you will follow my counsel, you will yield to me, and then go to King Arthur."

"Sir knight," said the two brothers, "we have fought long and lost much blood. Therefore we would be loath to fight with you."

"Then do as I tell you," said Sir Gawaine.

"We will agree to fulfill your wishes, but by whom shall we say we have been sent there?"

"Say by the knight who follows the quest of the white hart," said Sir Gawaine. "But what are your names?"

"Sorlouse of the Forest," said the elder.

"And my name," said the younger, "is Brian of the Forest."

Then they left and went to the king's court, while Sir Gawaine pursued his quest. And as Sir Gawaine followed the hart by the cry of the hounds, he came to a great river which the hart swam over. When the knight would have followed after, another knight stood on the other side and said, "Do not follow the hart unless you will joust with me."

"As for that," said Sir Gawaine, "I will not fail to follow my quest."

And so he made his horse swim over the water. Then the knights took their spears and ran together full hard. But Gawaine smote the knight off his horse and bade the fellow yield.

"No," said the knight, "not so, though you have the better of me on horseback. I pray you, valiant knight, alight on foot and let us match swords together."

"What is your name?" said Sir Gawaine.

"Allardin of the Isles," said the other.

Then both dressed their shields and smote together, but Sir Gawaine smote him through the helmet so hard that the knight fell down dead.

"Ah," said Gaheris, "that was a mighty stroke for a young knight."

Then Sir Gawaine and Gaheris rode after the white hart again and let slip at the hart three couples of greyhounds, who chased the hart into a castle and in the chief place of the castle slew the hart that Sir Gawaine and Gaheris followed after.

Then a knight came out of a room, with a sword in his hand, and slew two of the hounds in the sight of Sir Gawaine and chased the others out of the castle with his sword. And when he came again to the castle, he said, "O my white hart! I am grieved that you are dead, for my sovereign lady gave you to me. Your death shall cost dear if I live."

He went into his room and armed, and then came out fiercely, and met Sir Gawaine.

"Why have you slain my hounds?" cried Sir Gawaine. "They followed only their nature. I should prefer that you took out your anger on me rather than on the dumb beasts."

"You speak truly," said the knight. "I have been revenged on your hounds, and now I will settle with you before you go."

Then Sir Gawaine alighted and dressed his shield. And they struck fiercely and broke their shields and their hauberks so that the blood ran down to their feet. At last Sir Gawaine hit the knight so hard that he fell to the earth and cried for mercy and yielded to Gawaine. He prayed him, as he was a knight and a gentleman, to save his life.

"You shall die," said Sir Gawaine, "for the slaying of my hounds."

"I will make all the amends in my power," said the knight.

But Sir Gawaine would have no mercy, and unlaced the knight's helmet to strike off his head. Then the knight's lady came out of her room and fell over him so that Gawaine struck off her head by mistake.

"Alas!" said Gaheris. "That is shamefully done, and the disgrace will never leave you. You should give mercy unto those that ask for it, for a knight without mercy is without honor."

Sir Gawaine was so greatly astonished at the death of this fair lady that he knew not what he was doing. And he said to the knight, "Arise, I will give you mercy."

"No," said the knight, "I do not want your mercy now, for you have killed my love and my lady, whom I loved best of earthly things."

"Greatly am I grieved," said Sir Gawaine, "for I thought I was striking at you. But you must go to King Arthur, and tell him of your adventures, and how you were overcome by the knight that went in the quest of the white hart."

Then the knight swore to go to King Arthur. And Gawaine made him bear one dead greyhound before him on his horse and the other behind him.

"Before we part, tell me your name," said Gawaine.

"My name is Ablamore of the Marsh," said the knight. He then went toward Camelot.

V

And Sir Gawaine went into the castle and, preparing to stay there all night, began unarming.

"What are you doing?" said Gaheris. "Will you unarm in this country? Remember that you have many enemies around here."

At that moment four well-armed knights came in and assailed Sir Gawaine hard.

"New-made knight," they said, "you have shamed your knighthood, for a knight without mercy is dishonored. Also you have slain a fair lady, and that will be a great shame to you forevermore. Doubt not but that you shall have great need of mercy before you leave us."

Therewith one of them struck Sir Gawaine such a blow that he almost fell to the ground, and Gaheris smote him in return. Sir Gawaine and Gaheris were in great danger of their lives then. One of the four knights, an archer, with a bow smote Sir Gawaine through the arm so that the wound pained him greatly.

Both would have been slain, but that four ladies came and besought grace for Sir Gawaine. And at the request of the ladies the knights gave Sir Gawaine and Gaheris their lives, but made them yield to them as their prisoners. Then Sir Gawaine and Gaheris were very sorrowful.

"Alas!" said Sir Gawaine. "My arm pains me greatly;" and he complained piteously.

Early on the morrow one of the four ladies, who had

heard his groans, came to him secretly and asked, "Sir knight, what cheer?"

"None," said he.

"It is your own fault," said the lady, "for you have done a foul deed in slaying the lady. But are you not of King Arthur's kin?"

"Yes, truly," said Sir Gawaine.

"What is your name?" the lady asked. "You must tell me before you leave."

"My name is Gawaine, son of King Lot of Orkney, and my mother is King Arthur's sister."

"Ah, then you are a nephew of King Arthur," said the lady, "and I shall so speak for you that for his love you shall have leave to go to King Arthur."

And so she left and told the four knights that their prisoner was King Arthur's nephew, and that his name was Gawaine, King Lot's son, of Orkney.

One knight gave Gawaine the head of the white hart, because it was in his quest. Then they released Sir Gawaine under his promise that he should bear the dead lady with him, with her body hanging about his mane of his charger. And in this fashion he rode forth toward Camelot.

When Gawaine came into the court, Merlin requested King Arthur to have Gawaine sworn to tell all his adventures, and Gawaine told how he would give no mercy to the knight, and that because of this the lady was villainously slain.

Then the king and the queen were greatly displeased with Sir Gawaine for the slaying of the lady. And, by the insistence of Queen Guenever, Sir Gawaine was commanded to serve ladies the rest of his life and to fight their battles only. He was commanded to be ever courteous and never to refuse mercy to one that asked it.

Sir Gawaine was thus sworn never to be against ladies or gentlewomen, unless he fought for one lady, and his adversary for another. Thus ended the adventure of Sir Gawaine at the time of the marriage of King Arthur.

VI

When Sir Tor was ready, and mounted on horseback, he rode a long way after the knight with the white hound. Then suddenly he met with a dwarf, who smote his horse on the head with a staff, so that the horse went backward for more than a spear's length.

"Why smite you my horse?" asked Sir Tor.

"So that you will not pass this way," said the dwarf, "unless you first joust with the knights who await in yonder pavilions."

Then Sir Tor saw two pavilions with great spears, and two shields hung on trees near the pavilions.

"I may not delay," said Sir Tor, "for I am on a quest which I must follow."

"You shall not pass," said the dwarf, and blew his horn.

Then an armed knight came forth on horseback, riding fast toward Sir Tor. And both ran together hard, but Sir Tor bore the stranger from his horse, and the knight yielded to Tor's mercy.

"But, sir," he said, "I have a fellow in yonder pavilion that you must fight."

"He shall be welcome," said Sir Tor.

Then he saw another knight coming with great speed. A marvel it was, to see how the knight smote Sir Tor a great stroke in the midst of the shield, until his spear was shivered into pieces, and Sir Tor struck through the shield of the knight so that the spear went through his side but did not kill him.

Then Sir Tor alighted and struck him upon the helm, after which the knight besought him for mercy.

"I am willing to grant mercy," said Sir Tor, "but you and the other knight must go to King Arthur and yield as prisoners to him."

"By whom shall we say that we are sent there?" they asked.

"You shall say by the knight that followed the brachet. Now who are you?" asked Sir Tor.

"My name is Sir Felot of Langdoc," said the one.

"And mine is Sir Petipace of Winchelsea," said the other.

"Now go forth," said Sir Tor. "God speed you and me."

Then came the dwarf to Sir Tor. "I pray you to give me a gift," said he.

"I am willing," said Sir Tor.

"I ask no more," said the dwarf, "than that you will allow me to serve you. For I will serve no more cowardly knights."

"Then take a horse," said Sir Tor, "and ride with

me.   We ride after the knight with the white brachet."

"I can take you where he is," said the dwarf.

And so they rode through the forest until at last they saw two pavilions, with two shields, one white and the other red.

Sir Tor alighted with his spear, and with the dwarf came to the white pavilion, where he saw three damsels sleeping.

And then he went to the other pavilion, in which he found another fair lady sleeping.   And there was the white brachet baying at her.   Thereupon the lady awoke and went out of the pavilion with all her damsels.   But when Sir Tor saw the white brachet he took it by force and gave it to the dwarf.

"What are you doing?" asked the lady.   "Are you taking my brachet from me?"

"Yes," said Sir Tor.   "I have followed this brachet from King Arthur's court to this place."

"Well, sir knight," said the lady, "you will not go far with it before you will be encountered and have to fight for it."

"I shall await," said Sir Tor, "whatsoever adventure comes by the grace of God."

Then he mounted his horse and started on his way to Camelot, but it was so near night that he could go but little farther.

"Do you know of any lodging near by?" asked Sir Tor.

"I know of none near here except a hermitage," said the dwarf, "and you must take such lodging there as you find."

In a short while they came to the hermitage. There was bread there, and grass and oats for the horses. Very meager was their supper, but they rested all night. In the morning they heard a mass devoutly, and took their leave of the hermit. Sir Tor asked the hermit to pray for him, and he said that he would.

Thereupon Sir Tor mounted on horseback and rode toward Camelot for a long while. Then they heard a knight coming after them, crying loudly, "Knight, wait and give back my brachet that you took from my lady!"

Sir Tor turned and saw a knight, well horsed and well armed. Then Sir Tor dressed his shield and took his spear in his hand, and the other came upon him so fiercely that both men and horses fell to the earth.

Then they arose and drew their swords as eagerly as two lions. They smote through their shields so that pieces of them fell off, and they broke their helms and the thick mails of their hauberks so that their blood ran out. They both had many great wounds and were very weary.

But when Sir Tor saw that the other knight was fainting, he doubled his strokes so that the knight fell to the ground. Then Sir Tor made him yield.

"That will I not," said Abellius, "while my life lasts, unless you will give me the brachet."

"That will I not do," said Sir Tor, "for it was my quest to bring the brachet and you again to King Arthur's court, or kill you."

Then a damsel came riding upon a palfrey as fast as she could, and she cried with a loud voice unto Sir Tor.

"What do you want with me?" asked Sir Tor.

"I beseech you," said the damsel, "for King Arthur's love, grant me my request. I require it, gentle knight, as you are a gentleman."

"Now," said Sir Tor, "ask and I will give it."

"Gramercy," said the damsel, "I ask the head of this false knight Abellius, for he is the most outrageous knight alive, and the greatest murderer."

"I am very sorry," said Tor, "that I promised to grant your request. Let him make amends to you for any way in which he has grieved you."

"He cannot make amends," said the damsel, "for he has slain my own brother, who was a better knight than he. And he had no mercy upon him though I kneeled half an hour before him in the mire, begging him to save the life of my brother, who had done him no harm, but fought with him by adventure of arms as knights do. Yet, for all that I could do or say, he struck off my brother's head. Therefore I require you, as you are a true knight, to give me my gift, or else I shall shame you in the court of King Arthur; for Abellius is the falsest knight living, and a great destroyer of good knights."

When Abellius heard this, he was sore afraid and yielded himself up, and asked for mercy.

"I may not give you mercy now," said Sir Tor, "or I should not be keeping my promise. When I offered you mercy, you did not want it unless you could have the brachet that was my quest."

Thereupon Tor took off the helm of Abellius, but the knight arose and fled. Then Sir Tor sped after him and struck off his head.

"Now, sir," said the damsel, "it is almost night. I pray you come and lodge with me at my castle, close by."

"I am willing," said Sir Tor, for his horse and he had fared poorly since they had left Camelot. And so he rode with her and enjoyed her hospitality. The old knight who was her husband welcomed Sir Tor, and both the knight and his horse fared well. On the morrow Tor heard mass, and then took his leave of the knight and of the lady, who asked him to tell them his name.

"Truly," said he, "I am Sir Tor who was lately made knight. And this was my first quest of arms,— that I should bring again that brachet which the knight Abellius took away from King Arthur's court."

"O knight," said both the lady and her husband, "if you come again near here, come to our lodging, for it shall always be at your disposal."

Sir Tor left them, and came to Camelot on the third day by noon. And the king, and the queen, and all the court rejoiced to see him, and showed great joy that he was back again, for he had left the court with little save an old horse that his father, King Pellinore, had given him, and the armor and sword that were King Arthur's gift.

Then Merlin requested that the king and the queen have him tell of his adventures. When he had told his deeds they were well pleased.

"But," Merlin said, "these are slight deeds compared to what he shall do in the future. He shall prove to be a noble knight as valorous as any living, gentle and courteous, and true to his promises."

Thereupon King Arthur made Tor an earl and gave him vast lands.

VII

When King Pellinore had mounted his horse, he rode after the lady that the knight led away.   And as he rode in the forest he saw a damsel sitting in a valley by the side of a well, with a wounded knight in her arms.   Sir Pellinore hailed her.   And when she saw him she cried out, "Help me, knight, for Christ's sake!"

But King Pellinore would not tarry, so eager was he in his quest, though she cried more than a hundred times for help.

When the lady saw that Pellinore would not delay, she prayed to God to send the coward knight as little help as he had given, so that he might repent before he died.

And when the knight that lay there wounded died, the lady in sorrow killed herself with her love's sword.

Then as King Pellinore rode in that valley he met a poor laboring man.

"Did you see a knight riding by leading away a lady?" asked King Pellinore.

"Yes," said the poor man.   "I saw that knight, and the lady sorrowing greatly.   Yonder you will see two pavilions.   One of the knights of the pavilions challenged that knight because of the lady, and said that because she was his near cousin the other knight should lead her no farther.   The one said he would have the damsel by force, but the other said he would take care of her, since he was her kinsman, and would lead her to friends. In this quarrel I left them fighting," said the poor man, "and if you ride swiftly you will find them still fighting. The lady is in the keeping of the squires in the pavilions."

"May God reward you," said King Pellinore.

Then he rode at a gallop until he saw the two pavilions and the two knights still fighting. When he approached them, he saw the lady that was his quest.

"Fair lady," said Pellinore, "you must come with me to King Arthur's court."

"Sir knight," said the squires that were with her, "yonder are knights who are fighting for this lady. Go you and part them, and be agreed with them, so that you may have her at your own pleasure."

"You say well," said King Pellinore.

Then he rode between the fighting knights and asked why they quarreled.

"Sir knight," said the one, "I shall tell you. This lady is my near kinswoman, my aunt's daughter. And when I heard her complain that she was with that caitiff against her will, I fought with him."

"Sir knight," said the other, whose name was Ontzlake of Wentland, "this lady I got by my prowess of arms this day at King Arthur's court."

"That is untrue," said King Pellinore, "for you came in there suddenly, as we were all at the high feast, and took away this lady before any man could stop you. Therefore I was bidden to bring her again, and you also, unless one of us dies in the field. The lady must go with me to King Arthur, or I shall die for it, since I have promised this to my sovereign. Therefore fight no more for her, since neither of you shall have her at this time. And if you wish to battle for her, then fight with me, and I will defend her,"

"Well," said the knight, "make you ready, and we will fight you with all our power."

As King Pellinore began to alight Sir Ontzlake ran his horse through with his sword and said, "Now you are on foot as well as we."

And when King Pellinore saw that his horse was slain he was wroth. Fiercely and lightly he leaped from his horse, and in great haste drew out his sword and put his shield afore him.

"Knight, keep your head well," he said. "For you shall have a buffet for the slaying of my horse."

Then King Pellinore gave him such a stroke upon the helm that he cut the head down to the chin, and the man fell to the earth dead.

When Pellinore turned to the other knight, who was wounded, this fellow, who had seen the buffet that the other had, would not fight, but knelt down.

"Take my cousin, the lady, with you at your request," he said, "and I require you, as you are a true knight, put her to no shame or villainy."

"What!" cried King Pellinore. "Will you not fight for her?"

"No, sir," said the knight. "I will not fight with a knight of such valor as you are."

"Well," said King Pellinore, "you say well. For I promise you she shall have no villainy by me, as I am a true knight. But now, as I have no horse, I must take this steed of Ontzlake's."

"You do not need to do so," said the knight, "for I will give you a horse that will please you if you will lodge with me, for it is near night."

Said King Pellinore, "I am willing to abide with you all night."

And there Pellinore had right good cheer and fared on the best with good wine and pleasant entertainment. On the morrow after he had heard a mass and dined, a fair bay courser was brought to him, and his own saddle set upon him.

"Now what is your name?" asked the knight. "I would know, inasmuch as you have my cousin with you."

"Sir, I shall tell you. My name is Pellinore, king of the Isles and knight of the Round Table."

"Now I am glad," said the knight, "that such a noble man as you shall have the care of my cousin."

"What is your name?" asked King Pellinore.

"Sir," said the other, "my name is Sir Meliot of Logurs, and this lady, my cousin, is called Nimue. And the knight that is in that other pavilion is my sworn brother, Brian of the Isles. He is very loath to do any wrong, or to fight with any knight, unless he is sought so he would be shamed if he did not fight."

"It is strange," said King Pellinore, "that he will not fight with me."

"Sir, he will not fight unless requested to do so."

"Bring him one of these days to the court of King Arthur," said King Pellinore.

"Sir, we will come together."

"You will be greatly welcome there," said Pellinore.

Then Pellinore left with the lady, and brought her to Camelot. As they rode in a valley that was full of stones the lady's horse stumbled and threw her down. Her arm was so bruised that she almost swooned with the pain.

"Alas, sir," said the lady, "my arm is out of joint, and I must rest."

"Very well," said Pellinore.

And so he alighted under a fair tree where there was fair grass for his horse. Here he lay down and slept until it was night. And when he awoke he wanted to ride.

"Sir," said the lady, "it is so dark that you may as well ride backward as forward."

So they stayed there and made their lodging. Then Pellinore took off his armor, but a little before midnight they heard the trotting of a horse.

"Be still," said King Pellinore, "for we may hear of some adventure."

Then he armed again.

XIV

There before him, two knights met in the blackness. One came from Camelot, and the other from the North. They saluted each other.

"What news from Camelot?" asked the one.

"By my head," said the other, "I have been spying at the court of King Arthur, and almost all the world holds with King Arthur. There surely is the flower of chivalry. I am riding into the North now to tell our chieftains of the number of knights who owe allegiance to King Arthur."

"As for that," said the other knight, "I have brought with me the greatest poison that ever was concocted. And I shall go to Camelot with it. There we have a well cherished friend near King Arthur, who shall poison him—so has he promised our chieftains and has received great gifts to do it."

"Beware of Merlin," said the other knight, "for that magician knows all things by his devil's craft."

And the two traitors parted.

Then King Pellinore and the lady made ready and rode toward Camelot. And as they came near the well where the wounded knight and the lady were, Pellinore saw that all save the two heads of the bodies had been eaten by wild beasts. Then Pellinore mourned and wept, saying, "Alas, her life I might have saved! But I was so fierce in my quest that I would not stay."

"Why do you mourn so?" asked the lady.

"I do not know," said King Pellinore, "but my heart mourns for the death of this lady, who was a very fair damsel and young."

"Now you must follow my advice," said the lady. "Take this knight and let him be buried in a hermitage. Then take the lady's head and bear it with you unto King Arthur's court."

So King Pellinore took the dead knight on his shoulders and rode to the hermitage, where he asked the hermit to bury the corpse and say prayers for the departed soul.

"And take his armor for your trouble, holy sir."

"It shall be done," said the hermit, "as I will answer to God."

By noon they came to Camelot, and King Arthur and Queen Guenever were very glad of his return to the court. And there he was sworn to tell all the truth of his quest from the beginning to the end.

"Ah, Sir Pellinore," said the queen, "you were greatly to blame for not saving the lady's life."

"Madam," said King Pellinore, "I was so furious in my quest that I would not delay. And I shall repent it all the days of my life."

"Truly," said Merlin, "you ought sorely to repent it. For the lady was your own daughter, born of the Lady of the Rule. And that knight who was dead was her lover and would have wedded her. He was a good knight, who was coming to this court, and his name was Sir Miles of the Launds. A false knight and a coward, called Loraine le Savage, stole up behind him and slew him with a spear. In her sorrow the damsel, Eleine, slew herself with Miles's sword, because you would not stop and help her.

"For this misdeed you shall see your best friend fail you when you are in the greatest distress that ever you were or shall be in. And that penance has God ordained you for that deed; that he whom you most trust will leave you there and you shall be slain."

"I believe," said King Pellinore, "that this will

happen to me.　But God may change all destinies."

Thus when the quest of the white hart that Sir Gawaine followed was done and the quest of the hound pursued by Sir Tor, son of King Pellinore, and the quest of the lady that the knight took away, which King Pellinore at that time carried out, then King Arthur rewarded all his knights.

He gave lands to those that were not rich, and charged them never to commit outrage or murder, and always to be loyal.　He warned them against cruelty, told them to give mercy to all those that asked mercy, upon pain of forfeiture of their lordship of King Arthur forevermore, and always, upon pain of death, to give aid to ladies, damsels, and gentlewomen.　He bade that no man fight in a wrong quarrel, either for the law's sake or for worldly goods.　To observe these things were all the knights of the Round Table sworn, both old and young.　And every year they swore this vow again at the time of the high Feast of Pentecost.

Book the Fourth

MORGAN LE FAY AND THE THREE DAMSELS

I

Shortly after this time Merlin became enamored of the damsel, Nimue, that King Pellinore brought with him to the court, and she was one of the damsels of the lake.

Now Merlin would never let the maiden be alone, but followed her about everywhere. And Nimue was very kind to Merlin until she had learned all the things that she desired to know.

Merlin told King Arthur that he, Merlin, would not live long, and that in spite of all his crafts he would be put in the earth while yet alive. And Merlin told the king many other things that would come to pass. He warned Arthur always to keep his sword Excalibur and the scabbard safe. He said that Arthur should take care that the sword and the scabbard should not be stolen from him by a woman that he greatly trusted.

He knew that King Arthur would miss his trusted counselor Merlin. "Some time," he said, "to have me back again, you would give up all your lands."

"Well," said the king, "since you know what is going to happen, prepare against it and by your crafts put away that misfortune."

"No," said Merlin, "it is written that it must be."

Then he left King Arthur as soon as the damsel of the lake left the court. Merlin went evermore with her wheresoever she went, and she made Merlin swear that he would never perform any enchantment upon her.

So she and Merlin went over the sea, unto the land of Benwicke, where ruled King Ban, who was warring against King Claudas. Merlin spoke with King Ban's wife, Elaine, a fair and good lady. There also, Merlin saw young Launcelot.

The queen was very sorrowful about the mortal war that King Claudas had made on her lord and on her lands.

"Be comforted," said Merlin. "This child, Launcelot, within twenty years will revenge you upon Claudas, so that all Christendom will speak of it. And this same child shall be the man of greatest honor in this world. I know that his first name was Galahad, although you confirmed him in church as Launcelot."

"That is true," said Queen Elaine. "His first name was Galahad. But, O Merlin, shall I live to see my son a man of such honor?"

"Yes, lady," replied Merlin, "you shall live to see it, and live many winters after that."

"Soon after this the damsel of the lake and Merlin departed from Benwicke and journeyed toward Cornwall. On the way, as they went, Merlin showed his loved one many wonders. But when they came into Cornwall, she grew weary of his company and wished to get rid of him, but she was afraid because he was a devil's son.

Now it happened that Merlin showed her a wonderful rock which, when worked by enchantment, went under a stone. By her subtle craft the damsel of the lake induced Merlin to go under the stone to tell her of the marvels there, and then shut him in there so that he never came out, in spite of all his craft. Then she departed and left Merlin.

II

King Arthur rode to Camelot and there made a rich feast with mirth and joy. But after he returned to Carlisle news came to King Arthur that five kings, with a great host, had entered his land, and were burning and killing all that they found both in castles and in cities. The chieftains of this host, they said, were the King of Denmark, the King of Ireland his brother, the King of Wales, the King of Soleyse, and the King of the Isle of Longtainse.

"Alas!" said Arthur, "I have never had one month's rest since I was crowned king of this land. Now I vow never to rest until I meet with those kings in a fair field. For my true liege people shall not be destroyed if I can aid them."

Then the king wrote to King Pellinore and prayed him to make ready in all haste and follow him with such people as he might gather.

All the barons were secretly resentful that the king should depart so suddenly. But Arthur would not wait, but sent messages to those who were not at Carlisle and bade them come after him as quickly as they could.

Then the king came to Queen Guenever and said, "Lady, make ready to go with me, since I cannot be happy without you. You will make me more brave, no matter what adventure shall befall me, and I will not allow my lady to be in any jeopardy."

"Sir," said Guenever, "I am at your command and shall be ready whenever you wish."

So on the morrow the king and the queen departed with such knights as they had, and came into the North, to a forest near the river Humber, and there stayed.

When news came to the five kings that Arthur was near the Humber in a forest, a knight, a brother of one of the five kings, gave them this counsel:

"You know well that King Arthur has with him the flower of the world's chivalry, as was proved by his great battle with the eleven kings. Therefore let us hasten night and day until we come near him, for the longer he delays, the larger his host will be and the smaller ours. And he himself is so courageous that he has come to the field with only a few people. Therefore let us attack him before it is day, and not one of his knights shall escape."

III

The five kings assented to this counsel. And they passed with their host through North Wales, came upon King Arthur by night, and attacked his host while he and his knights were in their pavilions. And King Arthur was unarmed and had laid him to rest with Queen Guenever.

"Sirs," said Sir Kaye, "we should not be unarmed."

"We shall have little need," said Sir Gawaine and Sir Griflet, who lay in a little pavilion by the king.

Then they heard a great noise, and many cried, "Treason!"

"Alas!" said King Arthur. "We are all betrayed. To arms, my fellow knights!"

Soon they were armed at all points. Then a wounded knight came to Arthur, saying, "Sir, save yourself and my lady the queen. For our host is destroyed, and many of our people slain."

So the king and the queen, with three knights, rode toward the river Humber to pass over it. But the water was so rough that they were afraid to try to cross it.

"Now choose," said King Arthur to Guenever, "whether you will wait and take the adventure on this side. For, if you are taken, they will kill you."

"It were better for me," said Guenever, "to die in the water than to fall into the hands of your enemies and be slain there."

As they stood talking there, Sir Kaye saw the five kings coming toward them on horseback, by themselves, with their spears in their hands.

"Lo!" said Sir Kaye. "Yonder are the five kings. Let us go to them and match them."

"That were folly," said Sir Gawaine, "for we are but four and they are five."

"That is truth," said Sir Griflet.

"Fools!" said Sir Kaye. "I will undertake two of them, and you three can join spears with the other three."

And therewith the seneschal let his horse run as fast as he might and struck one of the kings through the shield and the body, so that the noble fell to the earth dead. When Gawaine saw that, he ran into another king so hard that he smote him through the body. Then King Arthur ran to another royal knight and smote him through the body with a spear, so that he fell down to the earth dead. Sir Griflet ran to the fourth king and gave him such a fall that he broke his neck. Anon Sir Kaye ran unto the fifth king and smote him so hard upon the helm that the stroke cleaved the headpiece and the skull to the shoulders.

"That was well done," said King Arthur, "and most worshipfully have you kept your promise. I shall therefore honor you as long as I shall live."

Then they set the queen in a barge on the Humber. And Guenever praised Sir Kaye always for his noble deeds and said, "If ever you love a lady, and she does not love you in return, she would be greatly to blame. Among ladies I shall bear your noble fame, for you fulfilled your word, and well."

And with that the queen departed.

Then the king and the three knights rode into the forest, for there they expected to hear of those who had escaped. And King Arthur found most of his people there and told them all that the five kings were dead.

"And therefore," he said, "let us stay together until it be day. And when the enemy sees that their chieftains are slain they will be so sad that they will not be able to help themselves."

It was as the king had said. For when they found the five kings dead the people sorrowed so that they fell down from their horses. Then King Arthur came, with a few men, and slew to the right and to the left, so that few escaped their swords. Thirty thousand men were slain.

When the battle was ended, King Arthur kneeled down and thanked God very meekly. Then he sent for Queen Guenever, who soon came to him. And they were very joyful because of their victory in that dangerous battle.

Then King Arthur was told that King Pellinore was within three miles with a great host.

"Go to King Arthur," Pellinore had said to the messenger, "and let him know how we have sped."

Soon King Pellinore arrived with a great army, and saluted the people and the king. There was great rejoicing made on every side. Then a search was made to find how many people of Arthur's army had been slain. Less than two hundred men and eight knights of the Round Table had perished in their pavilions. Then the king had built in the place where the battle was fought a fair abbey, and endowed it, calling it the Abbey of le Beale Adventure.

But when the remainder of the conquered foe at last came into their countries where the five kings ruled, and told the people how the kings had been slain, there was great sorrow. And when King Arthur's enemies, the King of North Wales and the King of the North, knew of the battle, they were heavy hearted.

IV

The king returned to Camelot in haste and, calling King Pellinore to him, said, "You know that we have lost eight good knights of the Round Table. By your advice we will choose again eight of the best that we may find in this court."

"Sir," said King Pellinore, "there are in your court right noble knights, both old and young. I should advise you to choose four old knights and four young."

"Which are the old?" asked King Arthur.

"Sir," said Pellinore, "King Urience, who married your sister Morgan le Fay; and the King of the Lake; and Sir Hervise de Revel, a noble knight; and Sir Galagars, for the fourth."

"This is excellent counsel," said Arthur, "and so shall it be."

"Then, of the young ones, sir," said Pellinore, "the first is Sir Gawaine, your nephew, who is as good a knight as any in this land; and the second is Sir Griflet le Fise de Dieu, a good knight and eager, who, if he lives, will prove an excellent knight; and the third, who seems well worthy to me, is Sir Kaye the seneschal, for often has he done nobly and at your last battle he honorably undertook to slay two kings."

"By my head," said King Arthur, "he is worthiest to be a knight of the Round Table of any that you have named, if he fought no more battles all the days of his life."

"Then," said King Pellinore, "for the fourth place,

I suggest two knights: Sir Bagdemagus and Sir Tor, my son, for you to choose which is the more worthy· Because Sir Tor is my son, I may not praise him. If he were not my son, I would say there is not in this land a better knight of his age than he, nor of better conditions, and more loath either to do or to take any wrong."

"By my head," said King Arthur, "he is as good a knight as any you have mentioned. That know I full well, for I have seen him proved. He says little but does much. For I know none in all this court, if he were as well born on his mother's side as he is on your side, that is like him in prowess and in might. And therefore I will have him at this time and leave Sir Bagdemagus until another choosing."

And when the knights were chosen by the assent of all the barons, there was found in the places every knight's name mentioned above. But when they were seated Sir Bagdemagus was very angry because Sir Tor was so advanced. Therefore suddenly he left the court of King Arthur, taking his squire with him, and they rode along in the forest until they came to a cross, where he alighted and said his prayers devoutly.

In the meantime his squire found it written upon the cross that Bagdemagus should never return again to the court until he had won a knight's body of the Round Table, body for body.

"See, sir," said the squire, "what I find written about you here. I bid you therefore return again to the court."

"That shall I never do," said Bagdemagus, "until I am worthy to be a knight of the Round Table."

And so he rode forth, by the way he found a branch of a holy herb that was the sign of the Holy Grail, a token such as no knight found unless his life were good.

He happened later to come to the rock where the damsel of the lake had put Merlin under a stone, and there he heard the wizard moaning sorrowfully. Sir Bagdemagus would have helped him, and went to the great stone, but it was so heavy that a hundred men could not have lifted it up. When Merlin knew that Bagdemagus was there, he told him that all his trouble was in vain, for he might never be helped but by the woman that put him there.

Then the knight departed, and did many adventures which proved him a good knight of valor. And when he came again to the court of King Arthur, he was made knight of the Round Table.

V

Now it happened that King Arthur and many of his knights went hunting in a great forest, and King Arthur, King Urience, and Sir Accolon of Gaul followed a great hart.

All three were well horsed, and they chased the hart so fast that within a short time they were ten miles from their knights. Their horses died, but when they they were all on foot, they still saw the weary hart before them.

"What shall we do?" King Arthur asked.

"Let us go on foot," said King Urience, "until we find a lodging."

Then they saw the hart lying on the bank of a great lake, with a brachet biting his throat, and many other hounds coming after. So King Arthur blew the prize [the note of the huntsman's horn that marks the death of a deer].

When Arthur looked about him, he saw before him a little ship all decked with silk down to the water's edge. The ship came straight to them and landed on the sands. When the king went to the bank and looked into the ship, he saw no earthly creature anywhere about it.

"Sirs," called the king to his two companions, "come and let us see what mystery is here."

So all three went into the ship, and they found it richly hung with silk. By this time it was dark night and there suddenly appeared a hundred torches which, set on all sides of the shipboards, gave great light. Then twelve fair damsels appeared and saluted King Arthur on their knees, calling him by name and welcoming him.

The king thanked them, and therewith they led the king and his two fellows into a fair room where a cloth was laid, and all the fittings of a table. There they were served with all wines and meats so that the king had great marvel, for he fared never better in his life. After dinner King Arthur was led into a room more beautiful than he had ever seen, and the two other knights were led into other rooms.

They fell asleep then, and slept soundly all that night. And in the morning King Urience awoke in Camelot in the room of his wife, Morgan le Fay. He wondered how he came there, for cn the evening before he had been some two days' journey away.

VI

When King Arthur awoke he found himself in a dark prison, and heard about him the complaints of many sad knights.

Then said King Arthur, "Who are you that mourn so here?"

"We are twenty good knights who are prisoners," said the voices, "and some of us have lain here seven years."

"Why are you here?" asked King Arthur again.

"We will tell you," said the knights. "The lord of this castle is named Sir Damas, and he is the falsest knight alive, a coward and a traitor. He has a younger brother, a good knight, whose name is Ontzlake. This traitor Damas, the elder, keeps from him a full fair and rich manor, and there has been much quarreling between them. Sir Ontzlake always offers to fight Sir Damas for his inheritance, body for body, or, if he will not, to fight any knight whom Sir Damas may find. But the elder brother is so evil and so hated that no knight will fight for him. Therefore Sir Damas has daily lain in wait, with many men with him, to take all the knights in this country. He has taken us by force and brought us each to his prison as we rode on our adventures."

"And are all these knights here?" Arthur asked.

"O sir, eighteen good knights have died in this prison from hunger. If any of us would have fought with his

brother Ontzlake, Sir Damas would have delivered us.
But, because this elder brother is so false and full of
treason, we would never fight for him, but would rather
die. And we are so weak with hunger that we may
hardly stand on our feet."

"God in His mercy deliver you," said King Arthur.

Then a damsel came and spoke to the king.

"Sir," said she, "if you will fight for my lord Damas,
you will be delivered from prison. Otherwise you will
never escape with your life."

"Now, that is hard," said King Arthur. "Yet I
would rather fight with a knight than die in prison. If
I may be delivered with all these prisoners, I will fight."

"The condition will be fulfilled," said the damsel.

"I am ready except for a horse and armor," said the
king.

"You shall not lack," said the maiden.

"It seems to me, damsel, I have seen you in the
court of King Arthur."

"No," replied the damsel. "I have never been there.
I am the daughter of the lord of this castle."

Yet was she false, for she was one of the damsels of
Morgan le Fay. Then she went to Sir Damas and told
him that the new knight would fight for him. And so
King Arthur was summoned, and when the knights of
Sir Damas saw how well formed he was, they said it would
be a pity that such a knight should die in prison.

So Sir Damas and Arthur were agreed that he should
fight for him upon this covenant, that all the other
knights should be released from prison. And Sir Damas

was sworn to King Arthur, who promised to fight this battle to the end. Then all the twenty knights were brought out of the dark prison into the hall and delivered, but all waited to see the contest.

VII

Now when Sir Accolon of Gaul awoke he found himself by the side of a deep well, in great peril of death. And there came out of that fountain a pipe of silver. And when Sir Accolon saw this he blessed himself and said, "Jesus save my lord, King Arthur, and King Urience, for the damsels in the ship have betrayed us. They were no women, but devils. If I may escape this misadventure, I shall destroy all these false damsels that use enchantments."

Then there came a dwarf with a great mouth and flat nose, and, saluting Sir Accolon, said that he came from Queen Morgan le Fay.

"And she greets you well and bids you be brave, for you shall fight at the hour of prime tomorrow with a knight. Therefore she has sent you here Excalibur, King Arthur's sword, and the scabbard. And she asks you, if you love her, to fight to the uttermost without mercy, as you have promised her. The damsel that brings her the head of the knight with whom you shall fight, she will make a rich queen forever."

"Now I understand you," said Sir Accolon. "I shall keep my promise, now that I have the sword. When saw you my lady, Queen Morgan le Fay?"

"Just now," said the hunchback.

Then Sir Accolon took the messenger in his arms and said, "Recommend me to my lady, Queen Morgan, and tell her that all shall be done as I promised her, or I will die for it. Now I suppose she has made all these enchantments for this combat?"

"You may well believe it," said the dwarf.

Then a knight and a lady came with six squires, saluted Sir Accolon, and prayed him to come and rest at the manor. Sir Accolon mounted a spare horse and went with the knight to a fair manor near a priory, and there he had passing good cheer.

Then Sir Damas sent to his brother Sir Ontzlake, and bade him be ready by the hour of prime the next day to fight with a good knight, for he had found a knight that was willing to do battle.

When this word came to Sir Ontzlake he was sad, for he had been wounded by a spear through both thighs. Now it happened that, by the means of Morgan le Fay, Sir Accolon was lodged with Sir Ontzlake. When Accolon heard how Sir Ontzlake was wounded, he said he would fight for him, because Morgan le Fay had sent him Excalibur and the scabbard to fight with some knight on the morrow. Then was Sir Ontzlake glad, and thanked Accolon heartily because he would do so much for him, and he sent word to Sir Damas that he had a knight who would be ready in the field by the hour of dawn to fight for him.

So, on the morrow, King Arthur was armed and well horsed.

"When shall we go to the field?" he asked.

"Sir," said Sir Dumas, "after you hear mass."

After mass a squire came on a great horse and asked Sir Damas if his knight was ready, for the other knight was already in the field.

Then King Arthur mounted on horseback, and all the knights and the people in the country roundabout were there. Twelve good men of the district were chosen to wait upon the two knights. To King Arthur, upon horseback, there came a damsel from Morgan le Fay, bringing a sword like Excalibur and the scabbard. And the damsel said unto King Arthur, "Morgan le Fay sends you your sword and her love."

And he thanked the damsel and thought it was so, but she was false, for the sword and the scabbard were counterfeit.

VIII

Then the knights let their horses run so fast that either smote the other in the midst of their shields with their spears, so that both horses and men went to the ground. Both started up then and drew their swords.

In the meantime, while they were fighting, the damsel of the lake who had put Merlin under the stone came into the field. She came for love of King Arthur, because she knew how Morgan le Fay had willed that the king should be slain that day. She therefore came to save his life.

The two knights went eagerly to their battle, but King Arthur's sword was not like Sir Accolon's, for with every stroke Accolon wounded King Arthur, so that it was a marvel that he stood upright, as the blood was falling fast. Then King Arthur began to suspect that his sword was changed, for it did not seem like his sword and he thought that the sword in Sir Accolon's hand must be Excalibur, for every blow with that sword drew blood from King Arthur.

"Now, knight," said Sir Accolon to King Arthur, "keep well from me."

The king did not answer him, but gave him such a buffet on the helm that he made him stoop and almost fall to the ground. Then Sir Accolon withdrew, and came on brandishing Excalibur on high. Greatly angered were they both, and dealt each other many sore strokes, but always Arthur was wounded, though his great courage made him hide his pain.

But Sir Accolon lost not a drop of blood, and because of Excalibur he grew ever stronger, while King Arthur was passing feeble. All the men that watched said they had never seen a knight fight so well as did King Arthur, considering his wounds. And all the people were sorry for him, but as the two brothers would not agree, the fight had to continue. When King Arthur withdrew a little to rest, Sir Accolon called him back to battle:

"This is no time to rest," he said.

And then he came fiercely toward King Arthur, who smote Accolon upon the helm so fiercely that his sword broke at the cross and fell in the grass among the blood. When Arthur saw the pommel and the handle in his hand, he feared that he was going to die, but still he held up his shield and lost no ground.

Then Sir Accolon began to speak again.

"Knight," he said, "you are overcome and can endure no longer. You are weaponless and have lost much blood, so I am loath to slay you. Therefore yield to me."

"No," said King Arthur, "I may not, for I have promised to fight you to the uttermost, by the faith of my body, while my life lasts. I had rather die with honor than live with shame. If it were possible for me to die a hundred times, I had rather die so often than yield to you. For though I lack a weapon, yet shall I lack no honor. And if you slay me weaponless, that shall be to your shame."

"Well," said Sir Accolon, "as for the shame, I will not spare. Now keep you from me, for you are but a dead man."

And therewith the knight gave Arthur such a stroke that he almost fell, for he would have had the king cry him mercy. But Arthur pressed upon his adversary with his shield and gave him with the pommel in his hand such a buffet that he went three strides back. When the damsel of the lake saw King Arthur's bravery, and knew the treason that had been made to slay him, she had great pity that so good a knight and so noble a man should be killed.

And so, when Sir Accolon struck the next blow, by the damsel's enchantment the sword Excalibur fell out of his hand to the earth. Then King Arthur leaped lightly to it and quickly got it in his grasp. And he saw that it was his good sword Excalibur.

"You have been from me all too long," he said. "And much damage have you done me."

Then he saw the scabbard hanging by Sir Accolon's side, and suddenly he pulled the scabbard away from Accolon and threw it as far as he might cast it from him.

"O knight," said the king, "this day have you done me great damage with this sword. Now are you come to your death. For you shall be as well rewarded with this sword, before we part, as you rewarded me."

Then King Arthur rushed upon the other knight with all his might, pulled him to the earth, and then snatched off his helm and gave him such a buffet on the head that the blood came out of his ears, nose, and mouth.

"Now will I slay you," said King Arthur.

"Slay me if it please you," said Sir Accolon, "for you are the best knight that ever I found, and I see well that God is with you. But because I promised to do this battle to the uttermost, and never to be recreant while I lived, therefore I will never yield, let God do with my body what he will."

Then King Arthur thought that he recognized him.

"Now tell me," he said, "of what country and of what court you are, or I will kill you."

Said the other, "I am of the court of King Arthur, and my name is Sir Accolon of Gaul."

Then was King Arthur more dismayed than before, for he remembered his sister Morgan le Fay, and the enchanted ship.

"O sir knight," said he, "I pray you tell me who gave you this sword."

Then Sir Accolon said, "Woe to this sword, for by it have I gotten my death!"

"That may well be," said Arthur.

"Now, sir," said the knight of Gaul, "I will tell you. This sword has been in my keeping most of these last twelve months. And yesterday King Urience's wife, Morgan le Fay, sent it me by a dwarf, so that I should slay King Arthur, her brother, with it."

"Why?" asked Arthur.

"He is the man whom she hates most in this world. Though she is married, she loves me most, and I love her. And if she could kill King Arthur by her crafts, she would then kill her husband lightly, and I would be king in this land, and she my queen. But all that is now over, for I am sure of my death."

"It would have been a great shame to have killed your lord," said King Arthur.

"That is true," said Sir Accolon. "But now I pray you that you will tell me from what court you come."

"O Sir Accolon, know that I am King Arthur, to whom you have done great harm."

When Accolon heard that, he cried out aloud, "O my gracious lord, have mercy on me! For I knew you not."

"Mercy shall you have," said King Arthur, "because I know that you did not recognize me. But I see by your talk that you have agreed to my death, and therefore are you a traitor. But I blame you less, for my sister Morgan le Fay by her false crafts made you agree and consent to her wicked lusts. But I shall be avenged upon her, if I live, so that all Christendom shall speak of it. God knows I have honored her and loved her more than any of my kin. I have trusted her more than my own wife and all my kin."

Then King Arthur called the keepers of the field.

"Sirs," he said, "come here, for we have almost killed each other. Had either of us known the other, there would have been no combat."

Then cried Sir Accolon to all the knights and men that were gathered together, "O my lords, this noble knight that I have fought with is the man of greatest prowess in the whole world. For it is himself, King Arthur, our most sovereign liege lord and king. I have fought against my king and lord."

Then all the people fell down on their knees and cried for King Arthur's mercy.

"Mercy shall you have," said King Arthur. "Here may you see what adventures happen to errant knights, for I have fought with one of my own nobles to my great damage and to his hurt. But now, sirs, because I have great need of a little rest, listen to my judgment of the matter between these two brethren. Sir Damas, for whom I have been champion and won the field of this knight, because you are a proud knight, and full of villainy, I will give to your brother the whole manor, with the appurtenance, under this manner of form: that Sir Ontzlake hold the manor of you, and yearly give you a palfrey to ride, for that will become you better to ride on than a courser."

"Also, I command you, Sir Damas," said King Arthur further, "never upon pain of death, to distress errant knights that ride on their adventures. Also, that you restore all their harness to these twenty knights, whom you have kept long in prison. And if any of them come to my court and complain against you, by my head, you shall die for it."

The twenty knights who heard this were exceeding glad.

"Also, Sir Ontzlake," said the king, "because you are called a good knight, and true and gentle in all your deeds, I will that in all goodly haste you come to me and to my court, that you may be a knight of mine. And, if your deeds warrant it, I shall so advance you by the grace of God that in a short time you shall live in ease as worshipfully as your brother Sir Damas now does."

"God thank you for your generosity and goodness," said Sir Ontzlake. "And I promise you that from henceforth I will be at all times at your command. For, sir, if I had not been hurt lately by an adventurous knight, I should have fought this battle with you."

"Would to God it had been so!" said Arthur. "For then I should not have been hurt as I am. My own sword was stolen from me by treason, and this battle was arranged beforehand to kill me by trickery and false enchantment."

"Alas," said Sir Ontzlake, "that any man or woman could find it in his heart to work treason against your noble person!"

"By the grace of God," said King Arthur, "I shall reward them in a short time. Now tell me, how far am I from Camelot?"

"Sir, you are two days' journey therefrom."

"I would fain be at some place of worship," said the king, "so that I might rest."

"Sir," said Ontzlake, "there is a rich abbey of nuns but three miles hence."

So the king took his leave of all the people and mounted on horseback with Sir Accolon. And when they came to the abbey surgeons and leeches examined his wounds and Sir Accolon's. Accolon died within four days, for he had bled so much that he could not live, but King Arthur recovered. And when Sir Accolon was dead the king sent him on a horse bier with six knights to Camelot and said:

"Bear him to my sister Morgan le Fay, and say that I send him to her for a present. Tell her also that I have my sword Excalibur and the scabbard."

IX

Now Morgan le Fay thought that King Arthur had been slain, so, when she saw King Urience sleeping in his bed, she called a damsel and said, "Go fetch me my lord's sword, for never saw I a better time to kill him than now."

"O madam," said the damsel, "if you slay my lord, you can never escape."

"Never you mind," said Morgan le Fay. "For I see that this is the best time to do it. Therefore hurry and fetch me the sword, before he awakes."

Then the damsel left and found the son, Sir Ewaine, sleeping on a bed in another room. She wakened him and bade him wait upon her ladyship, his mother and said:

"For she will slay the king, your father, asleep in his bed. I am sent to fetch her his sword."

"Well," said Sir Ewaine, "go your way and let me deal with this."

So the damsel brought the sword to Morgan with trembling hands. Morgan took the weapon, drew out the blade, and then walked boldly to the side of the bed.

As she lifted the sword high to strike, Sir Ewaine rushed in and caught his mother by the hand.

"Ah, fiend!" he said. "What are you doing? If you were not my mother, with this sword I would smite off your head. Men say that Merlin was begotten of a devil, but I may say that an earthly devil gave me birth."

"O fair son," said Morgan le Fay, "have mercy on me! I was tempted. Have mercy! I will never do so again. Betray me not."

"Swear to me," said Sir Ewaine, "that you will never attempt such a deed again!"

And Morgan swore this promise to her son.

When the news came to Morgan le Fay that Sir Accolon was dead and that King Arthur had his own sword again, although she was so sorrowful that her heart almost broke, she did not dare show any sign of her grief. But she knew that if she waited until her brother Arthur came there no gold could save her life.

So she went to Queen Guenever and asked leave of her to ride into the country.

"Wait," said Queen Guenever, "until your brother, the king, comes home."

"I may not," said Morgan le Fay, "for I have such news that I cannot wait."

"Well, then," said her liege lady, "leave when you will."

So, before it was day, Morgan took her horse and rode all that day and most of the next night. And the next noon she came to the abbey of nuns where King Arthur lay. Knowing that he was there, she asked where he was.

And they answered, "He is in his bed asleep, for he has had but little rest these three nights."

"Well," said she, "I charge you that none of you awake him until I do so myself."

She alighted then from her horse and thought to steal away Excalibur. So she went straight to his room. and there she found King Arthur asleep in his bed, with Excalibur unsheathed in his right hand.

When she saw that, she was very sad because she could not take the sword without wakening him. So she took the scabbard and went away on horseback.

When the king awoke and missed his precious scabbard, he was angry and asked who had been there. And they said his sister Queen Morgan le Fay had been there, and had put the scabbard under her mantle, and had gone.

"Alas!" said King Arthur. "You have not guarded me faithfully."

"Sir," said the nuns, "we dared not disobey your sister's commands."

Then said the king, "Bring the best horse that may be found, and bid Sir Ontzlake arm in all haste, and take another good horse, and ride with me."

As soon as the king and Sir Ontzlake were well armed they rode after this lady. And as they rode they came by a cross and found a cowherd there. They asked the poor man if a lady had been riding that way lately.

"Sirs," said the cowherd, "a lady came riding with forty horses. She rode to yonder forest."

Then they spurred their horses and followed after her fast. Soon King Arthur saw her, and rode after her as fast as he could ride. She saw him coming and rode at full speed through the forest until she came to a plain and a lake. She saw then that she could not escape.

"Whatsoever becomes of me," she said, "my brother shall not have this scabbard."

So she threw the magic sheath into the deepest water, where it sank, for it was heavy with gold and precious stones. Then she rode into a valley where many great stones were, and by enchantment turned herself and her horses and her men into a great marble stone. When King Arthur and Sir Ontzlake came there, the king could not tell the knights and his sister from each other.

"Ah," said the king, "here may you see the vengeance of God, that he has transformed them into objects as hard as their wicked hearts. I am sorry that this misadventure is befallen."

He looked for his scabbard then, but it could not be found. So he returned again to the abbey from which he had come.

But as soon as King Arthur had gone from the valley Queen Morgan turned herself and her men back into human shape.

"Sirs," she said, "now may we go wheresoever we will, for my brother Arthur has gone. Did you see my brother, King Arthur?"

"Yes," said her knights, "right well. And by his fierce countenance he would have caused us to run if we had been alive."

"I believe you," said Morgan.

Then as she rode she met a knight leading another knight on his horse before him, bound hand and foot, blindfold. When Morgan saw the knight so bound, she asked for the reason.

"Lady," said the captor, "I will drown him."

"Why," asked Morgan.

"Because I found him hidden away with my wife, and she shall have the same death soon."

"That would be a pity," said the queen. "And now, sir captive knight, what say you to this? Is it the truth?"

"No, truly, madam," said the other knight; "he is not speaking fairly of me."

"From whence do you come," Morgan le Fay asked, "and of what country?"

"I am of the court of King Arthur, and my name is Manassen. I am a cousin of Sir Accolon of Gaul"

"For the love of your cousin you shall be delivered," said the queen. "You shall have your adversary in the same situation as you are in."

And so Manassen was loosed, and the other knight bound. And Manassen armed himself in the other's harness, and so mounted on horseback, with the knight before him. Then he threw the knight into the fountain and drowned him, and, riding to Morgan again, he asked her if she wished to send a message to King Arthur.

"Tell him that I rescued you not for the love of him, but for the love of Sir Accolon. And tell him too that I fear him not while I can make me and them that are with me into likenesses of stones."

Then Morgan went into the country of Gore where she was richly received. She made her castles and towns passing strong, for always she feared King Arthur.

X

When the king had rested at the abbey, he rode to Camelot and found his queen and his barons right glad to see him. And when they heard of his strange adventures, they all marveled at the falsehood of Morgan le Fay, and many knights wished her to be burned. Then came Manassen to the court and told the king of his adventure.

"Well," said the king, "she is a kind sister. If I live, I shall be so revenged on her that all Christendom shall speak of it."

So on the morrow there came a damsel from Morgan to the king, and she brought with her the richest mantle that ever was seen in the court, for it was set full of precious stones, and the richest jewels that ever the king had seen.

And the damsel said, "Your sister sends you this mantle and desires that you will accept this gift of her. In whatever way she has offended you, she will make amends at your pleasure."

When the king beheld this mantle it pleased him much, though he said but little.

Then the damsel of the lake came to the king.

"Sir, I must speak with you in private," she said.

"Say on, what you will," said the king.

"Sir," said the lady, "do not put on this mantle, and do not let it touch you or any of your knights until you command the one who brought it to put it upon her."

"Well," said King Arthur, "it shall be done as you counsel me."

And then he said to his sister's messenger, "Damsel, I wish to see you put on this mantle you have brought me."

"Sir," said she, "it is not fitting that I should wear a king's garment."

"By my head," said Arthur, "you shall wear it before it comes on my back."

And so the king bade it be put on her, and immediately she fell down dead, and was burned to coals.

Then the king was greatly angered, and said unto King Urience, "My sister, your wife, will always betray me. And well I know that either you or my nephew, your son, is in league with her. But as for you, King Urience, I do not think that you conspire with her, for Sir Accolon confessed to me that she would have destroyed you as well as me. Therefore I hold you excused. But as for your son, I suspect him; therefore I charge you to put him out of my court."

When Sir Gawaine heard of it, he made ready to go with Ewaine, saying, "Whoever banishes my cousin Ewaine will banish me."

So the two knights left and rode into a great forest, and they came to an abbey, where they were well lodged. But when the king knew that Sir Gawaine had departed from the court, he and all his men were sorrowful.

"Now," said Sir Gaheris, Gawaine's brother, "we have lost two good knights, for the love of one."

XI

The two travelers heard mass in the abbey the next morning, and then rode forth until they came to a great forest.   Then Sir Gawaine saw in a valley near a tower twelve fair damsels, and two armed knights on two great horses.   And the damsels went to and fro by a tree. Then Gawaine saw that a white shield hung up on the tree, and that as the damsels came by it they would spit upon it.

Sir Gawaine and Sir Ewaine rode up and saluted them.   Then they asked why the damsels treated the shield in that way.

"Sirs," said the maidens, "we shall tell you.   There is a brave knight in this country who owns this white shield, but he hates all ladies and gentlewomen.   Therefore we put shame on the white shield."

Then Sir Gawaine said to the ladies, "It is not right for a good knight to despise all ladies and gentlewomen.

Perhaps he has some cause to hate women; and perhaps elsewhere he loves and is loved in return, if he is a man of such prowess. Now, what is his name?"

"Sir," said they, "his name is Marhaus, the son of the King of Ireland."

"I know him well," said Sir Ewaine. "He is as brave a knight as any living, for once I saw him proved at a jousting where many knights were gathered, and at that time no man there could withstand him."

"Ah," said Sir Gawaine, "I think you damsels are to blame. He will return soon, probably, and then it may be those knights of the tower must match him on horseback. I will stay no longer to see a knight's shield dishonored."

Sir Ewaine and Sir Gawaine rode on then, but soon saw Sir Marhaus come riding up on a great horse. When the twelve damsels saw Sir Marhaus, they fled into the tower so wildly that some of them fell by the way.

Then the one of the knights of the tower dressed his shield and cried, "Sir Marhaus, defend thee!"

They ran together then so that the knight broke his spear on Sir Marhaus, and the son of the King of Ireland struck him so hard that he broke his neck. Then the other knight of the tower turned toward Sir Marhaus, but he too was soon struck down, horse and man, stark dead.

Then Sir Marhaus rode to his shield and saw how it was defiled, and said, "Of this shame I am partly revenged. But, for her love that gave me this white shield, I shall wear it."

So he hung the defiled shield about his neck, and then, riding straight to Sir Gawaine and Sir Ewaine, asked them what they did there. They answered that they came from King Arthur's court to seek adventures.

"Well," said Sir Marhaus, "here am I ready, a knight adventurous, who will fulfill any adventure that you will desire of me."

"Let him go," said Sir Ewaine to Sir Gawaine, "for he is as good a knight as any living in this world. I am not willing that either of us should match with him."

"No," said Sir Gawaine, "not so. We should be ashamed if he were not tried, were he ever so good a knight."

"Well," said Sir Ewaine, "I will assay him before you, for I am weaker than you are. And if he smite me down, then you may revenge me."

So these two knights came together with great speed. Sir Ewaine smote Sir Marhaus on the shield so that his spear burst in pieces. Sir Marhaus bore horse and man to the earth, and hurt Sir Ewaine on the left side.

Then Sir Marhaus turned his horse and rode with his spear toward Sir Gawaine. When Arthur's knight saw that, he dressed his shield and they adventured their spears. They came together with all the might of their horses, and Gawaine's spear broke and Sir Marhaus' spear held. Then Sir Gawaine and his horse rushed down to the earth.

Lightly Gawaine rose to his feet, drew out his sword, and turned him toward the other on foot. Sir Marhaus

saw that and drew forth his sword, and came toward
Sir Gawaine on horseback.

"Sir knight," said Sir Gawaine, "alight on foot, or
I shall kill your horse."

"Gramercy," said Sir Marhaus, "you are right, for
it is not courteous for one knight to be on foot and the
other on horseback."

Thereupon Sir Marhaus set his spear against a tree
and alighted, and tied his horse to a tree. Then both
came together eagerly. Their shields flew into fragments,
their helms and their hauberks were broken, and each
wounded the other.

But Sir Gawaine, after it passed nine o'clock, became
stronger; and when noon came, his power was still
increased. Sir Marhaus wondered how the other's
might grew so great.

But, as evensong time drew near, Sir Gawaine's
strength lessened so that he could scarcely stand, while
Sir Marhaus grew stronger.

"Sir knight," said he, "you are a knight of as much
power and bravery as ever I knew. Our quarrels are
not great, and therefore it would be a pity to hurt you,
for I see that you are passing weak."

"Ah, gentle knight," said Sir Gawaine, "you say
the words that I should say."

Then they took off their helms, and swore to love
each other as brothers. Sir Marhaus prayed Sir Gawaine
and his brother to lodge with him that night. Then
they took their horses and rode to the lodging of the son
of the King of Ireland.

"Sir knight," said Sir Gawaine, as they, rode "I wonder that so valiant a knight as you are does not love ladies and gentlewomen."

"Sir," said Sir Marhaus, "they do not speak truthfully who say that, but I know who they are — the damsels of the tower. I hate them because they are most of them witches and enchantresses. No matter how brave a knight is, by their arts they will make him a coward to have the better of him. But to all good ladies and gentlewomen I owe my service as a knight."

And Gawaine and his brother had good entertainment there with Sir Marhaus. For when he knew that they were King Arthur's sisters' sons, he made them stay there seven nights until their wounds were healed.

"Now," said Sir Marhaus, when they were ready to leave, "I will bring you through the forest."

And so they rode for seven days before they met any adventure. But at last they came to a great forest called the "forest of Arroy," which was known all around there as the land of strange adventures.

"In this region," said Sir Marhaus, "no knight ever came without finding strange quests."

When they came into a deep valley, full of stones, they saw a fair stream of water, with a fair fountain at the head of it where three damsels sat. The knights rode up to them and saluted them. The eldest, who was threescore winters of age or more, had a garland of gold about her white hair. The second damsel, who was about thirty years old, wore a circlet of gold about her head. The third damsel was but fifteen years old, and she wore a fillet of flowers. The knights asked them why they sat at the fountain.

"We are here," said the damsels, "to teach errant knights strange adventures. If you seek adventure, each of you must choose one of us. And when you have done so, we will lead you to three highways, where each of you must choose a path and take his damsel with him. Twelve months from this day you must meet here again, if God spares your life. To this you must swear."

"It is an excellent plan," said Sir Marhaus.

"How shall each choose a damsel?"

"I shall tell you," said Sir Ewaine. "I am the youngest and weakest of you; therefore I will have the eldest maiden. For she has seen much and can help me when I need her."

"Then," said Sir Marhaus, "I will choose the damsel of thirty winters of age."

"Why, then," said Gawaine, "I thank you, for you have left me the youngest and fairest."

So each damsel took her knight by the rein of the bridle, and brought him to the three ways. And there they made their oaths to meet at the fountain that day twelvemonth, if they lived. So they parted, each knight with his lady behind him on his horse; Sir Ewaine took the way that lay west, Sir Marhaus the way south, and Sir Gawaine rode westward toward the north.

XII

Sir Gawaine followed the path until he came to a fair manor where an old knight lived. And Gawaine asked him if he knew of any adventures in that country.

"I shall show you some marvelous adventures tomorrow," said the old man.

On the next day they rode into the forest until they came to an open space where they found a cross. As they halted there the fairest man that ever any of them had seen came toward them, weeping and moaning. When he saw Sir Gawaine he saluted him and prayed God to send him much worship.

"Gramercy," said Sir Gawaine. "Also I pray to God that he send you honor and worship."

"Ah," said the knight, "sorrow and shame come to me after worship."

Then he passed on. And Sir Gawaine saw ten knights halt and make ready with their shields and spears to fight the one knight.

Then this one knight took a great spear, and one of the ten knights met him. But the woeful knight smote him so hard that he fell backward over his horse's tail.

The dolorous knight served each of them in this way, and smote them down, horse and man, with one spear. When they were all ten on foot, they attacked that one knight, who stood stone still and allowed them to pull him down off his horse and to bind him hand and foot. They tied him under his horse, and so led him with them.

"This is a doleful and a curious sight," said Sir Gawaine, "to see yonder knight so treated. And it seemed that the knight allowed them to bind him so, for he made no resistance."

"Verily," said his host, "that is true.   If he had resisted, they would all have been too weak to withstand him."

"Sir," said the damsel to Sir Gawaine, "it would be to your honor to help that dolorous knight, for I think he is one of the best knights that I have ever seen."

"I would gladly help him," said Sir Gawaine, "but it seems that he does not wish it."

"Then," said the damsel, "there is no need to help him."

As they talked they saw a knight appear, all armed save the head.   And opposite came a dwarf with a great mouth and a short nose, on horseback, all armed save the head.   When the dwarf came near, the knight inquired, "Where is the lady that should meet us here?"

Then she came out of the wood, and they began to fight for her.   For the knight said he would have the lady, and the dwarf said he would have her.

"Yonder is a knight at the cross," said the dwarf at last.   "Let us put it up to his judgment and as he decides so shall it be."

"I am willing," said the knight.

So then they with the lady came to Sir Gawaine and told him why they fought.

"Well, sirs," asked he, "will you put the matter into my hands?"

"Yes, sir," said both.

"Then, damsel," said Sir Gawaine, "stand between them, and whichever one of them you desire to go to, he shall have you."

When the damsel was set between them she left the knight and went to the dwarf. Then the dwarf took the lady and went his way singing, but the knight rode away mourning. Then came two knights well armed and one cried, "Sir Gawaine, knight of King Arthur, make ready in all haste to joust with me."

While one knight jousted with Gawaine, the other knight went to the damsel and asked her why she stayed with Gawaine.

"If you would rather stay with me," he said, "I will be your faithful knight."

"With you will I stay," said the damsel, "for I do not wish to stay with Gawaine. Just now one knight was here that defeated ten knights, but at last was cowardly led away by them. Let us two go our way while they fight."

Sir Gawaine fought with the other knight long; but at last they were both satisfied, and then the knight prayed Sir Gawaine to lodge with him that night. So Sir Gawaine went with his opponent. As they rode Gawaine asked, "Who is the knight that struck down ten others? When he had fought so manfully, he allowed them to bind him hand and foot and lead him away."

"Ah," said the other, "that is the best knight, I believe, in the world. He has had this happen to him now more than ten times. His name is Sir Pelleas, and he loves a great lady of this country, whose name is Ettarde. A three days' joust was proclaimed, and all the knights and gentlewomen of this district were there. He that proved to be the best knight was to have a

passing good sword and a circlet of gold; the circlet
the knight should give to the fairest lady that was at
those jousts. Sir Pelleas was the best knight there of
the five hundred nobles. Every man that Sir Pelleas
met he struck down, and he struck down twenty knights
each day of the tourney; wherefore they gave him the
prize. Then he went where the Lady Ettarde was, and
gave her the circlet. He said openly that she was the
fairest lady of all, and that he would prove it upon any
knight who denied it.

"He chose her for his sovereign lady, and swore
never to love any other, but she was proud and scorned
him. She said that she would never love him, although
he would die for her. Then all the ladies and gentlewomen scorned her, because there were many ladies
there fairer than she who would have loved Sir Pelleas
for his valor had he offered them love. But Pelleas
promised the Lady Ettarde to follow her into this
country, and never to leave her until she loved him.
Therefore he is here, living near a priory. Every week
she sends knights to fight with him, but when he has
defeated them he allows them to take him prisoner,
because he would see his lady. And always she shames
him. Sometimes she has her knights tie him to the
horse's tail, and often bind him underneath the horse.
Thus she shames him in every way she can think of.
This she does to make him leave this country and to cease
loving her, but he will not leave. He could, if he would,
defeat the men on foot as well as on horseback."

"Alas!" said Sir Gawaine. "It is a great pity. In

the morning I will seek him in the forest and give him what help I can."

So on the morrow Sir Gawaine took his leave of his host, Sir Carados, and rode into the wood. When he met Sir Pelleas making great moan, each of them saluted the other, and Gawaine asked him why he was sorrowing.

Then Pelleas told Gawaine his story.

"But I allow her knights always to treat me as you saw yesterday, hoping at last to win her love. For she knows that all her knights could not defeat me if I wished to fight with them. If I did not love her so well, I would rather die a hundred times than suffer this shame. I trust she will pity me at last, but, alas, I am unfortunate!"

"Now," said Sir Gawaine, "cease your mourning and I shall promise you by the faith of my body to do all I can to get you the love of your lady. I promise you."

"Ah, my good friend!" said Pelleas. "From what court do you come. Tell me, I pray you."

"I am of the court of King Arthur," then said Sir Gawaine, "and am his sister's son. King Lot of Orkney was my father, and my name is Sir Gawaine."

Then the other said: "My name is Sir Pelleas, born in the isles, and of many isles I am lord. And never have I loved lady or damsel until now. And, sir knight, since you are a nephew unto King Arthur and a king's son, I pray you, therefore, not to betray me but to help me. For I may never win her but by the help of some good knight. She is in a strong castle near here, within four miles, and she is lady over all this country. Thus I may never come to her unless I suffer her knights to take me. Yet have I never had one fair word from her. When I am brought before her she rebukes me, and then her men take me and my horse and my harness and put me outside the gates. She will not allow me to eat or drink. She will not take me, although I always offer to be her prisoner. I would desire no more, no matter how I suffered, if I could but see her daily."

"Well," said Sir Gawaine, "all this will I change if you will do as I counsel. I will have your horse and your armor, and will ride to her castle, and tell her that I have slain you. I will come to her and cause her to be fond of me; then shall I do my true part so that you will not fail to have her love."

Then Sir Gawaine swore to Sir Pelleas to be true and faithful unto him.

Then they changed their horses and harness, and Sir Gawaine departed and came to the castle, where the pavilions of the lady stood without the gates. And as soon as Ettarde saw Sir Gawaine she fled toward the castle, but Sir Gawaine called and bade her wait; for he was not the knight she thought.

"I am another knight, and have slain Sir Pelleas."

"Take off your helm," said the Lady Ettarde, "so that I may see your face."

And when she saw that it was not Sir Pelleas, she made him alight and led him into the great hall of her castle. Then she asked him whether he had slain Sir Pelleas.

And he said, "Yes."

Then Sir Gawaine told her his name, and his rank, and the court from which he rode.

"Truly," said she, "it is great pity that you have slain Sir Pelleas, for he was a good knight. But of all men alive I hated him most, for never could I be rid of him. Because you have killed him I shall be your love and do anything that may please you."

So she made Gawaine good cheer.

"I love a lady," said he, "but she will not love me."

"She is to blame," said Ettarde, "if she will not love you. For you are so well born and so brave that there is no lady in this world too good for you."

"Will you," said Sir Gawaine, "promise to do all that you may do to get me the love of my lady?"

"Yes," said she, "I promise you by the faith of my body."

"Now," said Sir Gawaine, "it is yourself that I love so well. Therefore I pray you to hold your promise."

"I may not choose," said the Lady Ettarde, "or I would be forsworn."

And so she promised him his desire. It was in the month of May that she and Sir Gawaine went out of the castle and supped in a pavilion. And there Gawaine, false to his trust, remained with the Lady Ettarde two days, in spite of the faithful promise he had made to Sir Pelleas. They had no fear of the dolorous knight, for the lady had placed her damsels in a pavilion next to her own, and in the third pavilion she had stationed part of her knights.

And on the third day, early in the morning, Sir Pelleas

armed, for he had not slept since Sir Gawaine left him. For Gawaine had promised by the faith of his body to come to his pavilion by the priory the next day after they parted.

Then Sir Pelleas mounted on horseback and came to the pavilions that stood without the castle. He found in the first apartment three knights in their beds, and three squires lying at their feet. Then he went to the second chamber and found four gentlewomen sleeping in four beds. And then he went to the third pavilion and found Sir Gawaine with his lady Ettarde.

Now, when Sir Pelleas saw that, his heart almost broke in its sorrow.

"Alas," he said, "that ever a knight should be found so false!"

He could no longer stay because of his sorrow, and so took his horse. But when he had gone half a mile he turned again to kill them both. But when he saw them again, both beside the fire dreaming, he said, "Though he be never so false, I will not kill him as he sleeps. For I will never destroy the high order of knighthood."

But he could not stay away. Therefore he returned with his sword naked in his hand, and went straight to them where they were lying, and laid the naked sword over their heads. Then he took his horse and rode away sorrowing.

And when Pelleas came to his own pavilions, he told his knights and squires what had happened.

Then he said, "For your true and faithful service, I shall give you all my goods. For I will never arise from my bed but will stay there until I am dead. And when I am dead take the heart from my body and bear it to Lady Ettarde between two silver dishes. Then tell her how I saw her in the pavilion with the false knight, Sir Gawaine."

Sir Pelleas then unarmed and went to bed, making the greatest sorrow that ever man heard.

When Sir Gawaine and the lady Ettarde awakened and found the naked sword over both their heads, then she knew that it was the sword of Sir Pelleas.

"Alas!" said she to Sir Gawaine. "You have betrayed me and Sir Pelleas, too. For you told me that you had killed him, and now I know that he is alive. If Sir Pelleas had been as discourteous to you as you have been to him, you would be a dead knight. But you have deceived me and betrayed me. May all ladies and damsels be warned by you and me."

Then Sir Gawaine made ready and went into the forest. It happened that the damsel of the lake, Nimue, met with a knight of King Pelleas who went sorrowing through the forest. Nimue asked him the cause of his sorrow, and the woeful knight told her that his master and lord would never arise from his bed but would stay there until he was dead because he had been betrayed by a knight and a lady.

"Bring me to him," said Nimue, "and I will warrant that he will not die of love. She that caused him to love will soon be in as evil a plight as he is now. She is a proud lady who will have no mercy for such a valiant knight."

When the knight brought the damsel of the lake to his lord and master, and she saw him lying in his bed, she thought she had never seen so fine a knight. Then she threw an enchantment upon him, and he fell asleep.

Then she rode to the Lady Ettarde, charging that no man should awaken Sir Pelleas until she returned. Within two hours she brought the Lady Ettarde thither, and both the ladies found him asleep.

"Lo!" said the damsel of the lake. "You ought to be ashamed to murder such a knight."

Then she cast an enchantment upon the scornful lady so that she loved Pelleas until she was almost out of her mind.

"Oh, woe is me!" said the Lady Ettarde. "Now I love him whom before I most hated of all men living."

"This is the righteous judgment of heaven," said the damsel of the lake.

When Sir Pelleas awoke and looked upon the Lady Ettarde, he hated her more than any woman alive, and said, "Away, traitress, never come in my sight."

And when she heard him say so, she wept and was sorrowful.

"Sir Pelleas," said the damsel of the lake, "take your horse and come with me out of this country, and you shall have a lady that shall love you."

"I am willing," said Sir Pelleas, "for this false Ettarde has caused me great sorrow."

Then he told the damsel of the lake how he had intended never to rise from his bed but to lie there until he was dead.

"And now I hate her as much as ever I loved her, thank Providence!"

"Thank me, rather," said his companion.

Soon Sir Pelleas armed, took his horse, and commanded his men to bring after him his pavilions and his stuff to whatever place the damsel of the lake would select. The Lady Ettarde died of sorrow, but the damsel of the lake made Sir Pelleas happy, and they loved each other all their lives.

XIII

As Sir Marhaus rode southward with the damsel of thirty years, they came into a deep forest. Night came on before they came to a courtyard, where they asked for lodging, but the man of the courtyard would not allow them to stay, no matter what they offered. He said, however, "If you will take the adventure of your lodging, I will take you where you can stay."

"What adventure shall I have for my lodging?" asked Sir Marhaus.

"That you will know when you go there," said the other.

"Whatever happens, I require you to take me there," said Sir Marhaus, "for I and my damsel are weary."

So the good man opened the gate, and within an hour brought his guest to a fair castle. There the poor man called the porter, and soon they were allowed to enter. The man explained to the lord of the castle that he had brought a knight errant and a damsel who needed lodging.

"Let them come in," said the lord. "Though they may repent that they took their lodging here with me."

So Sir Marhaus was let in with torchlight, and many young men welcomed him. Then his horse was led into the stable, and he and his damsel were brought into the hall. There stood a mighty duke, with many men about him. This lord asked Sir Marhaus his name and country and court.

"Sir," said he, "I am a knight of King Arthur's, and a knight of the Round Table. My name is Sir Marhaus, and I was born in Ireland."

And then said the duke, "I am right sorry that I took you in, for I do not love your lord, nor any knight of the Round Table. Rest tonight, but tomorrow I and my six sons will match with you if God will."

"Must I fight with you and your six sons at once?" asked Sir Marhaus.

"Yes," said the duke, "for I have made a vow. Sir Gawaine slew my seven sons, and therefore I vowed that no knight of King Arthur's court should lodge with me unless I fought with him and revenged the death of my seven sons."

"Sir," said Sir Marhaus, "I require you to tell me your name."

"I am the Duke of the South Marches."

"Ah," said Sir Marhaus, "I have often heard that you have been a great foe of my lord King Arthur and of his knights for a long time."

"That shall you learn tomorrow," said the duke.

"Shall I then fight with you?" Sir Marhaus asked.

"Yes," said the duke, "in that you shall not choose. Therefore go to your room, where you shall have all that belongs to you."

So Sir Marhaus was led to a room. In the morning the duke sent for him, bidding him make ready. Sir Marhaus arose and armed. After mass and breakfast they mounted on horseback in the court of the castle where they were to combat.

The duke was there all ready on horseback, armed, with his six sons near him and each had a spear in his hand. Then they encountered, and the duke and two of his sons broke their spears upon him, but Sir Marhaus held his spear and touched none of them.

Then came the four sons of the duke by couples, and two of them broke their spears, and so did the other two. But all this while Sir Marhaus did not touch them. Then Sir Marhaus ran to the duke and smote him with his spear so that horse and man fell to the earth. And so served he each of the sons afterward.

Then Sir Marhaus alighted and bade the duke yield or he would slay him. When some of the sons recovered and would have set upon Marhaus, he said to the duke, "Tell your sons to stop, or I will fight you all to the last."

When the duke saw that he could not escape death he told his sons to yield to Sir Marhaus. And they all knelt down and gave the pummels of their swords to Sir Marhaus, and he received them. By common assent all promised Sir Marhaus never again to be foes of King Arthur, and that at the next Pentecost the duke would come to Arthur's court with his six sons.

Then Sir Marhaus left. And within two days his damsel brought him where a great tournament had been proclaimed by the Lady de Vause. The best knight was to have a rich circlet of gold. There Sir Marhaus did so nobly that he struck down forty knights, and so the circlet of gold was awarded him.

He left the field with great honor. Seven days thereafter the damsel brought him to the place of an earl called Fergus, who was afterward a knight of Sir Tristram's. This earl was but a young man who had recently come into his lands.

Now this earl complained to Sir Marhaus that the giant Taulurd destroyed all his lands and that because of him he dared not ride abroad.

"Sir," asked Marhaus, "does he fight on horseback or on foot?"

"On foot," said the earl, "he is so large that no horse could carry him."

"Well," said Sir Marhaus, "then will I fight with him on foot."

In the morning the knight asked the earl to have one of his men bring him to the place where the giant was. There he saw the monster sitting under a holly tree, with many clubs of iron and many battle axes around him.

Sir Marhaus advanced toward the giant, holding his shield before him. The giant took a club of iron and came against his bold adversary as fast as he could drive. At the first stroke he cut Sir Marhaus' shield in pieces. The knight was in great danger, for the giant was a shrewd fighter, but at last Sir Marhaus struck off the monster's right arm above the elbow.

Then the giant fled, with the knight after him. Marhaus drove him to the water, but the giant was so tall that where he was wading the knight could not wade. Then Sir Marhaus made the man of Earl Fergus bring stones, with which he gave the giant many a hard knock, until the giant fell down into the water and was drowned.

Then Sir Marhaus went to the giant's castle and set free from the monster's prison twenty-four ladies and twelve knights. Great riches were there, so that Marhaus was never a poor man after that for the rest of his life.

Then he returned to Earl Fergus, who thanked him greatly and would have given him half his land, but the knight errant would take none. So Sir Marhaus stayed with the earl nigh half a year, for he had been sorely bruised by the giant. At last he took his leave. And as he rode by the way he met Sir Gawaine and Sir Ewaine. Later he met four knights of King Arthur's court: Sir Sagramowe le Desirous, Sir Osanna, Sir Dodinas le Savage, and Sir Felot of Listinoise. Sir Marhaus with one spear smote down these four knights and hurt them sorely. Then he left and went to keep his vow.

XIV

Sir Ewaine rode westward with his damsel of threescore winters of age, and she brought him to a tournament near Wales. At that tournament Sir Ewaine struck down thirty knights, and so the prize was given him. The prize was a gerfalcon and a white steed trapped with cloth of gold.

Sir Ewaine had many strange adventures by means of the old damsel that went with him. And she brought him to a courteous lady who was called the Lady of the Rock.

In that country there were two knights who were brothers, and they were called two perilous knights. One was Sir Edward of the Red Castle, and the other Sir Hugh of the Red Castle. By extortion these two brothers had taken a barony of lands from the Lady of the Rock. When Sir Ewaine lodged with this lady, she complained to him of these two knights.

"Madam," said Sir Ewaine, "they are to blame, for they are sinning against the high order of knighthood and the oath that they have made. If it please you, I will speak to them, because I am a knight of King Arthur's. I will tell them to be fair and if they will not listen to me, I will fight them in defense of your right."

"Thank you," said the lady, "and if I may not reward you, God will!"

On the next day the two knights were sent for, to speak with the Lady of the Rock. They did not fail to answer the summons, for they came with a hundred horses. When the lady saw them come, she would not allow Sir Ewaine to go out to them, but made him speak with them from a tower. The two perilous knights would not be persuaded, and answered that they would keep what they had won.

"Well," said Sir Ewaine, "then will I fight with one

of you, and prove that you do this fair lady wrong to take her land from her."

"That will we not do," said the two brethren, "for if we do battle we two will fight with one knight at once. Therefore, if you will fight both, we will be ready at whatever hour you will say. If you defeat us in plain battle, then the lady shall have her lands again."

"I agree," said Ewaine. "Therefore see that you be here tomorrow when I shall fight for the lady's right."

Then the knights departed and made ready. And that night Sir Ewaine was entertained sumptuously.

In the morning he arose early, heard mass, and broke his fast, then rode to the plain outside the gates, where the two brothers had halted and were awaiting him. Then they rode together with such force that Sir Edward and Sir Hugh broke their spears upon Sir Ewaine. And Arthur's knight smote Sir Edward so that he fell over his horse's tail, yet his spear broke not. Then Ewaine spurred his horse and, coming to Sir Hugh, overthrew him. But they soon recovered, drew their swords, and bade Sir Ewaine alight and fight to the uttermost.

Then Sir Ewaine suddenly alighted from his horse. He put his shield before him and drew his sword. They gave each other mighty strokes and the two brothers wounded Arthur's knight so grievously that the Lady of the Rock feared that he would die. Thus they fought together for five hours like madmen.

At last Sir Ewaine struck Sir Edward upon the helm so hard that his sword carved through to his collar bone. Then Sir Hugh's courage weakened when Ewaine started to kill him also, and he kneeled down and yielded. Then Ewaine courteously received Sir Hugh's sword, took him by the hand, and went into the castle with him.

Then the Lady of the Rock was glad, but Sir Hugh sorrowed for his brother's death. The lady's lands were restored to her, and Sir Hugh was commanded to be at the court of King Arthur at the next Feast of Pentecost.

So Sir Ewaine dwelt with the lady half a year, for it was long before his wounds healed. Then when the end of the year drew nigh, when Sir Gawaine and the others should meet at the crossway, all of them remembered the promise that they had made. Sir Marhaus and Sir Ewaine brought their damsels with them, but Sir Gawaine had lost his damsel.

At the end of the year all three knights met at the fountain with the damsels. The damsel that had gone with Sir Gawaine came also, but she could say but little good of him.

Then the knights left the damsels and rode through a great forest, where they met a messenger who came from King Arthur and who had been seeking them for almost a year throughout all England, Wales, and Scotland. The messenger was charged, if he could find Sir Gawaine and Sir Ewaine, to bring them to the court again. Then all were glad, and they prayed Sir Marhaus to ride with them to King Arthur's court.

Within twelve days they came to Camelot, and the king was passing glad of their return, and so indeed were all at court. Then King Arthur bade them tell all the adventures that had come to them in the year. The honor of Sir Marhaus was well known; for there in the court were the knights that he had fought aforetime, and he was named one of the best knights then living.

Before the Feast of Pentecost the damsel of the lake came and brought with her Sir Pelleas. At that high feast there was a great jousting of knights, and Sir Pelleas had the prize of all the knights that were at that jousting, and Sir Marhaus was named next. But Sir Pelleas was so strong that few knights could keep their seat after a buffet from his spear.

And at that feast Sir Pelleas and Sir Marhaus were made knights of the Round Table, for there were two places vacant, because two of the noble company had been slain during those twelve months. King Arthur had great joy of Sir Pelleas and Sir Marhaus; but the once dolorous knight never after loved Sir Gawaine, although he spared him for the love of King Arthur. But often, at the jousts and tournaments, Sir Pelleas would not stay near Sir Gawaine.

Many days later Sir Tristram fought with Sir Marhaus on an island. They had a great battle there, but at last Sir Tristram slew Sir Marhaus. And Sir Tristram himself was so sorely wounded that scarcely could he recover, but stayed at a nunnery half a year.

Sir Pelleas was a worshipful knight and was one of the four who won the Holy Grail. And the damsel of the lake arranged that he never fought with Sir Launcelot du Lake. For when Sir Launcelot was at any jousts or tournaments she would not allow Pelleas to be there on that day unless it were on Launcelot's side.

Book the Fifth

THE EMPEROR LUCIUS

I

One day when King Arthur had rested for a long time after his wars, twelve ancient men came into the hall where he sat with his knights. Each man bore in his hand a branch of olive, to show that he came as an ambassador and messenger from the Emperor Lucius, who was at that time dictator of the public welfare of Rome.

These messengers, after coming into the presence of King Arthur, made obeisance to him in reverence, and spoke as follows:

"The high and mighty Emperor Lucius sends you greeting, O King of Britain. And he commands you to acknowledge him as your lord, and to send him the taxes which this country owes the empire, and which your father and all his predecessors paid, as records show. You, as a rebel, not acknowledging him as your lord, are withholding these taxes, contrary to the decrees made by the noble Julius Caesar, conqueror of this realm and the first Emperor of Rome. If you refuse Lucius his demand, know for certain that he will make war upon you and upon your lands, and will punish you and your subjects, so that it shall be a perpetual example to all kings and princes who would withhold their taxes from that noble empire which governs the whole world."

When the ambassadors had delivered their message the king commanded them to withdraw while he held council with his barons.

Some of the young knights, hearing this message, wished to attack the ambassadors and kill them, saying that it was an insult to all the knights there to allow them to speak to the king in that manner.

But the king commanded that none of his subjects, upon pain of death, should do the messengers any harm, and commanded a knight to take the embassy to their lodgings, and to see that they had all that was necessary for their best cheer and that no dainty should be spared. For the Romans were great lords, and, though their message did not please the king, yet must he remember his honor.

After this the king called all his lords and knights of the Round Table into council upon this matter and asked them to speak their minds freely.

Then Sir Cador of Cornwall spoke first and said, "Sir, I am pleased with this message, for we have rested many days idly. And now I hope you will make sharp war on the Romans, and I do not doubt but that we shall gain honor."

"I well believe," said King Arthur, "that this matter pleases you. The demand grieves me, for I will never pay taxes to Rome. Therefore I pray you to counsel me. I understand that Belinus and Brenius, knights of Britain, have had the empire in their hands for many days; and also Constantine, the son of Queen Helaine. It is evident that we owe no tribute to Rome but that we, who are descendents, have a right to claim the title of the empire."

Then said King Anguish of Scotland, "Sir, you ought of right to be above all other kings, for there is none like you in all Christendom for knighthood and dignity. And I counsel you never to obey the Romans. For when they reigned over us they distressed our ancestors and put this land to great extortions. I therefore make my vow to avenge myself on them. To strengthen your forces, I will furnish twenty thousand good men of war who, with myself, shall await on you when it pleases you."

And the King of Little Britain offered him thirty thousand, for which King Arthur thanked him. Then every man agreed to make war and to aid as much as he could. The Lord of West Wales promised thirty thousand men. Sir Ewaine, and Sir Idres' son, with their cousins, offered thirty thousand men. Then Sir Launcelot and all the others promised men.

So, when King Arthur understood their desire, he thanked them heartily. And then he called the ambassadors so that they could hear his answer. And in the presence of all his noble knights and lords he said to them:

"Return to Emperor Lucius, your lord and procurer for the common weal of the Romans, and say to him that his demand and commandment mean little to me. I know of no truage or tribute that I owe to him or to any earthly creature or prince, Christian or heathen. But I claim to have the sovereignty of the empire, to which I am entitled by the right of my predecessors, once kings of this land. Say further to your Emperor Lucius that I have fully decided to go with my army, with strength and power, to Rome, by the grace of God to take possession of the empire and subdue those that are rebels. Therefore I command this Lucius, and all those in Rome, that they give me their homage and acknowledge me as their emperor and governor."

Then King Arthur commanded his treasurer to give the ambassadors great and large gifts and to pay all their expenses. He assigned Sir Cador to lead them out of the land.

So the Roman senators took their leave, and went aboard ship at Sandwich, and passed forth by Flanders, Almaine, the mountains, and all Italy, until they came to Lucius. Then they gave him King Arthur's answer. When the emperor understood it, he was greatly enraged.

"I had supposed," he said, "that Arthur would have obeyed me."

"O sir," said one of the senators, "know that I and my fellows were afraid to behold his countenance. I fear that you have made a rod for yourself, for he intends to be lord of this empire. He is quite a different man from what you thought him to be, and has the most noble court in the world. No other kings or princes can compare with his noble maintenance."

"How do you know this?" Lucius asked.

"Why, sir," said the senator, "on New Year's Day

we saw hin in his great estate which was the most royal
that ever we saw in all our days. He was served at the
table with nine kings and the noblest company of princes,
lords, and knights that there is in all the world. And
Arthur in his person is the most manly man alive, and
likely to conquer all the world, for his courage is great.
Therefore I advise you, sir, to keep well your guards in
the mountains, for certainly King Arthur is a lord to be
feared."

"Well," said Lucius, "before Easter I intend to pass
the mountains, and so into France. And there I intend
to relieve this marvel of his lands with Genoese and
other mighty warriors of Tuscany and Lombardy. And
I shall send for all those who are subject and allied to the
empire of Rome to come to my aid."

Then Emperor Lucius sent old wise knights to the
following countries: first to Ambage and Arrage, to
Alexandria, to Inde and to Hermony, where the river
Euphrates runs into Asia, to Africa and Europe, to
Ertaine and to Elamy, to Araby, to Egypt, and to
Damaske, to Damiet and to Cayer, to Capadoce and
to Tarce, to Turkey, Pounce, and Pampoille, to Surrie
and Galacy. All these lands were subject to Rome!
So also were Greece, Cyprus, Macedone, Calabar,
Cateland, and Portingale, with many thousands of
Spaniards.

Then all these kings, dukes, and admirals assembled
about Rome, with sixteen kings at once, and a great
multitude of people. When the emperor understood
that they were coming, he made ready all his Romans

and all the people between him and Flanders. And he took with him fifty giants, and they were ordained to keep and guard his person and to break the front of the battle of King Arthur.

Thus Emperor Lucius departed from Rome and came down the mountains of Savoy to destroy the lands that King Arthur had conquered. And the Roman host came to Cologne and besieged a castle there, and won it soon, and garrisoned it well with two hundred Saracens or infidels. After that the Romans destroyed many fair countries which King Arthur had won from King Claudas.

And Lucius came with all his host, which was distributed threescore miles in breadth, and commanded them to meet him in Burgoyne, for he intended to destroy the realm of Little Britain.

II

King Arthur had commanded all of his retinue to be ready at the Feast of Saint Hilary to hold a parliament at York.

At that parliament it was concluded that all the navy of the land should be ready within fifteen days at Sandwich. And King Arthur there showed to all his army how he purposed to conquer the empire which he ought to have by right.

Arthur appointed two governors of the realm, Sir Boudwin of Britain, and Sir Constantine, son of Sir Cador of Cornwall, who after the death of King Arthur was sovereign of the realm. In the presence of all the lords Arthur resigned the rule of the realm and Guenever his queen unto them. Because of this Sir Launcelot du Lake was angry, for he left Sir Tristram with King Mark for the love of La Beale Isoude.

Then Queen Guenever lamented the departing of her lord and others, and swooned so that her ladies carried her to her room. Then the king with his great army departed, leaving the queen and the realm under the control of Sir Boudwin and Sir Constantine.

And when he was on his horse, Arthur said with a high voice, "If I die on this journey, I wish Sir Constantine should be my heir and crowned king of this realm as next of my blood."

Then he entered the sea at Sandwich with all his army and with a great multitude of ships, galleys, and small craft, sailing on the sea.

III

And as the king lay in his cabin he fell into a sleep, and dreamed a marvelous dream:

It seemed to him that a dreadful dragon devoured many of his people. The beast came flying out of the west. His head was enameled with azure, and his shoulders shone like gold. His belly was like mails of a marvelous hue, and his tail was full of tatters; his feet were full of fine sables, and his claws like fine gold. And a hideous flame of fire flew out of his mouth, as if the land and water had all flamed into fire.

Then it seemed to King Arthur that there came out of the east a grim boar, all black in a cloud, and his hoofs were as big as a post. He was rugged looking and the foulest beast that ever man saw. He roared and growled so hideously that it was a marvel to hear him.

Then the dreadful dragon advanced and came in the wind like a falcon, giving great blows to the boar. And the boar hit him again with his grisly tusks so that his breast was all bloody and the hot blood made all the sea roundabout red.

Then the dragon flew away, but came down on the boar with such might that the blow ground all the flesh and bone to powder, which was scattered over the sea.

So ended the dream. Then King Arthur awoke, and was worried about his vision. He sent for a wise philosopher, commanding him to tell him the meaning of his dream.

"Sir," said the philosopher, "the dragon that you dreamed of was your own person. The colors of his wings are the countries which you have conquered, his tail signifieth the noble knights of the Round Table. The boar that the dragon killed coming from the clouds is some tyrant who torments the people, or else you yourself must fight with some horrible giant, whose like you never saw before in your days. Fear nothing from this dreadful dream, therefore, but, as a conqueror, be comforted."

Soon after this they saw land, and sailed until they arrived at Barfleet in Flanders. And when they were there King Arthur found many of his great lords ready, for they had been commanded to wait upon him.

Then a husbandman of the country came to tell him how there was in the land of Constantine, near Britain, a great giant. Now this giant had slain, murdered, and devoured many people in that region. His food for seven years had been the children of the peasants of that country.

"All the children," said the husbandman, "are now slain and consumed. Lately this monster has taken the Duchess of Britain as she rode with her men, and has led her to his lodging which is in a mountain, to keep her prisoner until her life's end. Although people followed her, more than five hundred in number, they could not rescue the duchess, but they left her shrieking and crying pitifully. I suppose, sir, that by now the giant has slain her, although she is your cousin Howel's wife, and near you in kin. Now, as you are a righteous king, pity this poor lady and revenge us all as a valiant conqueror."

"Alas!" said King Arthur, "Great mischief is this. I should gladly lose the best country that I have if I could have been a furlong ahead of this beast, and rescued that sweet lady. Can you take me there, fellow, where this giant stays?"

"Yes, sir," said the good man. "Yonder where you see two great fires, there shall you not fail to find him and more treasure, I suppose, than is in all the realm of France."

When King Arthur understood the situation, he went into his tent and called unto him Sir Kaye and Sir Bedivere. He commanded them secretly to make ready his horse and harness and to arm themselves, for after evensong he wished to ride on pilgrimage with them only to Saint Michael's Mount.

Then they made them ready, armed, and took their horses and their shields. They departed thence and rode forth as fast as they could go until they came to within a furlong from that mount. There they alighted, and the king commanded them to wait there, for he said he himself would go up to that mount.

He ascended the steep slope until he came to a great fire, where he found a widow wringing her hands and moaning as she sat by a newly made grave. King Arthur saluted her and asked why she made such lamentation.

Then she answered, "Sir knight, speak softly, for yonder is a devil. If he hears you speak, he will come and destroy you. What are you doing here on this mountain? For if there were fifty of you instead of one, you would not be able to resist this devil."

"Tell me the whole truth of it," said King Arthur.

"Why, fair sir, here a duchess lies dead, who was the fairest lady of the world, wife of Sir Howel of Britain. He hath murdered her."

"Dame," said the king, "I come from the great conqueror, Arthur, to settle with that tyrant for Arthur's people."

Said the widow: "He cares not for kings or treaties. But if you have brought King Arthur's wife, Dame Guenever, the monster will be more glad than if you gave him half of France."

"I must be on my way to him," said Arthur.

"Beware, sir. Do not approach too near this giant, for he has overcome and conquered fifteen kings and has made him a coat full of precious stones, embroidered with their beards. The kings sent them to save their people this last Christmas. If you wish to speak with him, you will find him at yonder great fire at his supper."

"Well," said the knight, "for all your words of fear, I will give him my message."

Then King Arthur went forth near the crest of that hill and saw where the monster sat at supper, gnawing a human limb and warming his broad legs by a fire. And three damsels were turning three broaches on which twelve infants were being roasted like young birds.

When the champion saw that, his heart bled for sorrow. And he hailed the monster, saying, "May He that controls all the world give you short life and shameful death, and the devil have your soul! Why have you murdered these young innocent children and this duchess? Arise, you glutton! For this day shall you die!"

Then the giant started up and took a great club in his hand, and struck at the king so that his coronal fell to the earth. And King Arthur hit him so that he cut the giant's body. Then the monster in great anguish threw away his club of iron and, catching the king in his arms, crushed the king's ribs.

The three damsels knelt down and called upon our Lord Jesus to help the noble champion.

Then King Arthur wrestled with the giant so that he was at one time under and the next on top. Wallowing and struggling, they rolled down the steep hillside until they came to the beacon, and ever as he could Arthur struck the fiend with his dagger. Then they came rolling to the place where the two knights were that kept the king's horse.

When these knights saw their chieftain fast in the monster's arms, they came and loosed him. Then King Arthur commanded Sir Kaye to smite off the giant's head and to bear it to Sir Howel.

"Tell the duke," said Arthur, "that his enemy is slain. And afterward let the fiend's head be placed on high so that all the people may see it. Go into the mountain and fetch me my shield and my sword, and also the great club of iron. As for the treasure, take that also, for there you will find riches without measure. If I have the monster's kirtle and his club, I desire no more. That was the fiercest giant that ever I met, except the one I overcame in the Mount of Araby."

Then the knights fetched the club and the kirtle, took some of the treasure, and returned again to the host. When this duel was known through the countryside, the people came and thanked the king.

"Give the thanks to God who rules over all," said Arthur. "And divide among you whatever goods you find."

After that King Arthur commanded his cousin Howel to have a church built on that hill in the worship of Saint Michael.

On the next morning the noble king, with his great
army, came to a valley in the country of Champagne,
where they pitched their pavilions.   While the king was
at his dinner two messengers came in, one of whom was
the Marshal of France, and said to the king, "The
Emperor Lucius has entered France and has destroyed
a great part thereof.   Now he is in Bourgoyne and has
made a great slaughter of the people, and has burned
whole towns and boroughs.   If you do not come hastily,
the beseiged people must yield up their bodies and
goods."

IV

Then did King Arthur call Sir Gawaine, Sir Bors,
Sir Lionel, and Sir Bedivere and command them to go
straight to Lucius the emperor.

"Say to him that he must leave my land quickly.
And if he will not, bid him make ready for battle and not
distress the poor people."

Then these noble knights departed on horseback,
and when they came to the green wood they saw in a
meadow many pavilions of silk of different colors pitched
beside a river.   And toward the emperor's pavilion,
which was in the middle with an eagle displayed above,
our knights rode.

Then Sir Gawaine and Sir Bors rode to give the
message, leaving Sir Lionel and Sir Bedivere concealed.
Then the two gave their message, and commanded Lucius
in King Arthur's name to leave his land or make ready
for battle.

Then Lucius answered, "Return to your lord and tell him that I shall subdue him and all his lands."

Then was Sir Gawaine angry.

"I had rather fight against you than be lord over all France," he said.

"And I," said Sir Bors, "would rather fight you than hold in fee all Britain and Bourgoyne."

"Lo, how these proud Britons boast!" said a knight named Sir Gainus, a cousin of the Roman emperor. "They brag, forsooth, as if they bore up the whole world."

Then Sir Gawaine was grieved by these words. He drew out his sword and smote off Sir Gainus' head. After this the two messengers turned their horses and rode over waters and through woods until they came to the place where Sir Lionel and Sir Bedivere were concealed.

The Romans followed fast after them on horseback and on foot. When Sir Bors turned his horse and saw a Roman knight coming fast, he smote him through the body with a spear, so that he fell down stark dead on the ground.

Then came Calibure there, one of the strongest of Pavy, and struck down many of King Arthur's knights. When Sir Bors saw him do so much harm, he went toward him and smote him through the breast, so that he fell dead.

Then Sir Feldenak wished to revenge the death of Gainus on Sir Gawaine, but Sir Gawaine saw him coming and struck the Roman on the head. Then he returned where his fellows were concealed, and there was an encounter. For the concealed knights attacked the Romans, slew and hewed them downright, and forced them to flee to their tents.

Then the foreign foe gathered more forces. And foot-men came on. There was a new battle then, and so many people that Sir Bors and Sir Berel were taken.

But when Sir Gawaine saw that, he took with him the good knight Sir Idrus, and said he would never see King Arthur again unless he rescued them. And Gawaine drew out Galatine, his good sword, and followed them that led those two knights away. And he struck the knights that led Sir Bors, and delivered him. Sir Idrus rescued Sir Berel in like manner.

Then the battle began to be waged fiercely, and our knights were in much danger; so Sir Gawaine sent for help unto King Arthur.

"For I am sore wounded and hurt," he said.

The messenger came to the king with Sir Gawaine's message.

Then the king assembled his army. But before he was ready the prisoners were come, for Sir Gawaine and his fellows had put the Romans to flight. The knights returned without the loss of any of their number, save that Sir Gawaine was sore wounded. Then King Arthur had his wounds examined and leeches tried to heal them.

This was the beginning of the first fighting between the Britons and the Romans, and there were slain of the

Romans more than ten thousand. That night among King Arthur's host there was great joy and feasting. On the morrow after, Arthur sent all the prisoners to Paris, under the guard of Sir Launcelot and Sir Cador, with many other knights.

V

The Emperor of Rome heard that these prisoners should be sent to Paris, so he sent certain knights and princes with threescore thousand men to lie in ambush to rescue his knights and lords that had been taken captive.

On the next day Sir Launcelot and Sir Cador, who were in charge of conveying the prisoners, were about to pass through a wood. Sir Launcelot sent certain knights to see if there were any in the wood to hinder their passage. And when these knights came into the wood they saw the great ambuscade. They returned then and told Sir Launcelot that threescore thousand Romans lay in wait there.

Then Sir Launcelot, with such knights as he had, and men of war to the number of ten thousand, went to meet the concealed host. They fought with them manfully there, and slew many of the Roman knights.

Of the Roman and Saracen party the King of Lyly and three great lords, Aladuke, Herawd, and Heringdale, were slain. But Sir Launcelot fought so nobly that no man could endure a blow from his hand, for wheresoever he came he slew on every side, showing his great might. The Romans and Saracens fled from him as sheep before the wolf or the lion, and he put all that remained alive to flight.

So long they fought that the news came to King Arthur, and so he armed and came to battle. When he saw how his knights had vanquished the enemy, he embraced each of them, and said, "No king, save myself, ever had so many noble knights."

"Sir," said Sir Cador, "we did not fail each other, but Sir Launcelot's prowess was wonderful. His cousins, also, did this day many valiant feats of war."

When Sir Cador told which of the knights were slain, Sir Berel, Sir Moris and Sir Maurel, and others, the king wept.

"Your courage almost destroyed you," the king said, "for if you had returned, you would have lost no honor, for I call it folly for knights to stay when they are over-matched."

"No," said Sir Launcelot and the others, "for dishonor can never be redeemed."

VI

Arthur's valiant knights won the field and brought their prisoners safely to Paris, but a senator escaped from the battle in the wood and came to the Emperor Lucius.

"Sir," he said to the emperor, "I advise you to withdraw. What are you doing here? You will win nothing in these marches but innumerable blows, for today one of King Arthur's knights was worth a hundred of ours in the battle."

"For shame!" said the emperor. "You speak like a coward. Your words grieve me more than all the loss that I have had this day."

Then Lucius sent forth a king called Sir Liomy, with a great army, and bade him hasten, for he the emperor would follow hastily. King Arthur was warned secretly, and sent his people to Sessoyne, and took up the towns and castles from the Romans.

He commanded Sir Cador to take the rearward of the British host and to have with him certain knights of the Round Table. And Sir Launcelot, Sir Bors, Sir Kaye, with Sir Maroke, waited upon the royal person. The king separated his host into divers parts, so that his enemies could not escape.

When the Emperor Lucius entered the valley of Sessoyne he could see where King Arthur had displayed his banners. Lucius saw that he was surrounded by his enemies and that he must fight or yield, for he could not flee. Then Lucius said openly to his Romans, "Sirs, I admonish you to fight well this day and acquit yourselves as men. Remember how Rome rules the whole world. Suffer not these Britons to abide against us."

Then Lucius had his trumpets blown so that the ground trembled. Shouts were heard on all sides, and great blows were struck everywhere. Many men were overthrown, hurt, and slain, and great feats of war were shown that day. It would take long to recount the noble feats of every man, since they would fill a volume.

King Arthur rode into the battle, exhorting his
knights to do well, and he fought as nobly as a man
could.   He drew out Excalibur, his good sword, and
fought where the Romans were thickest.   Then Arthur
slew a great giant named Galapas, who was a man of
mighty bulk and height.   He shortened Galapas by smiting off both legs at the knees, crying, "Now you are
a better size to deal with than you were."

And after Arthur struck off the monster's head the
body killed six Saracens as it fell.

Sir Gawaine fought nobly and slew three great
generals in that battle.   And all the knights of the
Round Table fought most bravely.   But at last King
Arthur saw where Lucius fought and did great wonders.
He rode up to him, and each struck the other fiercely.
At last Lucius struck King Arthur in the face and made
a great wound.   And when King Arthur felt himself hurt,
he struck the Roman again with Excalibur so it cut his
head from the summit of his helmet down to beneath the
breast.

Then the emperor fell down dead.   When it was
known that Lucius was slain, all the Romans and their
army were put to flight.   King Arthur with his knights
followed the chase and slew downright all whom they
could reach.   Thus was the victory given the noble
conqueror King Arthur.

On Lucius' side more than a hundred thousand were
slain.   And King Arthur searched for the dead bodies
of the men of his retinue, and buried those that were
slain, every man according to his degree.   And he caused

surgeons to examine the wounds of all those who were hurt. He bade them spare no salves or medicines until they were all whole.

Then the king rode straight to the place where Emperor Lucius lay dead, and with him he found the Soldan of Surrie slain, and the King of Egypt and the King of Ethiope, who were two noble kings. Likewise seventeen other kings of divers regions were dead, and threescore senators of Rome, all noble men, whom King Arthur had embalmed with many aromatic gums. Then they were wrapped in sixty folds of cloth of sendal and laid in chests of lead. And upon all these bodies were set their shields with their arms and banners so that it should be known of what country they were.

He found three senators who were still alive, and to them he said, "To save your lives, I bid you take these dead bodies and carry them with you to great Rome. Present them to the Potestate for me, and show him my letters. Tell him that I in my person shall soon be at Rome, and I warn its citizens to take care how they shall demand tribute from me."

"Furthermore, when you come to Rome, I command you to say to the Potestate and all the Council and the Senate, that I send these dead bodies instead of the tribute they demanded. And if they are not content with these dead, I shall pay more taxes at my coming, for I owe no other tribute and none other will I pay."

"We understand, sir," said the three senators.

"And further I charge you to say that I command

them, upon pain of their heads, never to demand nor ask of me either lands or tribute. Methinks these dead should suffice for Britain, Ireland, and all Almaine with Germany."

Then the three senators aforesaid departed with their sad convoy, with the body of Lucius lying on a car covered with the arms of the empire. There followed two bodies of kings in chariots, and after them the remains of the senators. And so the senators went to Rome, and showed their legation the message sent the Potestate and Senate, recounting the battles done in France and how the field was lost and innumerable people were slain. Then the senators advised their countrymen to move no more in war against the noble conqueror King Arthur.

"For his might and valor are not to be doubted, when one remembers the noble kings and the great multitude of knights of the Round Table, to whom no earthly prince can compare."

VII

King Arthur and his noble knights, after the great fight against the Romans, entered Lorraine, Brabant, and Flanders. They returned then to high Almaine, and so over the mountains into Lombardy, and afterward into Tuscany, where there was a city which would not yield. So King Arthur besieged it and assaulted its stout walls for a long time.

And within the citadel the people defended themselves valiantly. Then the king called a knight, Sir Florens, and told him that the army lacked food, and that, not far from there, were great forests and woods where many of his enemies kept cattle.

"Make ready," Arthur said to the knight, "and go there, and take with you my nephew Sir Gawaine, and Sir Whichard, and Sir Clegis, Sir Clemond, and also the captain of Cardiff. Bring with you all the cattle that you can find."

Then these knights made ready and rode over hills, through forest and woodland, until they came to a fair meadow full of sweet flowers and grass. And they rested there with their horses all that night. And at dawn on the next morrow Sir Gawaine stole away from his fellows to seek adventure.

Soon he was aware of an armed knight walking his horse easily by a woodside, with his shield on his shoulder. The knight rode a strong courser, with only a page with him bearing a mighty spear, and the knight bore on his shield three griffins of gold in sable carbuncle.

When Sir Gawaine saw this gay stranger, he rode straight up to him and asked him from whence he came. The other answered that he was a Tuscan.

"You proud knight," said he to Sir Gawaine, "why are you so bold? Here is no prey for you. You shall be my prisoner before you leave."

Then said Sir Gawaine, "You boast greatly and speak haughty words. But for all your boasting, I counsel you to make ready before mishap comes to you."

VIII

Then they took their spears and ran at each other with all the might they had, and smote each other through the shields into the shoulders. And they drew out their swords and struck great strokes until sparks flew from their helmets.

Then was Sir Gawaine abashed. With Galatine, his good sword, he smote the stranger through his shield and thick hauberk made of thick mails, and all bruised and broke the precious stones, and wounded his enemy until men could see both liver and lungs. Then the knight groaned and went after Sir Gawaine again. And with a cross stroke he cut a vein that grieved Sir Gawaine greatly, and he bled fast.

"Bind your wound," said the stranger then to Sir Gawaine, "for your blood covers your horse and your fair arms. All the leeches of Britain cannot stop your blood, for wounds made by this sword can never be stopped."

Then answered Sir Gawaine, "I care little. Your boasting words I do not fear, nor shall I lose courage. You will suffer grief and sorrow before we leave. But tell me in haste who may stop my bleeding?"

"That may I do," said the strange knight, "and so I will if you will help me that I may be christened and believe in God. It will be great merit for your soul."

"I am content," said Sir Gawaine, "if God will help me to accomplish all your desire. But first tell me what you seek here alone, and of what land and allegiance you are?"

"Sir," said the knight, "my name is Priamus, and my father is a great prince, who has been rebel to Rome. My father is descended from Alexander the Great, and the warlike Hector, Duke Joshua, and Maccabaeus were of our line. I have inherited Alexandria and Africa and all the isles, yet I will believe in the Lord that you believe in, and for your labor I will give you enough treasure. I was so proud that I thought no man my peer. I was sent to this war with seven-score knights, and now I have fought with you and you have given me my fill of fighting. Wherefore, sir knight, tell me who you are and from whence you come."

"I am no knight," said Sir Gawaine. "I have been brought up for many years with the noble prince King Arthur. I take care of his armor and his other array, and point his doublets. Last Christmas he made me yeoman, and gave me horse and harness and a hundred pounds in money. And if fortune be my friend, I think that I may be helped by my liege lord."

"Ah," said Priamus, "if his knaves are so keen and fierce, then his knights must be passing good. Now, whether you are knave or knight, tell me your name."

"By heaven," said Sir Gawaine, "I tell you the truth. My name is Sir Gawaine, and I am known in King Arthur's noble court, and am one of the knights of the Round Table. He dubbed me a duke with his own valiant hands. And God's goodness lent me my strength."

"Now am I better pleased," said Priamus, "than if you had given me all the province and rich Paris. I had rather be torn with wild horses than that any varlet or page should have defeated me. But now, sir knight, I warn you, that the Duke of Lorraine is near here with all his army. He has the noblest men of arms in all Dolphine, the lords of Lombardy, with the garrison of Godard and Saracens of Southland, to the number of threescore thousands of good men of war."

"What is then your counsel?" asked Sir Gawaine.

"Why, sir, if we leave and make haste, it will harm us both, for we are sore hurt and wounded and liable never to recover. But see that my page does not blow his horn, for if he does a hundred good knights who wait upon my person are near here. If they should take you, no ransom of gold or silver could acquit you."

Then Sir Gawaine rode over a river to save himself, and the knight followed after him. They rode forth till they came to the fellows of Gawaine who were in the meadow where they had been all night. When Sir Whichard was aware that his friend was wounded, he ran to him, sorrowfully weeping, and asked him who it was that had so wounded and maimed him. Then Gawaine told how he had fought with the stranger knight, and how each of them had hurt the other, and how the other knight had salves to heal them.

"But I can tell you other tidings, too," he said, "for soon we must fight many enemies."

Then Sir Priamus and Sir Gawaine alighted and let their horses graze in the meadow; then they unarmed, and the hot blood ran down freshly from their wounds. And Priamus took from his page a phial full of the four waters that came out of Paradise, and with certain balm anointed their wounds. He washed them with that water, and, within an hour after, they were both as whole as ever they were.

Then with a trumpet the knights were all assembled for counsel. There Priamus told them what lords and knights had sworn to rescue him, and that without fail they should be attacked by many thousand. He therefore counseled them to withdraw.

"It would be a great shame to us," then said Sir Gawaine, "to retreat without fighting. I advise that we take arms and make ready to meet the Saracens. And with the help of God we shall overthrow them. And Sir Florens shall stay in this field, and we shall not forsake yonder fellows."

"Now cease your words," said Sir Priamus, "for I warn you that you shall find many perilous knights in yonder woods. They surpass you in number, for you have not more than seven hundred."

"Nevertheless," said Sir Gawaine, "we shall meet them and see what they can do, and the best shall have the victory."

IX

Then Sir Florens called Sir Floridas with a hundred knights to him, and drove forth the herd of cattle. Then seven hundred men of arms followed him. Sir Ferrant of Spain on a fair steed came leaping out of the wood and came to Sir Florens and asked him why he fled. Sir Florens then took his spear and rode against the mocking foe and struck him so hard that he broke his neck bone.

Then all the other misbelievers thought to avenge the death of Sir Ferrant, and advanced against the Christians, so there was a great fight, and many were slain and lay dying on the cold ground. Sir Florens with his hundred knights fought right manfully, and when Priamus the good knight perceived the great struggle, he went to Sir Gawaine and bade him go and help the knights who were sore beset with their enemies.

"Sir, grieve you not," said Sir Gawaine, "for the honor shall be theirs. I shall not once move my horse toward them until I see that there are more than our knights are strong enough to match."

Then he saw an earl, called Sir Ethelwold, and the Duke of Dutchmen come leaping out of a wood with many thousands, and Priamus' knights, too, and they came straight into the battle. Then Sir Gawaine encouraged his knights and bade them be unafraid, for all should soon be theirs.

Then the British host began to gallop and meet their enemies fiercely. Men were slain and overthrown on every side. And then the knights of the Round Table smote down to the earth all them that withstood them, and soon the enemy began to retreat.

"By heaven," said Sir Gawaine, "this makes my heart glad, for now they are less in number by twenty thousand."

Then a giant named Jubaunce came into the battle and fought and slew many of the British knights, among them Sir Gherard, a knight of Wales. Then our knights took heart to them and slew many Saracens.

And then Sir Priamus came in with his pennon, riding with the knights of the Round Table, and fought so manfully that many of their enemies lost their lives. And there Sir Priamus slew the Marquis of Moisesland. Sir Gawaine with his men slew many Saracens and at last had the field. But in that combat Sir Chestelaine, a child and ward of Sir Gawaine, was slain; for this he was very sorrowful, but the child's death was soon revenged.

When the battle was ended, many lords of Lombardy and many Saracens were left dead upon the field. Sir Florens and Sir Gawaine took many cattle, much gold and silver, and great treasure and riches. When they returned to King Arthur who was still besieging the city, they presented their prisoners to the king and told him of their adventures and of their conquest over their enemies.

"Now God be thanked," said King Arthur. "But what man is he standing by himself there? He seems no prisoner."

"Sir," said Sir Gawaine, "this is a good man of arms. He has matched me, but he will be grateful to God and to me if he may become a Christian. If he had not aided us, we should never have returned. Therefore I pray you that he may be baptized, for no nobler man lives, nor a better knight."

Then the king had him baptized, called him by his first name, Priamus, and made him a duke and knight of the Round Table.

Then the king assaulted the city again, and there was a rearing of ladders and a breaking of walls. The ditch was filled so that men with little trouble might enter the ramparts. Soon after, a duchess and Clarisine the countess, with many ladies and damsels, came out and knelt before the king, asking him for the love of God to receive the city and not to take it by assault, for in that case many guiltless people would be slain.

Then the king veiled his visor and said graciously, "Madam, none of my subjects shall harm you or any of your damsels, nor any who belong to you, but the duke must follow my decision."

The king commanded them to leave the assault immediately. Soon the duke's eldest son brought out the keys and, kneeling down, delivered them to the king, asking mercy. Then the king seized the town by the assent of his lords, and took the duke and sent him to Dover, there to remain prisoner all his life, and assigned certain rents for the dowry of the duchess and for her children.

Thereupon he appointed lords to rule those lands and made laws for the country. After that he journeyed toward Rome, and sent Sir Floris and Sir Floridas before him with five hundred men of arms. They came to the city of Urbine and laid in ambush there as many as they thought was best to leave. They then rode toward the town, from which many people came and skirmished with the advance riders. Then those in ambush came out and won the bridge. Thereafter they gained the town, and set upon the walls the royal banner of Britain.

Then came King Arthur upon a high hill and saw his banner displayed upon the walls of the city and knew then that the fortress was won. Soon he sent commands that none of his liege men should injure a lady, wife, or maid. When he entered the city, he passed through and came to the castle. There he comforted those who were sad, and made captain there a knight of his own country.

And when the people of Milan heard that the city of Urbine had been taken, they sent to King Arthur great sums of money and besought him as their sovereign lord to have pity upon them, promising him to be his true subjects forevermore. They yielded homage to him and fealty for the lands of Pleasaunce, and of Pavie, Petersaint, and the port of Tremble, and they promised to give to him yearly during his life a million of gold.

Then King Arthur rode into Tuscany, and there he won towns and castles and wasted all that he found in his way who would not obey. And he went to Spolute and to Viterbe, and rode from there into the vale of Vicecount, among the vines.

And from there he sent to the senators of Rome to know whether or not they would acknowledge him as their lord. But soon after, on a Saturday, all the senators who were left alive came unto King Arthur, and all the noblest cardinals who at that time lived in the city of Rome, and they all prayed him for peace and offered him riches. They besought him as governor to give

them seven weeks in which to assemble all the barony
of the Romans, and then, with the holy sacrament
which belongs to that high and exalted position, to crown
him as emperor.

"I consent to what you have devised," said King
Arthur. "And at Christmas will I be crowned there,
and will hold my Round Table with my knights there."

Then the senators made all things ready for his
coronation.

On the appointed day, as the romance reads, Arthur
came to Rome, and was crowned there by the Pope's
own hands with all the solemnity that could be made.
And Arthur stayed there for a while, and set up courts
in all his lands from Rome to France. And he gave
lands and realms to his servants and knights, to each
one according to his deserts, so that none of them complained, either rich or poor.

And he gave Sir Priamus the duchy of Lorraine.
The newly baptized knight thanked the king and said
that he would serve him and be his true subject all the
days of his life. After that King Arthur made some
knights and dukes and earls and gave his men great
riches and honor. When this was done all his lords and
knights, and all the great men of estate, assembled
before him and said, "Noble emperor, blessed be the
eternal God! Your war is finished, and your conquest is
achieved. We know no man so great or mighty that he
dare make any war against you now. Therefore we
heartily pray your noble grace to return home. Also
we pray you to give us leave to go home to our wives,

from whom we have been long away. We would rest now, since your expedition is ended with great honor."

Then King Arthur answered, "You speak the truth. To tempt God is not wise. Therefore in all haste make ready and we will return to England."

Then there was great hurry and confusion in the preparations. After the permission to leave was given, King Arthur returned and commanded that upon pain of death no man should rob by the way. He must not take food or any other thing unless he paid for it.

Thus Arthur came over the sea and landed at Sandwich, and here Queen Guenever came to meet him, right glad of his return. He was nobly received by all the people in every city, town, and borough, and great gifts were presented to him at his homecoming to welcome him.

Book the Sixth

SIR LAUNCELOT DU LAKE

I

Soon after the noble and worthy King Arthur came from Rome to England, the knights of the Round Table had many jousts and tournaments. Some good knights increased so in honor that they surpassed all their fellows in prowess and noble deeds. Especially was this true of Sir Launcelot du Lake.

In all tournaments and jousts and deeds of arms, both for life and for death, he surpassed all other knights. And he was never overcome unless by treason or enchantment.

So Sir Launcelot increased greatly in worship and honor after King Arthur came from Rome. Therefore Queen Guenever favored him above all other knights, and certainly he loved the queen in return more than all other ladies and damsels all the days of his life. For her he did many great deeds of arms, and saved her from the fire by his noble chivalry.

Sir Launcelot was long contented with tournaments but afterward decided to prove himself in strange adventures. So he bade his brother Sir Lionel get ready, and the two of them would ride in quest of adventure.

So they armed and mounted their horses, and rode into a deep forest. When they came out into a great plain, about noon, Sir Launcelot wished to sleep, for

the weather was hot.   Then Sir Lionel saw a great apple
tree that stood by a hedge.

"Brother," he said, "there is a fair shadow yonder.
There may we rest ourselves and our horses."

"Very well, good brother," said Sir Launcelot.   "In
the last seven years I have not been so sleepy as I am
now."

So they alighted there and tied their horses to trees.
Sir Launcelot lay down under an apple tree and thrust
his helmet beneath his head for a pillow and fell asleep
immediately, but Sir Lionel stayed awake.

In the meantime three knights came riding as fast
as ever they could ride, and there followed after those
three one figure on horseback.   And when Sir Lionel
beheld him, he thought he had never seen so great a
knight, nor one so well equipped.

Soon this strong knight overtook one of the three
flying riders, and there struck him down to the ground.
And then he rode up to the second knight and gave him
such a stroke that horse and man fell down upon the
earth.   Afterward he overtook the third fellow and smote
him over his horse's tail more than the length of his
spear.

Then he alighted, reined his horse, and bound all
the three knights fast with the reins of their own bridles.
When Sir Lionel saw him do this, he made ready to
challenge him.   He sought out his horse silently, hoping
not to awaken his brother Launcelot.

When Sir Lionel had mounted his courser and had
overtaken this strong knight, he bade him turn.   And

the stranger knight turned and smote Sir Lionel so hard
that he bore horse and man to the ground.   Then he
alighted and bound him fast and threw him over his
own horse.   This he did to all four of them and rode
away with them to his own castle.   When he came
there, he unarmed them and, after beating them all
naked with thorns, put them in a deep prison where
there were many more knights, who moaned miserably.

II

When Sir Ector de Maris knew that Sir Launcelot
had left the court to seek adventures, he was angry
with himself and made ready to go and seek Sir Launcelot.
After he had ridden for a long time through a great
forest, he met a man who was like a forester.

"Fair fellow," said Sir Ector, "do you know in this
country any adventures which are near?"

"Sir," said the forester, "this region I know well.
Here within this mile is a strong, well-ditched manor,
near which on the left hand there is a fair ford for horses
to drink.   And over that ford a fair tree grows, on which
many fair shields hang that belonged once to good knights.
On this tree hangs also a basin of copper and brass.   If
you strike three times upon that basin with the end of
your spear, you will hear news soon, unless you have
more fortune than has any other knight who has passed
through this forest."

"Gramercy," said Sir Ector.

So he left and came to this tree, on which he saw
many fair shields.   Among them he saw his brother's

shield, Sir Lionel's, and many more he recognized as belonging to knights of the Round Table. This grieved his heart, and he promised there to revenge his brother Sir Lionel.

So Sir Ector beat upon the basin as if he were mad, and then he gave his horse a drink at the ford. Soon a knight came up behind him and bade him come out of the water and make ready to fight. And Sir Ector turned swiftly, shook his spear, and struck the other knight so hard that his horse turned about three times.

"That was well done," said the strong knight.

Therewith he rushed his horse upon Sir Ector and caught him under his right arm and bore him out of the saddle. He then rode away with him into his hall, and threw him down in the middle of his floor. This knight, who was Sir Turquine, then said to Ector, "Because you have done this day more to me than any knight for twelve years, I will grant you your life if you swear to be my prisoner all your days."

"No," said Sir Ector, "I will never promise you that."

"I am sorry for that," said Sir Turquine.

And he took the young man and unarmed him, beat him all naked with sharp thorns, and put him down into a dark dungeon. When Sir Ector saw Sir Lionel there, he was sorrowful.

"Alas, brother!" he said. "Where is our brother Sir Launcelot?"

"Brother, I left him asleep under an apple tree when I went away, and I cannot tell what is become of him."

"Alas!" said the knights. "Unless Sir Launcelot

help us, we may never be delivered, for we know no knight who is able to match our master Sir Turquine."

III

While Launcelot lay sleeping, there came by him four queens of high estate, riding on four white mules. So that the heat of the sun should not hurt them, four knights rode with them, bearing a canopy of green silk on four spears between them and the sun.

As they rode by they heard a great horse neighing, and saw a sleeping knight who lay all armed in the shadow of a tree. When those queens looked on his face they knew that the knight was Sir Launcelot. Then they began to quarrel about him, for each of them said she would have him for her love.

"We shall not quarrel," said Morgan le Fay, King Arthur's sister. "I will put an enchantment upon him so that he shall not awake for six hours, and then I will lead him away unto my castle. And when he is surely within my power, I will take the spell from him, and then let him choose which of us he will have for his fair friend and lady."

So this enchantment was put upon Sir Launcelot. They laid him upon his shield and so bore him on horseback between two knights, and brought him unto the Castle Chariot. There they laid him in a cold room, and at night they sent unto him a fair damsel with his supper ready for him. By that time the spell was past, and when the girl came in she saluted him and asked how he was.

"I cannot tell, fair damsel," said Sir Launcelot, "for I know not how I came into this castle, unless by some magic spell."

"Sir," said the maiden, "be cheerful, and, if you are such a knight as all say you are, I will tell you more tomorrow at dawn."

"Gramercy," said Sir Launcelot, "for your good will."

So the girl left, and there he lay all that night without seeing any one. In the morning early came the four queens richly dressed. All bade him good morrow.

"Sir knight," said the queens, "you must understand that you are our prisoner, and we here know well that you are Sir Launcelot du Lake, King Ban's son. We know that you are the noblest knight now living, and that no lady has your love but one, and that is Queen Guenever. Now shall you lose her forever, and she you. Therefore you must now choose one of us four."

"And who are you, fair ladies?" asked the knight.

"I am Queen Morgan le Fay, ruler of the land of Gore. And here is also the Queen of Northgales, and the Queen of Eastland, and the Queen of the Out Isles. Now choose one of us to be your fair lady. If you will not do this, here shall you stay in this prison until you die."

"This is a hard case," said Sir Launcelot, "that either I must perish or else choose one of you. Yet had I rather die in this prison with honor than have one of you to be my friend and lady, whether I wish it or no. Therefore you are answered, for I will have none of you, since you are false enchantresses. And as for my lady Dame Guenever, were I at my liberty as I was, I would prove it upon you or upon yours that she is the truest lady living unto her lord."

"Well," the queens asked, "is this your answer, that you will refuse us?"

"Yes, upon my life," said Sir Launcelot. "I refuse you."

So they departed, and left him there alone, in great sorrow.

IV

Just at noon the damsel came to him with his dinner, and asked him how he fared.

"Truly, fair maiden," said Sir Launcelot, "in all my life I never fared so ill."

"Sir," said the damsel, "I am sorry, but if you follow my advice I will help you out of this distress, and you shall have no shame or villainy if you give me a promise."

"Fair damsel, that I will grant you, for sore am I afraid of these queens and witches, for they have destroyed many a good knight."

"Sir," said she, "that is true. Because of the renown they hear of you, they would have your love and service. They say that your name is Sir Launcelot du Lake, the flower of all the knights living, and they are passing angry with you that you have refused them.

"But, if you promise me to help my father on Tuesday next, in the tournament between him and the King of

Northgales, I will aid you. Last Tuesday my father lost the field through three knights of King Arthur's court, and if you will be there on next Tuesday and help my father, by the grace of God I will deliver you."

"Fair maiden," said Sir Launcelot, "tell me your father's name and then I will give you an answer."

"Sir knight, my father is King Bagdemagus, who was foully treated at the last tournament."

"I know your father well as a noble king and a good knight, and, by the faith of my body, I shall be ready to do your father and you service on that day."

"Thank you, sir," said the damsel. "Tomorrow see that you are ready early and I will free you. Take your armor and your horse, shield, and spear. Near here, within ten miles, is an abbey of white monks, and there I pray you to wait. To that place will I bring my father."

"All this shall be done," said Sir Launcelot, "as I am a true knight of King Arthur."

And so the damsel departed. On the morrow she came and found him ready. Then she brought him out of twelve locks, and led him to his armor. When he was all armed and arrayed, she took him to his own horse. Lightly he saddled him, and took a great spear in his hand, and so rode forth.

"Fair damsel," he said, "I shall not fail you, by the grace of God."

Then he rode away into a great forest all that day, but he could find no highway. Night fell, and then in a valley he saw a pavilion of red sendal.

"By my faith," said Sir Launcelot, "in that pavilion will I lodge all this night."

So he alighted and tied his horse to the pavilion. then he unarmed, and found there a rich bed on which he soon fell asleep.

V

Within an hour the knight to whom the pavilion belonged came back and so he laid him down beside Sir Launcelot.

And when Sir Launcelot felt him, he started up and leaped at the knight. Then they got their swords in their hands. And out of the door of the pavilion went the knight, followed by Sir Launcelot. The knight of the pavilion was wounded, and then he yielded to Sir Launcelot.

"Sir," said the knight, "that is my pavilion, and there this night my bride and lady had agreed to come to me. Instead I am now likely to die of this wound."

"I am sorry," said Sir Launcelot, "for your hurt, but I was afraid of treason, for I was lately beguiled. Come on your way now to the pavilion, and take your rest, and I will try to stanch your blood."

And so they both went into the pavilion, and Sir Launcelot checked the flow of blood. Then came the knight's lady, a very fair damsel. And when she saw that her lord Sir Belleus was wounded, she cried out against Sir Launcelot, and lamented her lord's hurt.

"Peace, my lady and my love," said Sir Belleus, "for this knight is a good man and a knight adventurous."

And then he told her how he was wounded.

"And when I yielded to him," he said, "he showed me his mercy, and has checked my wound."

"Sir," said the lady, "tell me who you are."

"Fair lady," said he, "my name is Sir Launcelot du Lake."

"So I thought by your speech," said the lady. "For I have seen you oftentimes, and I know you better than you think. But now you must promise me, of your courtesy, for the pain that you have caused my lord Sir Belleus and me, that when he comes to King Arthur's court you will have him made a knight of the Round Table, for he is a good knight, and a mighty lord of lands."

"Fair lady," said Sir Launcelot, "have him come to the court at the next high feast, and see that you come with him. I shall do all in my power, and if he prove a mighty knight, then shall you have your desire."

As they stood talking dawn came. Then Sir Launcelot armed, mounted his horse, and took his leave. They showed him the way toward the abbey, and to that place he rode within the space of two hours.

VI

As soon as Sir Launcelot came into the abbey yard King Bagdemagus' daughter arose and went to a window. When she saw it was Sir Launcelot, quickly she sent men to him to lead his horse into a stable. And he was brought into a fair chamber, and there unarmed. The lady sent him a long gown, and then she herself came.

She made Sir Launcelot passing good cheer, and

said he was the knight in the world who was most welcome to her. Then sent she in haste for King Bagdemagus her father, who lived twelve miles from that abbey, and before evening he came with a following of knights.

When the king had alighted from his horse, he went straight to Sir Launcelot's chamber, where he found his daughter. Then the king embraced Sir Launcelot. Sir Launcelot told the king how he had been betrayed, and how his brother Lionel had departed he knew not where, and how the princess had delivered him out of prison, for which he would serve her as long as he lived, and all her kindred and friends.

"Then," said the king, "am I sure of your help on Tuesday next coming?"

"Yes, sir," said Sir Launcelot. "I will not fail you, for so have I promised my lady, your daughter. But what knights of my lord King Arthur were with the King of Northgales?"

And the king said, "It was Sir Mador de la Porte, and Sir Mordred, and Sir Gahalatine; against those three neither I nor my knights could fight."

"Sir," said Sir Launcelot, "I hear that the tournament will be within three miles of this abbey. Send to me three knights of yours whom you most trust, and see that these three kinghts all have white shields, and one for me also, with no painting on the shields. And we four will come out of a little wood in the midst of both parties, and we will fall in front of our enemies and trouble them all that we may. In this way no one will know who I am."

So they rested that night, which was the Sunday. The king then left and sent to Launcelot three knights, with four white shields. And on Tuesday they lodged in a little leafy wood near where the tournament should be. And there were scaffolds built, so that the lords and ladies might see the tournament and judge the winner.

Then the King of Northgales came into the field with eightscore helmets, and the three knights of King Arthur stood by themselves. Then came into the field King Bagdemagus with fourscore helmets. In the first encounter twelve of King Bagdemagus' party and six of the King of Northgales' party were slain, and the knights of Launcelot's friend were far set back.

VII

Then came Sir Launcelot du Lake, and he thrust in with his spear into the thickest of the combat. He smote down with one spear five knights, and he broke the backs of four of them. In that throng he cast down the King of Northgales and broke his thigh with that fall. The three knights of King Arthur's court saw all this valor of Launcelot.

"Yonder is a fierce guest," said Sir Mador de la Porte.

So they encountered, and Sir Launcelot bore him down, horse and man, so that his shoulder went out of joint.

"Now it is my turn to joust," said Sir Mordred, "since Sir Mador has fallen."

Sir Launcelot saw him coming, and with a great spear gave him such a buffet that his saddlebow broke. And so Mordred flew over his horse's tail so that his helmet pitched into the earth a foot or more. And there he lay in a swoon.

Then Sir Gahalatine came in with a spear, and Sir Launcelot drove against him with all his strength, so that both their spears broke in their hands, whereupon they drew out their swords and gave each other many grim strokes. Then was Sir Launcelot angry out of measure, and he smote Sir Gahalatine on the helmet so that both his nose and his mouth burst out bleeding. His head hung low, then, and his horse ran away with him, and he fell down to the earth.

Sir Launcelot took a great spear in his hand, and before that great spear broke he bore down to the ground sixteen knights. Then Sir Launcelot seized another great spear and smote twelve more knights. After that the knights of the King of Northgales would joust no more, and the prize was given unto King Bagdemagus.

As each party left for his own place, Sir Launcelot rode forth with King Bagdemagus unto his castle. There he found good cheer both with the king and with his daughter. And they gave him great gifts. On the morrow he took his leave and told King Bagdemagus that he would go seek his brother Sir Lionel who had left him while he slept.

"If you have need at any time of my service," Sir Launcelot said to the king's daughter, "I pray you let me know, and I shall not fail you, as I am a true knight."

And so Sir Launcelot departed and by adventure came into that same part of the forest where he had been taken sleeping. In the midst of a highway he met a damsel riding upon a white palfrey.

"Fair damsel," said Sir Launcelot, "know you in this country any adventures?"

"Sir knight," the damsel made answer, "there are many adventures near at hand if you dare to meet them."

"Why should I not?" Sir Launcelot asked. "For that reason came I here."

"Well," said the maiden, "you seem to be a good knight, and if you dare to meet another good knight I shall bring you where is the best champion and the mightiest that ever you found, if you will tell me your name and of what country and court you are."

"Damsel, I am willing to tell you my name. It is Sir Launcelot du Lake."

"Sir, that is well. Certainly adventures will befall you now, for near here dwells a knight who will not be overmatched unless by you. His name is Sir Turquine, and I understand that he has in prison threescore and four good knights of King Arthur's court that he has won with his own hands. But, when you have finished this task, you must promise me, as you are a true knight, to go with me and help me and other damsels who are distressed daily by a false knight."

"All your desire, damsel, I will fulfill if you will bring me where this knight stays."

"Then, fair sir, come on your way."

So they brought him to the ford and to the tree where the basin hung. Sir Launcelot let his horse drink, and then beat on the basin with the end of his spear so hard and with such force that he made the bottom fall out of it. Thus he beat for a long time, but nothing happened. Then he rode along the gates of the manor for half an hour before a great knight came along, driving a horse before him on which an armed knight lay bound. And as they came nearer and nearer, Sir Launcelot thought that he recognized the bound knight, and at length he saw that it was Sir Gaheris, the brother of Sir Gawaine, a knight of the Round Table.

"Now, fair damsel," said Sir Launcelot, "I see fast bound a knight who is a fellow knight of the Round Table. He is Sir Gawaine's brother, and I promise you right now, by the leave of God, to rescue that knight and unless his master is the better knight I will deliver all the prisoners out of danger, for now am I sure that he has two brothers of mine as captives."

By that time the other had seen Launcelot, so they raised their spears.

"Now, fair knight," said Sir Launcelot, "put that wounded knight from your horse and let him rest a while. Then let us two prove our strength together. For if, as I have been informed, you have shamed and harmed knights of the Round Table, you must now defend the yourself."

"If you are of the Round Table," said Sir Turquine, "I defy you and all your knights."

"You boast too much," said Sir Launcelot.

VIII

Then they put their spears in their rests and came together with their horses as fast as it was possible for them to run. And each smote the other in the middle of their shields so that both their horses' backs broke under them. At this both knights were astonished. As quickly as they could alight from their horses, they took their shields before them and drew out their swords and came together eagerly. They gave each other so many blows that neither their shields nor their harness could hold their blows.

Within a short while both were wounded and bled grievously. Thus they fought for two hours or more, grimly striking each other wherever they might find any bare place. At last both were breathless and stood leaning on their swords.

"Now, fellow," said Sir Turquine, "hold your hand a while and tell me what I shall ask you."

"Say on," quoth Sir Launcelot.

"You are," said Sir Turquine, "the biggest man that ever I met withal, and the best breathed, and like one knight that I hate above all other knights. And if you are not he, I will lightly accord with you, and for your love I will deliver all the prisoners that I have (threescore and four now). So, if you will tell me your name, you and I will be fellows together and I will never fail you while I live."

"That is well said," said Sir Launcelot, "but, since it is only in this way that I may have your friendship, let me know what knight it is whom you hate above all others."

"Truly," said Sir Turquine, "his name is Launcelot du Lake, for at the dolorous tower he slew my brother Sir Carados, who was one of the best knights then living. And therefore I hate him most of all knights, for if I may once meet him one of us shall make an end of the other, and to that I make a vow. For Sir Launcelot's sake I have slain a hundred good knights, and as many have I utterly maimed so that they never after might help themselves. Many have died in prison, but yet I have threescore and four, and all shall be delivered if you will tell me your name, if you are not Sir Launcelot."

"Now, sir," said Sir Launcelot, "at your request I will tell you that I am Sir Launcelot du Lake, King Ban's son of Benwicke, and knight of the Round Table. I defy you to do your worst."

"Ah," said Sir Turquine, "Launcelot, you are most welcome to me of any knight that ever was, for we will never part until one of us is dead."

Then they hurtled together like two wild bulls, thrusting and slashing with their shields and swords, so that sometimes they both fell on their faces. Thus they fought for two hours and more, and never would rest. And Sir Turquine gave Sir Launcelot so many wounds that all the ground there as they fought was besprinkled with blood.

Then at last Sir Turquine waxed faint and bore his shield full low from weariness. When Sir Launcelot saw that, he leaped upon him as fiercely as a lion, and got him by the banner of his helmet. Then he pulled him down on his knees, and razed off his helm, and smote his neck in two. And when Sir Launcelot had done this he went to the damsel and said to her, "Maiden, I am ready to go with you where you wish me to go, but I have no horse."

"Fair sir," said the damsel, "take this wounded knight's horse and send him to this manor and command him to go and deliver all the prisoners."

And so Sir Launcelot went to Sir Gaheris and prayed him to lend him his horse.

"Fair lord," said Sir Gaheris, "take my courser at your own command, for you have saved both me and my horse. And I say that you are the best knight in the world, for you have lately slain in my sight the mightiest man and the best knight (except yourself, sir) that ever I saw. I pray you to tell me your name."

"Sir, my name is Sir Launcelot du Lake. When you come into the manor, I am sure that you will find there many noble knights of the Round Table, for on yonder tree I have seen many shields that I know. There was Sir Kaye's shield, and Sir Brandel's shield, and those of Sir Marhaus, and Sir Galind, and Sir Brain de Listinoise, and Sir Aliduke, with many more that I do not remember. And I saw also the shields of my two brothers, Sir Ector de Maris and Sir Lionel. Wherefore I pray you to greet them all from me, and say to them that I bid them take from there such stuff as they find. Ask my brothers to go to the court and stay there until I come. For by the high Feast of Pentecost I hope to be there, but now I must ride with this damsel to keep my promise.

And so Sir Launcelot left Sir Gaheris. And Sir Gaheris went to the manor, and found there a yeoman porter, keeping many keys. Instantly the knight threw the porter on the ground. Then he took the keys and opened the prison and let out all the captives, who loosed each other's bonds. When the poor knights saw Sir Gaheris they all thanked him, for they thought because he was wounded that he had slain Sir Turquine.

"No," said Sir Gaheris, "Sir Launcelot it was who slew him Sir Turquine his own hands. I saw it with my own eyes. And he greets you all, and asks you to hasten to the court. And as for Sir Lionel and Sir Ector de Maris, he requests them to await him at the court."

"That shall we not do," said his brothers. "We will find him if we live."

"So will I," said Sir Kaye. "I will find him before I come to the court, as I am a true knight."

Then all the knights sought the house where the armor was kept and armed themselves. Then each man found his own horse and all that belonged to him. When all this was done, there came a forester with four horses laden with venison. So Sir Kaye said, "Here is good meat for us for one meal, for we have not had a good feast for many a day."

Then the venison was roasted, and after supper some stayed there all night. But Sir Kaye and Launcelot's two brothers rode to find Launcelot if they could.

IX

As Sir Launcelot rode with the damsel on a fair highway, she said, "Sir, near this road stays a knight who distresses all ladies and gentlewomen. He either robs them or injures them."

"What!" cried Sir Launcelot. "Is there a knight who is a thief and an insulter of women? He does great shame to the order of knighthood and lives contrary to his oath. It is a great pity that he lives. Fair damsel, you shall ride, yourself alone, and I will keep myself hidden. If he trouble you, I will rescue you and teach him to conduct himself as a knight should."

Then the maiden rode by the way at a soft, ambling pace, and that knight soon came on horseback out of the wood with his page. He took the damsel from her horse, and then she cried out. With that Sir Launcelot came as fast as he could until he reached that knight.

"O you false knight and traitor to knighthood!" he cried. "Who taught you to distress ladies and gentlewomen?"

When the knight heard Sir Launcelot rebuke him, he did not answer but drew his sword and rode forward. Sir Launcelot threw his spear from him, drew out his sword, and struck the knight such a buffet on the helmet that he cut his head to the throat.

"Now have you the payment you have long deserved," said Launcelot.

"That is true," said the maiden, "for, just as Turquine watched to destroy knights, so did this fiend wait to

distress and prey upon ladies and gentlewomen. And
his name was Sir Piers du Forest Savage."

"And now, damsel," said Sir Launcelot, "do you wish
any more service of me?"

"No, sir," said she, "not at this time. But may
Almighty God preserve you wheresoever you go, for
you are the most courteous knight alive and the most
tender to all helpless ladies. But, sir knight, one thing
it seems you lack. You are a wifeless knight. I have
heard that you never loved a maiden, and that is a great
pity. But it is said that you love Queen Guenever, and
that she has ordained by enchantment that you never
shall love any other but her and that no other damsel
shall make you happy. Therefore many women of high
estate in this country are sorrowful."

"Fair damsel," said Sir Launcelot, "people may speak
of me whatsoever it please them. But I think I will
never be wedded. For, if I were, then should I be bound
to stay with my wife, and leave arms and tournaments,
battles and adventures. I will not love lightly, chiefly
for dread of God. For knights that are slaves to their
senses will not be happy or fortunate in the wars. Either
they will be overcome by a simpler knight than they,
or they will by misfortune and their own cursedness
slay better men than they are."

So Sir Launcelot and the damsel left each other, and
he rode on then into a deep forest for more than two days.

On the third day as he rode over a long bridge there
started up suddenly a foul churl and smote his courser
on the nose so that he turned about. Then the churl

asked Sir Launcelot why he rode over that bridge without his leave.

"Why should I not fare this way?" Sir Launcelot asked. "Surely I must cross over."

"You shall not," said the churl.

Then the fellow lashed at him with a huge club shod with iron. Immediately Sir Launcelot drew his sword and quickly cut open the churl's head.

At the end of the bridge was a fair village, and all the people came and cried out to Lauucelot.

"Sir," they said, "a worse deed have you never done, for you have slain the chief porter of our castle."

Sir Launcelot let them say what they would, and went straight to the castle. When he came there, he alighted and tied his horse to a ring in the wall. And there he saw a fair green court, toward which he turned, for he saw it was a fair place to fight in. As he looked about, he saw many people in the doors and windows who said, "Fair knight, unfortunate are you."

Then came two great giants to him well armed except for their heads, with two horrible clubs in their hands. Sir Launcelot put his shield before him, and turned away the stroke of one giant, and with his sword cut his head in two. When his fellow saw that, he ran away as if he were mad, in fear of that horrible stroke. Sir Launcelot ran after him as fast as he could, struck him on the shoulder, and cut him in two.

Then the knight went into the hall, and there came before him threescore ladies and damsels. All kneeled to him and thanked God and him for their deliverance.

"For, sir," they said, "most of us have been here for seven years prisoners to the monsters. And here we have wrought all manner of embroidery for our meat, though we are all great gentlewomen born. Blessed be the time that you were born! For you have done the greatest deed that ever any knight did in this world. Of this we will bear record. We all pray you to tell us your name so that we may tell our friends who delivered us out of prison."

"Fair damsels," said he, "my name is Launcelot du Lake."

"Ah, sir," said they, "well may you be he. None but you could have had the better of these two giants. For many fair knights and good have tried it, and have ended their lives here. Many times have we wished for you. These two giants dreaded no man alive but you."

"Now may you tell your friends who has delivered you," said Sir Launcelot, "and greet them from me. If I come into any of your districts, I shall be glad to see you. Such treasure as there is in the castle I give to you as a recompense for your grievance. And I wish that the lord who is the owner of this castle should receive it again as his right."

"Fair sir," said they, "the name of this castle is Tintagil. The duke who owned it some time ago wedded the fair Igraine. Later Uther Pendragon wedded her and became the father of King Arthur."

"Well," said Sir Launcelot, "I understand now to whom this estate belongs."

So he left them after commending them to God.

Then he mounted his horse and rode into many strange and wild countries, and through many waters and valleys. Poorly was he lodged at night until at last he happened by fortune to come to a house where he found an old gentlewoman who took care of his needs. There he and his horse were well nourished.

When it was time to sleep, his hostess brought him to a garret over a gate. Then Sir Launcelot unarmed, put his armor near him, and went to bed. Soon after he fell asleep came some one on horseback who knocked at the gate in great haste. And when Sir Launcelot heard this he arose and looked out of the window and saw by the moonlight three knights who came riding after one man. All three lashed at him at once with their swords, and that one knight turned on them and defended himself with knightly courage.

"Truly," said Launcelot, who witnessed this encounter, "that one knight will I help, for it would be a shame for me to see three knights fight one. If he were slain, I should be partner to his death."

So he took his harness and went out of a window by a sheet. Then he said, "Turn to me, knights, and stop your fighting with that other knight."

Then all three left the knight, who was Sir Kaye, and turned to Sir Launcelot. A great battle began, for they all three alighted and struck many great blows at the rescuer and assailed him on every side. Then Sir Kaye tried to help.

"No, sir," said Sir Launcelot, "I will have none of your help. If you want my aid, let me fight them alone."

Sir Kaye, when he understood the knight's wish, let him have his will, and so stood aside. Soon within six strokes Sir Launcelot had struck them to the earth.

"Sir knight," they all three cried, "we yield to you as a matchless man of might."

"As for that," said their master, "I will not take your yielding unless you will yield to Sir Kaye the seneschal. Upon that covenant will I save your lives."

"Fair knight," said they, "that we are loath to do because we chased Sir Kaye here and would have overcome him had you not been here. Therefore to yield to him would be unreasonable."

"Well, as to that," said Sir Launcelot, "think well, for you may choose whether you will die or live. You must yield to Sir Kaye, or else not all at."

"Fair knight," said they, "to save our lives we will do as you command."

"Then," said Sir Launcelot, "on Whitsunday next coming go to King Arthur's court. And there you must bow to Queen Guenever, ask her to put all three of you in her grace and mercy, and say that Sir Kaye sent you there to be her prisoners."

"Sir," said they, "if we live it shall be done, by the faith of our bodies."

There every knight swore upon his sword; and so Sir Launcelot let them depart. And then he knocked at the gate with the pummel of his sword. His hostess came then, and so both Sir Launcelot and Sir Kaye entered.

"Sir," said the lady, "I thought you were in your bed."

"So I was," said Sir Launcelot, "but I arose and leaped out of my window to help an old fellow of mine."

When they came into the light, Sir Kaye saw that it was Sir Launcelot. Then he knelt down and thanked him for his kindness, for twice had he saved Kaye from death.

"Sir," said Sir Launcelot, "nothing have I done but what I ought to do. And you are welcome. Here shall you take your rest."

When Sir Kaye was unarmed he asked for food. And when meat was brought him he ate with a great appetite. And when he had supped they went to bed.

On the morrow Sir Launcelot arose early and left Sir Kaye sleeping. He took Sir Kaye's armor and his shield and armed him. Then he went to the stable and took his horse, commended his hostess to God, and departed.

Soon after that Sir Kaye arose and missed his friend. Then he saw that the other had his armor and his horse.

"Now, by my faith," he said, "I know well that Sir Launcelot will anger some of King Arthur's court. For knights will be bold and think that it is I, and that will deceive them. But because of his armor and shield I am sure that I shall ride in peace."

Soon thereafter Sir Kaye thanked his hostess and left.

X

Launcelot rode for a long time in a great forest and at last came to a country full of fair rivers and meadows.

Before him he saw a long bridge, on which were three pavilions of silk of divers colors. Outside of the pavilions hung three white shields on truncheons of spears, and great long spears stood upright close by.

At every pavilion's door three fresh squires stood, but Sir Launcelot passed them by and did not speak.

"It is the proud Sir Kaye," said the three knights when he had passed. "He thinks no knight so good as he, although the contrary is oftentimes proved."

"By my faith," said one of these knights, whose name was Sir Gaunter, "I will ride after him and try him for all his pride. And you may see how I speed."

So this Sir Gaunter armed him, hung his shield upon his shoulder, and mounted a great horse. He took his spear in his hand and galloped after Sir Launcelot. Soon he came near him.

"Abide, proud Sir Kaye," he cried, "for you shall not pass."

So Sir Launcelot turned, and they came together with all their might. Sir Gaunter's spear broke, but Sir Launcelot smote him down, horse and man. When Launcelot stood on the ground, the brothers said to each other, "Yonder knight is not Sir Kaye, for he is bigger than he."

"I wager my head," said Sir Gilmere, "that yonder knight has slain Sir Kaye and has taken his horse and his harness."

"Whether it be so or not," said Sir Reynold, the third brother, "let us mount upon our coursers and rescue our brother Gaunter upon pain of death. We all shall have

trouble enough to match that knight, for I think it is
Sir Launcelot, or Sir Tristram, or Sir Pelleas."

So they took their horses and came near Sir Launcelot.
And Sir Gilmere put forth his spear and ran to him, and
was smitten down so that he lay in a swoon.

"Sir knight," said Sir Reynold, "you are a strong
man. And I suppose you have slain my two brethren,
for which my heart is angry against you. Except to
save my honor I would not fight you, but I must, so
guard yourself!"

Then they drove together with all their might and
broke both their spears to pieces. They drew their
swords then and lashed together eagerly. Soon Sir
Gaunter arose and came to his brother Sir Gilmere and
bade him arise, saying, "Let us help our brother Sir
Reynold, who is not matching yonder good knight."

Therewith they leaped on their horses and rushed
toward Sir Launcelot. When he saw them come he
struck Sir Reynold so that he fell off his horse to the
ground. Then he struck at the other two brothers and
with two blows smote them to the earth. Sir Reynold
then began to start up with his head all bloody, and
came straight to Sir Launcelot.

"Now let be," said the disguised knight. "I was not
far away when you were made knight, Sir Reynold. I
know you are a good knight, and loath am I to slay you."

"Gramercy for your goodness," said Sir Reynold.
"I will say for my brothers and myself that we will not
be loath to yield to you if we know your name. We
know well that you are not Sir Kaye."

"As for that, sir, be it as it may. You must yield to Dame Guenever, and see that you be with her at Whitsunday and yield you unto her as prisoners. Say that Sir Kaye sent you to her."

Then they swore it should be done, and Sir Launcelot passed on while the three brothers helped each other as well as they might.

XI

Sir Launcelot rode into a deep forest and there by a dell he saw four knights of King Arthur's court under an oak. They were Sir Sagramour le Desirous, Sir Ector de Maris, Sir Gawaine, and Sir Ewaine. When these four knights had spied Sir Launcelot, they thought by his arms that it was Sir Kaye.

"Now, by my faith," said Sir Sagramour, "I will prove the might of Sir Kaye."

He got his spear in his hand and came toward Sir Launcelot. Our knight saw him coming and struck Sir Sagramour with his spear so hard that horse and man fell to the earth.

"Lo, my fellows," said Sir Ector, "yonder you may see what a buffet he has. That knight is much bigger than Sir Kaye ever was. Now shall you see what I may do to him."

So Sir Ector got his spear in his hand and galloped toward Sir Launcelot, and was smitten through the shield and shoulder so that horse and man went to the earth, but ever the strange knight's spear held.

"By my faith," said Sir Ewaine, "that is a strong

knight, and I am sure he has slain Sir Kaye. And I see by his great strength that it will be hard to match him."

Then Sir Ewaine took his spear and rode toward Sir Launcelot. But our knight met him on the plain and gave him such a buffet that he swooned.

"Now I see," said Sir Gawaine, "that I must encounter with that stranger knight."

So he got a good spear in his hand and advanced toward Sir Launcelot. They let their horses run as fast as they might, and each smote the other in the midst of their shields. But Sir Gawaine's spear broke, and Sir Launcelot charged so upon him that his horse fell over on his back, and much trouble had Sir Gawaine to get off his horse. Sir Launcelot went on his way smiling.

"God give him joy that made this spear!" Sir Launcelot said. "For there never came a better in my hand."

Then the four knights came together and comforted each other.

"What say you to this jest," Sir Gawaine asked, "that one spear has felled four of us?"

"We commend him to the devil," said they all, "for he is a man of great might."

"You may well say it," quoth Sir Gawaine, "for I lay my life on it that it is Sir Launcelot. I know by his riding. Let him go, for when we come to court we shall know."

And they had great trouble to get their horses again.

XII

Now let us speak of Sir Launcelot, who rode a great while on in a deep forest until he saw a black brachet, apparently following the tracks of a deer that had been hurt. So the knight rode after the brachet.

On the ground was a large stain of blood, and, as Sir Launcelot rode after, the brachet kept looking behind her. She went on through a great marsh, with the knight following. Then the brachet came to an old manor and ran over the bridge, which was old and rickety.

Sir Launcelot rode over the bridge and came into the midst of a great hall. There he saw a knight lying dead, and the brachet licked his wounds. Then a lady came out, weeping and wringing her hands.

"O knight, too much sorrow have you brought me," she said.

"Why say you so?" quoth Sir Launcelot. "I never did harm to this knight, for hither by trace of blood this brachet brought me. Therefore, fair lady, be not displeased with me, for I am sore grieved for your sorrow."

"Truly, sir," said she, "I believe it could not be you that killed my husband, for he who did the deed is wounded and may never recover."

"What was your husband's name?" he asked.

"Sir," said she, "his name was Sir Gilbert, one of the best knights of the world. I know not the name of him who killed him."

"Now God send you better comfort," said Sir Launcelot.

So he left and went into the forest again, where he met a damsel who knew him well, and she said with a loud voice, "Glad am I to find you, my lord, and now I ask you, on your knighthood, to help my brother, who is sore wounded and can never stop bleeding, for today he fought with Sir Gilbert and killed him. There is a lady, a sorceress, who dwells in a castle near by. Today she told me that my brother's wounds would never be whole until I could find a knight who would go into the Chapel Perilous. And there he would find a sword and a bloody cloth that the wounded knight was wrapped in. If my brother's wounds were touched with the sword and the cloth, he would be healed."

"That is a marvelous thing," said Sir Launcelot. "But what is your brother's name?"

"Sir," said she, "his name is Sir Meloit de Logurs."

"I am more sorry, then," said Sir Launcelot. "He is a knight of the Round Table, and for him I will do all in my power."

Then, sir," said she, "follow this highway and it will bring you to the Chapel Perilous. And here I shall stay until God sends you hither again. If you are not successful, I know no knight living who may achieve the adventure."

So Sir Launcelot departed, and when he came to the Chapel Perilous he alighted and tied his horse to a little gate.

As soon as he was within the churchyard he saw on

the front of the chapel many fair, rich shields turned upside down, and many of the shields Sir Launcelot recognized as belonging to knights he had known. Thirty knights a yard taller than any man he had ever seen stood by him, and all of them grinned and gnashed their teeth at him. Their faces frightened him greatly, so he put his shield before him. Then he took his sword in his hand ready for battle. The thirty great knights were in black armor, ready with their shields, and with swords drawn.

When Sir Launcelot advanced to attack them, they scattered on every side of him and gave way. Then he waxed all bold and entered the chapel. There he saw no light but a dim lamp burning, and a corpse covered with a cloth of silk. Then Sir Launcelot stooped down and cut a piece of that cloth away.

It seemed to him then that the earth quaked a little under him, and this made him afraid. A fair sword was lying by the dead knight, and when he got this in his hand he hastened out of the chapel. As soon as he was in the chapel yard all the knights spoke to him grimly and said, "Sir Launcelot, lay that sword from you, or you shall die."

"Whether I live or die," said the knight, "with no great words will you get it again. Fight for it if you dare."

Therewith he passed through them, and beyond the chapel yard a fair damsel met him.

"Sir Launcelot," she said, "leave that sword behind you, or you will die because of it."

"I will not leave it," said Sir Launcelot, "for any word."

"No," said she, "and if you left that sword you would never see Queen Guenever again."

"Then would I be a fool to leave this sword," said Sir Launcelot.

"Now, gentle knight," said the maiden, "I entreat you to kiss me once."

"No," said the knight, "God forbid."

"Well, sir," said she, "if you had kissed me, your life would be over. But now, alas, I have lost all my labor, for I ordained this chapel for your sake and for Sir Gawaine. And once I had Sir Gawaine in my power, and at that time he fought with that knight, Sir Gilbert, who lies dead there in yonder chapel, and smote off his left hand."

"Why would you have my life?" said Sir Launcelot.

"I tell you that I have loved you for seven years, Sir Launcelot, but no woman may have your love except Queen Guenever. But, since I could not have your body alive, I should have been happy to have had your dead body. And I would have embalmed it so that I could keep it all the days of my life. Daily I should have kissed you in spite of Queen Guenever."

"Now may heaven preserve me from your subtle crafts!" said Sir Launcelot.

Then he took his horse and left her. And when the fair knight had departed the lady was so sorrowful that she died within fourteen days. Her name was Hellawes the sorceress, lady of the Castle Nigramus.

Then Sir Launcelot met the damsel, sister of Sir Meliot. When she saw him she clapped her hands and cried for joy. Then they rode to a castle nearby, where Sir Meliot was lying. Sir Lancelot recognized him, though he was pale as death from bleeding. When Sir Meliot saw the knight, he kneeled and cried, "O lord Sir Launcelot, help me!"

Then our knight went unto him and touched his wounds with Sir Gilbert's sword, and he wiped his wounds with a part of the bloody cloth in which Sir Gilbert's body was wrapped. In a few moments Sir Meliot was healed, and there was great joy among them. They made Sir Launcelot as welcome as they could. Then on the morrow he took his leave, and bade Sir Meliot go to King Arthur's court.

"It draws near the Feast of Pentecost, and there, by the grace of God, you shall find me," he said, as they parted."

XIII

Sir Launcelot rode through many strange countries, over marshes and valleys, until he came to a fair castle.

And as he passed the castle he thought he heard two little bells ring; then a falcon with long lines about her feet came flying over his head toward a high elm. As she flew to perch on the elm the lines caught over a bough. And when she would have taken her flight, she hung fast by the legs. Sir Launcelot saw how the falcon hung, and he was sorry for her.

In the meantime a lady came out of the castle and

called to Launcelot, "O Launcelot! As you are the flower of all knights, help me to get my hawk, for if the bird is lost my lord will destroy me. The hawk slipped away from me, and if my lord knows of it he is so hasty that he will kill me."

"What is your lord's name?" Sir Launcelot asked.

"Sir," she said, "his name is Sir Phelot, a knight who belongs to the King of Northgales."

"Fair lady," said Sir Launcelot, "since you know my name and ask me on my knighthood to help you, I will do what I may to get your hawk, yet truly I am a poor climber, and the tree is passing high, with but few boughs to help me."

And therewith Launcelot alighted and tied his horse to the tree. He prayed the lady to help him, and then put off all his clothes except his shirt and breeches. Then he climbed up to the falcon, tied the lines to a great rotten branch, and threw the hawk down with the branch. Soon the lady got the hawk in her hand.

Then Sir Phelot came out of the grove suddenly, armed, with his naked sword in his hand.

"O knight, Sir Launcelot," said he, "now have I found you as I would have you."

And the knave stood at the bottom of the tree to slay the rescuer of the hawk.

"Ah, lady," Sir Launcelot asked, "why have you betrayed me?"

"She has done as I commanded her," said Sir Phelot. "And therefore there is no other way, for the time is come when you must die."

"Great dishonor is it," said Sir Launcelot, "for an armed knight to slay an unarmed man by treason."

"You will get no other grace," said Sir Phelot.

"Truly," said Sir Launcelot, "this shall be your shame. But, since you will not do otherwise, take my armor and hang my sword upon a bough so that I may get it, and then do your best to slay me if you can."

"No," said Sir Phelot, "for I know you better than you think. Therefore you will get no weapon if I may keep you from one."

"Alas," said Sir Launcelot, "that any knight should die without a weapon!"

Then he looked above and under him, and over his head he saw a dead branch all leafless. Launcelot broke it near the body of the tree and then came lower and waited. Suddenly he leaped on the farther side of the horse from the knight.

Then Sir Phelot lashed at him eagerly, trying to kill him, but Sir Launcelot put away the stroke with the dead branch. Then Launcelot struck him on the side of the head so that he fell in a swoon on the ground, and he took Sir Phelot's sword out of his hand and struck his head off.

"Alas, why have you slain my husband?" cried the lady.

"I am not at fault," said Sir Launcelot, "for with falsehood would you both have slain me with treason, and now it has returned upon you."

Then she fainted as though she would die. Sir Launcelot got all his armor as well he could, and put it on for fear of more trouble, for he knew that the knight's castle was near. And as soon as he could he took his horse and left, thanking God that he had escaped that adventure.

XIV

So Sir Launcelot rode through wild ways and marshes. And as he rode in a valley he saw a knight with a naked sword chasing a lady to kill her. And just as the knight was ready to kill her she cried to Sir Launcelot and prayed him to rescue her. When he saw the trouble, he took his horse and rode between them.

"Knight, for shame!" he said. "Why will you kill this lady? You shame yourself and all knights."

"What have you to do between me and my wife?" asked the other. "I will kill her in spite of you."

"You shall not," said Sir Launcelot, "for I will fight you first."

"Sir Launcelot," said the knight, "you have no right, for this lady has betrayed me."

"It is not so," said the lady. "Truly, he speaks wrongly of me. Because I love my cousin he is jealous of us. But, sir, as you are called the greatest knight in the world, I entreat you to save me, for, whatsoever you say, he will kill me, for he is without mercy."

"Do not fear," said Sir Launcelot, "for he will not dare."

"Sir," said the knight, "I shall be ruled as you will have me."

Then Sir Launcelot rode on one side and the lady on

the other side.   He had gone but a little way when the knight stopped.

"Some men of arms are riding after us," he said, and bade Sir Launcelot turn and look behind him.

As Sir Launcelot turned, the knight suddenly struck off the lady's head.   When Launcelot saw what he had done, he was wroth.

"Traitor, you have shamed me forever," said Sir Launcelot.

Then suddenly he alighted from his horse and drew out his sword to kill the other.   But the man fell flat on the earth and, catching Sir Launcelot by the hips, cried for mercy.

"For shame," said Launcelot, "you cowardly knight! You may have no mercy.   Arise and fight with me."

"No," said the knight.   "I will not arise until you grant me mercy."

"I will proffer you fair terms," said Sir Launcelot. "I will unarm me and have nothing else but my sword in my hand, and if you can slay me, you will be even forever."

"No, sir," said the knight, "that will I never do."

"Well," said Launcelot, "take this lady and the head, and bear it with you.   Here you must swear upon my sword to bear it always upon your back and never rest until you come to Queen Guenever."

"Sir," said the knight, "that will I do, by the faith of my body."

"Now," said his accuser, "tell me your name."

"Sir, my name is Pedivere."

"In a shameful hour were you born," said Sir Launcelot.

So Pedivere left with the dead lady and her head, and found the queen with King Arthur at Winchester. There he told all the truth.

"Sir knight," said the queen, "this is a horrible and shameful deed. As penance I decree that you must bear this lady with you on horseback to the Pope of Rome, and of him receive penance for your foul deeds. You must never rest one night unless the dead body is lying beside you on the bed."

Sir Pedivere took an oath there to do this thing and left. When he came to Rome the Pope bade him return to Queen Guenever. But in Rome his lady was buried by the Pope's command. After this Sir Pedivere became a holy man and a hermit.

XV

Sir Launcelot came home two days before the Feast of Pentecost, and King Arthur and all the court were glad of his coming. And when Sir Gawaine, Sir Ewaine, Sir Sagramour, and Sir Ector de Maris saw Sir Launcelot in Sir Kaye's armor, then they knew well it was he who smote them all down with one spear. Then there was laughing and smiling among them.

All the knights that Sir Turquine had taken prisoner kept coming home, and they all honored and worshipped the man who had saved them. When Sir Gaheris heard them speak, he said, "I saw all the battle from the beginning to the ending."

And then he told King Arthur how the struggle had gone and how Turquine was the strongest knight that ever he had seen except Sir Launcelot. Almost threescore knights confirmed this record. Then Sir Kaye told the king how Sir Launcelot had rescued him when he was in danger of being killed, and how he had made the three knights yield, not to him, but to Sir Kaye. There at the court they all stood as witnesses of the truth of his story.

"And, by my faith," said Sir Kaye, "because Sir Launcelot took my harness and left me his I rode in good peace, and no man would fight with me."

Thereupon came the three knights who fought with Sir Launcelot at the long bridge, and they yielded to Sir Kaye. But Kaye said that he had never fought with them. Then he pointed out the man who had overcome them, and when they understood who he was they were glad.

When Sir Meliot de Logurs came to the court he told King Arthur how Launcelot had saved him from death. All the other deeds of Launcelot were told, how four queens who were sorceresses had kept him in prison, and how he was delivered by the daughter of King Bagdemagus.

All the great deeds of arms that Sir Launcelot did with the King of Northgales and King Bagdemagus were told, and the truth about the tournament was related by Sir Gahalatine and Sir Mador de la Porte and Sir Mordred, for all three had been at that jousting tournament.

Then came in the lady who knew Sir Launcelot when he wounded Sir Belleus at the pavilion, and at the request of Sir Launcelot Belleus was made knight of the Round Table.

At that time Sir Launcelot had the greatest name of any knight in the world, and he was the most honored by both high and low.

Book the Seventh

SIR GARETH

I

When King Arthur's Round Table was fully attended, he commanded that the solemn and high Feast of Pentecost should be held at a city and castle which in those days was called Kinkenadon, upon the sands that were near the Welsh boundaries.

King Arthur's custom at the high Feast of Pentecost, and more so than at any other holy season in the year, was never to eat until he had heard or seen some great adventure or marvel. Because of that custom, all manner of strange adventures came to King Arthur at that feast.

Sir Gawaine, a little before noon of the day of Pentecost, saw from a window three men on horseback, and a dwarf on foot. The three men alighted, and the dwarf kept their horses. One of the men was taller than the others by a foot and a half. Sir Gawaine went to the king.

"Sir," he said, "go to your feast, for here at hand is a strange adventure."

So King Arthur went to the table with many other kings, and all the knights of the Round Table, except those who were prisoners or recently slain. It was the custom that at the high feast the whole number, a hundred and fifty, should be assembled, for that was the full Round Table.

Then two men richly dressed came into the hall, and upon their shoulders leaned the fairest young man that the knights had ever seen. He was large, tall, and broad in the shoulders, with a handsome face and the fairest, largest hands that any had seen. But he bore himself as though he could not walk unless he leaned on the shoulders of his attendants.

When King Arthur saw him, room was made and all were silent. The attendants went straight to the high dais with him without saying a word. And then this big young man drew back and easily stretched up erect.

"God bless you," he said to King Arthur, "and all your fair fellowship, and especially the knights of the Round Table. I have come here to ask you to grant me three requests. These are not unreasonable and you may honorably grant them to me without great hurt or loss to you. The first gift I will ask for now, and the other two gifts on the same day a year from now wherever you hold your high feast."

"Now ask," said King Arthur, "and you shall have your petition."

"Sir," said he, "this is my petition for this feast: that you give me meat and drink for these twelve months, and then will I ask my other two boons."

"My fair son," said King Arthur, "ask more, I pray you. For this is but a simple request. I know that you must come from men of honor, and unless I am greatly deceived you will prove to be a man of great valor."

"Sir," said the young man, "be that as it may. I have asked all that I wish."

"Well," said King Arthur, "you shall have meat and drink enough. I never refused that to any, either my friend or my foe. But what is your name?"

"I cannot tell you, sir," said the fair young man.

"It is strange," said the king, "that you know not your own name, and yet you are one of the best youths that ever I saw."

Then the king took him to the steward, Sir Kaye, and charged him that he should give the youth all manner of food and drink.

"And I charge you that he have everything he wishes," said the king, "as though he were a lord's son."

"There is little need," said Sir Kaye, "to spend so much on him, for I am sure he is baseborn and never will make a knight. For if he had been gently born he would have asked horse and harness of you. His request shows what he is. And since he has no name, sir," said Sir Kaye, "I will give him a title: 'Beaumains,' which is to say Fair Hands. And into the kitchen I will bring him, and there he shall have food every day, so that he will be as fat by the twelve months' end as a pork hog."

Then the two men that had brought the youth departed and left him to Sir Kaye, who scorned and mocked him.

II

Sir Gawaine was angry at that, and especially did Sir Launcelot bid Sir Kaye stop his mocking.

"For I dare lay my head as wager," said Launcelot, "that the lad will prove a man of great worship."

"No," said Sir Kaye, "it could not be. His request showed what he is."

"Beware," said the other knight. "You treated the good knight Sir Brewnor, brother to Sir Dinadan, like this. You called him La-Cote-Male-Taile, or the Evil-Shapen Coat, and were sorry afterward."

"Like that," said Sir Kaye, "this will never prove, for Sir Brewnor always desired honor, and this one desires bread and drink. Upon pain of my life, he was brought up and fostered in some abbey. Wherever it was, they lacked meat and drink, and so he is come here for sustenance."

But Sir Kaye bade him get a place and then sit down to eat.

Then Beaumains went to the hall door and sat down among the boys and lads, where he ate sadly.

After the feast Sir Launcelot bade Beaumains come to his room, where he should have meat and drink enough. Sir Gawaine did likewise, but the newcomer refused them all. He would do nothing but as Sir Kaye commanded him. It was natural for Sir Gawaine to offer the stranger lodging, meat, and drink; for the prompting came of his blood, and was nearer akin to him than he knew. Sir Launcelot offered these things because of his great gentleness and courtesy.

The youth was put in the kitchen, and every night slept as the scullery boys did. He endured all this for twelve months and never displeased man or child, but was always meek and mild. But whenever he knew of any jousting of knights he tried to see it if he could.

And always Sir Launcelot gave him gold to spend, and new clothes. So also did Sir Gawaine.

Whenever any feats of skill were performed he would be there. And none could cast the bar or stone nearly as well as he.

"How do you like my boy of the kitchen?" Sir Kaye would ask at such times.

So it passed until the Feast of Pentecost came. And that time the king held it at Carlion, and most royally, as he did yearly. But the king would eat no meat on Whitsunday until he had heard of some adventure. Then came a squire to the king.

"Sir, you may go to the table now," said the squire, "for here comes a damsel with some strange adventure."

Then the king was glad and took his place. Immediately a maiden came and saluted him, praying for aid.

"For whom?" asked Arthur. "What is the adventure?"

"Sir," said she, "my lady, who is of great worship and renown, is besieged by a tyrant so that she may not go out of her castle. Because here in your court are the noblest knights in the world, I come to you and pray you for aid."

"Who is your lady, and where does she live? Who is he that is besieging her?" the king asked.

"Sir king," said the damsel, "my lady's name you shall not know at this time. But she is a lady of great worship and of great lands. And as for the tyrant that destroys her lands, he is called the Red Knight of the Red Lands."

"He is unknown to me," said the king.

"Sir," said Sir Gawaine, "I know him well, for he is one of the most perilous knights of the world. It is said that he has the strength of seven men. Once I escaped from him barely with my life."

'Fair damsel," said the king, "there are knights here who would do all in their power to rescue your mistress. But, because you will not tell her name nor where she dwells, none of my knights shall go with you by my will."

"Then must I speak further," said the maiden.

III

At these words Beaumains came before the king while the damsel was still there.

"Sir king," he said, "I have been these twelve months in your kitchen and have had my full sustenance. And now I would make my two requests."

"Ask upon my peril," said the king.

"Sir, these two boons I crave: first, that you will grant me this adventure with the damsel, for it belongs to me."

"You shall have it," said the king. "I grant it to you."

"Then, sir, this is the other gift: that you shall bid Sir Launcelot du Lake make me a knight, for from him I will have my honor and duty, or from none. I pray you let him ride after me and make me knight when I ask him."

"All this shall be done," said the king.

"For shame!" said the damsel then.   "Shall I have no one but your kitchen page?"

Then was she angry, and took her horse and departed.

Then some one came to Beaumains and told him that his horse and armor were ready, and that there was a dwarf at hand with all things that he needed.   All the court wondered where the rich gear came from.   When he was armed, Beaumains strode into the hall and took his leave of King Arthur and of Sir Gawaine, and of Sir Launcelot, whom he prayed to come after him.   And so he departed and rode after the damsel.

When Beaumains was armed, there were few so fine as he.

IV

Many went after him to behold how well he was horsed and trapped in cloth of gold.   But he had neither shield nor spear.

Then Sir Kaye said openly in the hall, "I will ride after my boy of the kitchen, to see whether he will know me for his better."

"Stay at home, Sir Kaye," said Sir Launcelot and Sir Gawaine.

But Sir Kaye made ready, took his horse and spear, and rode after the boy.   Just as Beaumains overtook the damsel, the seneschal came and said, "What, Sir Beaumains, do you not know me?"

Then the young man turned his horse and knew it was Sir Kaye who had mocked him so often.

"Yes," said Beaumains, "I know you for an ungentle knight of the court, and therefore beware of me."

Therewith Sir Kaye ran straight at him, and Beaumains came as fast upon him with the sword in his hand. He put away the seneschal's spear with his sword, and thrust him through the side so that Sir Kaye fell down as though dead.

Then the youth alighted and took his fallen foe's shield and spear and started upon his own horse and rode his way. All that saw Sir Launcelot, and so did the damsel. Then Beaumains bade his dwarf start upon Sir Kaye's horse, and he did.

When Sir Launcelot was come up with him the youth offered to joust with him, and both made ready. They came together so fiercely that either bore the other down to earth, and sore were they bruised. Then the older knight arose and helped the younger to get clear of his horse.

Then Beaumains put his shield before him and proffered to fight with his friend on foot. And so they rushed together like two wild boars, thrusting, lunging, and slashing for an hour. And Sir Launcelot marveled at the strength of the youth, for he fought more like a giant than a knight. Sir Launcelot was afraid that the youth would surpass him.

"Beaumains," he said, "your quarrel and mine is not so great but that we may leave off."

"Truly that is so," said Beaumains, "but it does me good to feel your power. And yet, my lord, I have not shown you my greatest strength."

V

Said Sir Launcelot, "I promise you, by the faith of my body, I fought with you with all my strength. Therefore have no fear of any earthly knight."

"Do you think I may stand against a proved knight?" asked Beaumains.

"Yes," said Sir Launcelot; "fight as you have today and I will be your warrant."

"Then I pray you give me the order of knighthood, sir."

"In that case you must tell me your name," said his sponsor. "Also of what kin you be born."

"Sir, if you will not disclose it, I will tell you," said young Beaumains.

"No," said the elder, "that I promise you, by the faith of my body, until it is openly known."

"Then, sir," said he, "my name is Gareth of Orkney, and I am brother to Sir Gawaine."

"Ah, sir," said Sir Launcelot, "I am now more glad than I was, for I thought always that you were of great blood and that you did not come to the court merely for meat and drink."

Then Sir Launcelot gave him the order of knighthood, and afterward Gareth prayed him to depart and let him go on his adventure. So Sir Launcelot left him and came to where Sir Kaye lay. He had him borne home on his shield, and his wounds almost killed him. After that all men scorned Sir Kaye, especially Sir Gawaine, and Sir Launcelot said that it was not the seneschal's part to rebuke a young man when he did not know what his kin was and why he came to the court.

When the new-fledged knight, Beaumains, had overtaken his damsel, she said, "What are you doing here? You smell of the kitchen. Your clothes are all foul with the grease and tallow that you got in Arthur's kitchen. Do you think that I honor you for the knight that you killed? No, truly, for you killed him by accident. Therefore return, you dirty kitchen page! I know you well, for Sir Kaye named you Beaumains. What are you but a lazy lubber, a turner of broaches, and a washer of dishes?"

"Damsel," said the poor knight, "say to me what you like, I will not leave you no matter what you say, for I have promised King Arthur to achieve your adventure, and I shall finish it to the end, or die."

"For shame, kitchen knave! Will you finish my adventure? You shall soon be met by one whom, for all the broth that ever you ate, you could not once look in the face."

"I will try," said Beaumains.

Then as they rode in the wood there came a man, hurrying as fast as he could.

"Where are you going?" asked Beaumains.

"O lord, help me!" said he. "For near here are six thieves who have taken my lord and bound him, and I am afraid that they will kill him."

"Take me there," said Beaumains.

And so they rode together until they came to the place where the knight was bound, and then Beaumains rode upon the thieves. His first stroke killed one, and his second another. At the third stroke he slew the third thief. Then the other three fled, and Beaumains rode after and overtook them. Then those three thieves turned and assaulted Sir Beaumains. But at last he killed them, then returned and unbound the knight.

And the knight thanked him and prayed him to ride along to his castle near there, where he would richly reward him for his good deeds.

"Sir," said Beaumains, "I wish no reward. Today I was made knight by the noble Sir Launcelot, and therefore I will have no prize but as God will reward me. Moreover, I must follow this damsel."

When he came near again, she bade him ride far from her.

"For you smell of the kitchen," she said. "Do you think that I am glad? This deed that you have done is by chance. You will soon see a sight that will make you turn again quickly."

Then the knight who was rescued from the thieves rode after the damsel, and prayed her to lodge with him that night. And because it was already dark the damsel rode with him to his castle. There they had great cheer. At supper the knight put Sir Beaumains' place near the damsel.

"Shame!" said she. "Sir knight, you are not courteous to honor a kitchen page more than me. It becomes him more to cut a swine than to sit before a maiden of high parentage."

The knight was ashamed of her words, and so put

Beaumains at a side table and sat with him there. All that evening they had good entertainment.

VI

On the next day the damsel and Beaumains, after thanking the knight, took their leave. They rode until they came to a great forest, where there was a great river and but one passage. There two knights were ready on the farther side.

"What do you say?" asked the damsel. "Will you match yonder two knights, or will you turn again?"

"No," said Sir Beaumains, "I would not turn again if there were six more."

Then he rushed into the water, and in the midst of the stream Beaumains and one of the stranger knights both broke their spears. Then they drew their swords and both smote each other eagerly. At last Sir Beaumains smote the other on the helmet so that he fell down into the current and was drowned.

Then Beaumains spurred his horse to the land, where the other knight fell upon him and broke his spear. So they drew their swords and after they had fought together long, Sir Beaumains clove the other through his helmet to the shoulders. Then he rode to the damsel and bade her lead him on the way.

"Alas," said she, "that ever a kitchen page should have the fortune to destroy two such brave knights! You think you have fought bravely, but that is not so. The first knight's horse stumbled and therefore he was drowned in the swift current; it was never by your force and might.   The last knight, by mishap, you came up behind and shamefully you killed him."

"Damsel," said Sir Beaumains, "say what you will. But whomsoever I have to fight, I trust to God to serve him before he depart.   And therefore I care not what you say, if I may help your lady."

"Shame, shame, foul kitchen knave! You shall see knights who will change your boasting."

"Fair maiden, speak to me kindly.   For, whoever the knights be, I do not care nor do I fear them."

She said, "I speak for your own good.   You may still return with honor.   For I know that if you follow me you will be slain, since I see that all you do is by accident and not by the prowess of your hands."

"Well, damsel, say what you will.   But wherever you go I will follow you."

So Sir Beaumains rode with the maiden until evensong, and always she chid him and would not stop. Then they came to a black land, where there was a black hawthorn on which a black banner hung.   And on the other side hung a black shield.   And near it stood a long black spear, and a great black horse covered with silk stood by a black stone.

VII

There sat a knight all in black armor, and his name was the Knight of the Black Lands.

When the damsel saw the sable knight, she bade Sir Beaumains flee down the valley, for his horse was not yet saddled.

"Thank you for nothing," said Sir Beaumains, "for always you would have me a coward."

With that the black knight came to the damsel.

"Fair maiden," he asked, "have you brought this knight from King Arthur's court to be your champion?"

"No, fair knight," said she, "this is but a kitchen knave who has been fed in King Arthur's kitchen for alms."

"Why comes he in such array?" the knight asked. "It is great shame that he bear you company."

"Sir, I cannot be rid of him," said the damsel. "For he rides with me in spite of me. Would to heaven you would put him from me, or kill him if you can! For he is an unhappy knave, and through misadventure I saw him slay two knights at the passage of the water, and other marvelous deeds he did by accident."

"It astonishes me," said the black knight, "that any man of worship will fight with him."

"Sir, they do not know him," said the damsel. "And because he rides with me they think he is some man of worship."

"That may well be," said the black knight. "Nevertheless, whatever you say, he is a very likely person, and seems to be a strong man. I grant you this much, I will put him down on his feet. His horse and his armor he shall leave with me, but it would be a shame for me to do him any more harm."

When Sir Beaumains heard him say this to her, he said, "Sir knight, you are full liberal with my horse and my harness. I will let you know they cost you naught, and whether you like it or not I will pass this land in spite of you. You will get no horse and harness from me unless you win them with your hands. Therefore let me see what you can do."

"Dare you say that?" said the black knight. "Now leave the lady, for it does not become a kitchen knave to ride with a gentlewoman."

"You lie!" said Sir Beaumains. "I am a gentleman born and of higher lineage than you, and that I will prove upon your body."

Then in great wrath they came together with their horses with a noise as of thunder. The black knight's spear broke, and Sir Beaumains thrust him through both his sides. Therewith his spear broke, and the truncheon stuck still in the black knight's ribs. But the black knight drew his sword and smote many eager strokes of great force, and wounded Sir Beaumains. But the black knight within an hour and a half fell down from his horse in a swoon and died there.

And when Beaumains saw him so well armed he alighted, put on the armor, took his horse, and rode after the damsel.

When he came near, she said, "Away, kitchen knave, get out of the wind, for the smell of your greasy clothes grieves me. Alas! that ever such a man as you should slay as good a knight as you have conquered! But all this is by accident. Near here is a knight who will pay you back all your debt; therefore I advise you to run away."

"It may chance," said Sir Beaumains, "that I shall

be killed, but I warn you, fair damsel, that I will not flee away nor leave your company for all that you can say. It would be as well for you to keep still as to chide me all day. For I will not go until I finish this journey unless I am killed or truly beaten. Therefore ride on your way, for I will follow you whatever happens."

VIII

As they rode together they saw a knight come by them all in green, both his horse and his harness.

And when he came near the damsel he asked her, "Is that my brother the black knight that you have with you?"

"No, no," said she, "this kitchen knave has slain your brother."

"Alas!" said the green knight. "It is great pity that so noble a knight as he was should be slain by a knave's hand. Ah, traitor, you shall die for slaying my kin! He was a noble knight, and his name was Sir Percard."

"I defy you," said Sir Beaumains, "for I will have you know that I slew him in knightly fashion and not shamefully."

Then the green knight rode up to a green horn which hung upon a thorn. He blew three deadly notes, and three damsels came and armed him.

Then he took a great horse and a green shield and a green spear. And they ran together with all their might, and broke their spears in their hands. Then they drew out their swords and gave many sad strokes. Each of them wounded the other cruelly. At last Sir Beaumain's

horse struck the green knight's courser on the side so
that he fell to the ground. The green knight easily got
off his horse and stood upon his feet.

Sir Beaumains alighted then, and they rushed together
like two mighty champions until both had many wounds.
Thereafter the damsel came and said to the green knight,
"My lord, for shame! Why stand you fighting with
that kitchen knave so long? Alas! It is a shame that
ever you were made knight, to see such a filthy boy match
such a valiant knight as you."

When he heard these words the green knight was
ashamed, and he gave Sir Beaumains such a mighty
stroke that he cut his shield. When the young knight
saw his shield in pieces, he was ashamed of that stroke
and of the damsel's insult. Angrily he gave the green
knight such a buffet upon the helmet that the knight fell
on his knees and groveled on the ground.

The green knight cried then for Sir Beaumains'
mercy, and yielded to the supposed kitchen knave, praying him to grant him his life.

"All this is in vain," said Sir Beaumains, "for you
shall die unless this damsel who has come with me pray
me to save your life."

Then he unlaced the green knight's helmet, to slay
him.

"For shame, you kitchen page," cried the damsel,
"I will never pray you to save his life."

"Then shall he die," said Sir Beaumains.

"Be not so rash, you unclean knave," said the
damsel, "as to slay him."

"Alas!" said the green knight. "Do not allow me to die, when a fair word may save my life. Spare me, fair knight, and I will forgive the death of my brother, and forever become your man, and my thirty knights forever shall do you service."

"In the name of the Evil One!" said the damsel. "That such a foul kitchen knave should have you and thirty knights' service!"

"Sir knight," said the young victor, "all this will not avail unless my damsel asks me for your life."

Then he raised his hand to kill him.

"Let be," said the damsel. "You wicked knave, do not kill him. If you do, you shall repent it."

"Damsel," said Sir Beaumains, "your charge is to me a pleasure. And at your command his life shall be saved."

Then he said, "Sir knight with the green armor, I release you at this maiden's request, for I will not make her angry. I will fulfill all that she bids me do."

Then the green knight kneeled down and did him homage with his sword.

Then said the maiden, "I am sorry, green knight, for your homage and for the death of your brother, the black knight. Of your help I had great need, since I am sore afraid to pass this great forest."

"No, do not be afraid," said the green knight, "for you shall lodge with me tonight, and tomorrow I will help you through the huge wood."

So they took their horses and rode to his manor, which was near by.

IX

And always the maiden rebuked Sir Beaumains and would not suffer him to sit at her table. But the green knight put him at a side table.

"I cannot understand," said the green knight to the damsel, "why you rebuke this noble knight as you do. For I warn you, damsel, he is a noble knight, and I know no other man who can match him. Therefore you do wrong to insult him, for he will do you right good service. Whatsoever he pretends to be, you will find at the end that he is come of noble blood and of king's lineage."

"Shame, shame," said the maiden, "for you to say of him such worship!"

"Truly," said the other, "it would be shame for me to say of him any dishonor, for he has proved himself a better knight than I am, yet have I met with many knights in my life, and never before this time have I found a knight his match."

And so that night they went to their rest. And all through the hours the green knight commanded thirty knights to watch Sir Beaumains secretly to keep him from all treason.

On the morrow they arose, and heard mass, and broke their fast. And then they took their horses and rode on their way. And the green knight took them through the forest.

"My lord Sir Beaumains," then said the green knight, "I and my thirty knights will always be at your command, both early and late, wheresoever you will send us."

"It is well said," quoth Sir Beaumains, "and when I call upon you, you must yield yourself and all your knights unto King Arthur."

"If you so command us, we shall be ready at all times," said the green knight.

"Shame on you!" said the damsel. "That any good knight should be obedient to a kitchen knave!"

Then parted the green knight and the damsel. And then said she to Beaumains, "Why do you follow me, kitchen boy? Cast away your shield and your spear, I counsel you, and flee away betimes. Or you shall soon say 'Alas!' For if you were as mighty as ever was Sir Launcelot, Sir Tristram, or the good knight Sir Lamorak, you might not go beyond a pass hereby that is called the Pass Perilous."

"Damsel," said Beaumains, "he who is afraid may flee. For it would be shameful to turn again when I have ridden so long with you."

"Well," said the maiden, "you shall soon see whether you will turn or not."

X

Soon they saw a tower as white as snow, well fortified all about, and double ditched. Over the tower gate hung fifty shields of divers colors.

Under that tower there was a fair meadow, and therein were many knights and squires in pavilions and upon scaffolds. There at that castle on the morrow a great tournament was to be held. And the lord of that tower was in his castle and looked out of a window. And he saw a damsel and a page, and a knight armed at all points.

"So heaven help me," said the lord of the tower, "with that knight will I joust, for I see that he is a knight errant."

So he armed himself and took his horse hastily. And when he was on horseback, his shield and his spear, his horse and his harness, and all that belonged to him were bright red. And when he came near Sir Beaumains he thought that he was his brother, the black knight.

"Brother," cried he then aloud, "what do you here?"

"No, no," said the damsel, "it is not your brother. This is but a kitchen knave who has been brought up for alms in King Arthur's court."

"Nevertheless," said the red knight, "I will speak with him before he leaves."

"Ah," said the damsel, "Sir Kaye named him Beaumains, and this knave has slain your brother. This horse and harness belonged to your brother the black knight. I saw him overcome also your brother the green knight with his own hands. Now you may be revenged upon him, for I cannot get rid of him."

With this both the knights parted. And they came together with all their might so that both of their horses fell to the earth. And lightly they got off their saddles, and put their shields before them, and drew their swords. And each gave to the other many sad strokes, now here and now there, thrusting, lunging, cutting, and hurling like two boars for the space of three hours.

Then the damsel cried out to the red knight, "Alas,

noble red knight, think what honor has been yours! Never let a kitchen knave overcome you!"

Then the red knight became angry and doubled his strokes, and wounded Sir Beaumains so that the blood ran down to the ground and it was a wonder to see that strong battle. Yet at the last Sir Beaumains struck him to the ground. But when Beaumains would have slain the red knight, he cried for mercy.

"Noble knight, do not kill me," he said, "and I will give you fifty knights who are at my command. And I forgive you all the shame you have done to me, and the death of my brother the black knight."

"All this will not help you," said Sir Beaumains, "unless my damsel asks me to save your life."

And therewith he pretended to get ready to strike off the red knight's head, but the damsel said, "Beaumains, do not kill him, for he is a noble knight. Be not so rash—you had better save him."

Then Sir Beaumains bade the red knight stand up and thank the maiden for his life. Whereupon the knight prayed Sir Beaumains to see his castle and to lodge there all that night. The damsel accompanied them and they had great cheer there.

But always the girl spoke many insulting words to Sir Beaumains, at which the red knight wondered. And while Beaumains slept the red knight had three score knights watch Sir Beaumains so that he should have no shame or villainy.

On the morrow they heard mass and broke their fast. Then the red knight came before Sir Beaumains with his threescore knights.   He proffered him his hom-age and fealty at all times.

"I thank you," said Sir Beaumains.   "Only this shall you grant me, when I call upon you, to come before my lord King Arthur and yield you unto him to be his knight."

"Sir," said the red knight, "I will be ready with all my knights at your command."

So Sir Beaumains and the damsel departed, and ever she rode before him chiding him.

XI

"Damsel," said Sir Beaumains, "you are uncourteous to rebuke me as you do, for it seems to me that I have done you great service.   And ever you threaten me that I shall be defeated by knights that we meet but always they lie in the dust or in the mire.   And therefore I pray you rebuke me no more.   When you see me beaten or yielding as a coward, then you may bid me go from you shamefully.   But I tell you that I will not depart from you otherwise."

"Well," said the damsel, "right soon you will meet with a knight who will pay you all your wages, for he is the man of the most worship in all the world, except King Arthur."

"I am willing," said Sir Beaumains.   "The more honor he has, the more shall it be to my honor to fight with him."

Then they saw before them a fair city, but between them and the city for a mile and a half there was a fair meadow that was new-mown, wherein were many pavilions goodly to behold.

"Lo," said the damsel, "yonder is the lord who owns that city. And his custom, when the weather is fair, is to lie in this meadow to joust and tourney. And always there are about him five hundred knights, and all gentlemen of arms. And there are all the games that any gentleman can devise or think."

"That lord," said Sir Beaumains, "would I gladly see."

"You shall see him soon enough," said the damsel.

As they rode near, she saw the pavilion where he was.

"See," asked she, "yonder pavilion that is all of the color of Ind? All manner of things about it, both men and women, and horses trapped, shields and spears, are all of the same hue. And there rests Sir Persaunt of Ind, the most lordly knight that ever you looked upon."

"That may well be," said Sir Beaumains, "but, no matter how brave a knight he is in this field, I will stay until I see him under his shield."

"Fool!" said she. "You had better fly in time."

"Why," said Beaumains, "if he be such a knight as you make him out, he will not set upon me with all his men, or with his five hundred knights at one bout. And if there comes no more than one at once, I shall never fail him while my life lasts."

"Shame," said the damsel, "that ever such a kitchen-smelling knave should make such a boast!"

"Damsel," said Sir Beaumains, "I had rather fight five battles than to be so rebuked."

"Sir," said she, "I wonder who you are and of what kin you come. Boldly you speak and boldly you have fought. Therefore I pray you save yourself while you have time. For your horse and you have had great labor, and I fear we are delaying overlong from the siege toward which we are faring. Our goal is but seven miles hence, and all perilous passages have we passed save only this one. And here I fear that you will catch some hurt. Therefore I wish that we were away from here and that you should not be bruised by this strong knight. But I tell you that this Sir Persaunt of Ind is nothing in might or strength to the knight that is besieging my lady."

"As for that," said Sir Beaumains, "have no doubt, damsel, that by the grace of God I shall so deal with this knight Sir Persaunt that within two hours after noon shall deliver him. And then shall we come to the siege by daylight."

"Oh, mercy!" said the damsel. "I have marveled what manner of man you may be. For you must come of noble blood. Never did a woman offer more foul or more shameful treatment to a knight than I have done to you, but ever courteous have you been to me and that came never but of gentle blood and lineage."

"Damsel," said Sir Beaumains, "a knight has little strength who may not have patience with a damsel. For, whatsoever you said to me, I took no heed to your words. For the more you said, the more you angered me, and my wrath I wreaked upon them with whom I fought. And therefore all your insults furthered me in my battles and caused me to prove myself in the end, for peradventure, though I had meat in King Arthur's kitchen, damsel, yet I might have had enough in other places. All that I did to prove and to try my friends, and the result will be known some other day. And, whether I be a gentleman born or not, I let you know, fair maiden, I have done you gentleman's service. And perhaps better service yet will I do for you before I depart from your side."

"Alas!" said she. "Fair Beaumains, forgive me all that I have said and done against you."

"With all my heart," said the knight, "do I forgive you. For you did nothing but as you ought to do, since all your evil words helped me. And, maiden, since you speak thus fair to me, it pleases me greatly. And now I think there is no knight living whom I cannot conquer."

XII

Sir Persaunt of Ind had seen them as they came into the field, and he sent to them to know whether they came in war or peace.

"Say to your lord," said Sir Beaumains, "I will use no force unless he wishes."

"Well," said Sir Persaunt, when the messenger had told him all the answer, "then will I fight him to the uttermost."

And so he armed and rode against the errant knight.

And when Sir Beaumains saw him he made ready, and there they met with all the might that their horses had. They broke their spears in three pieces, and their horses rushed so together that they both fell dead to the earth. Then the knights put their shields before them and drew out their swords. They gave each other many great strokes so that often they came together with such force that they both fell groveling on the ground.

Thus they fought for two hours and more so that their shields and their hauberks were hacked to pieces, and the knights were wounded in many places. At last Sir Beaumains struck the knight of Ind through the side of the body, and then he retreated here and there, but maintained his battle a long time.

Then Sir Beaumains smote Sir Persaunt on the helmet so that he fell sprawling to the earth, and he leaped over him and unlaced his helmet to kill him.

Then Sir Persaunt yielded and asked for mercy. The damsel came and prayed Sir Beaumains to spare his life.

"I am willing," said the young victor, "for it would be a pity that this noble knight should die."

"Gramercy, gentle knight and damsel," said Sir Persaunt, "for certainly now I know well it was you that killed the black knight my brother at the black thorn. He was a full noble knight; his name was Sir Percard. Also I am sure that you are he that won my other brother, the green knight; his name was Sir Pertolope. Also you defeated the red knight my brother, Sir Perimones. And now, sir, since you have won these knights, this shall I do to please you. You shall have my homage and fealty, and a hundred knights will always be at your command, to go and ride where you will command us."

Then they went to Sir Persaunt's pavilion, where they drank wine and ate spices.

XIII

On the next day the damsel and Sir Beaumains heard mass and broke their fast; then took they their leave.

"Fair damsel," asked Sir Persaunt, "where are you leading this noble knight?"

"Sir," said she, "this knight is going to the siege of my sister at the Castle Dangerous."

"Well," said Sir Persaunt, "that is the Knight of the Red Lands, who is the most perilous knight that I know now living, and a man that is without mercy. They say that he has seven men's strength. God save you from that knight, Sir Beaumains, for he does great wrong to that lady. And that is a great pity, for she is one of the fairest gentlewomen of the world, and I think that your lady here is her sister."

"Yea," said the damsel, "I am the sister Linet, and my lady's name is Dame Lyones."

"Now I will tell you," said Sir Persaunt. "This Red Knight of the Red Lands has laid siege almost two years. And many times he might have taken Dame Lyones if he had wished, but he prolonged the time because he wished Sir Launcelot du Lake to fight with him, or Sir Tristram, or Sir Lamorak de Galis. For this reason the red knight tarries at the siege."

"Now, my lord Sir Persaunt," said the damsel Linet, "I require you that you will make this gentleman knight before he fights with the red besieger."

"I will with all my heart," said Sir Persaunt, "if it would please him to take the order of knighthood from so simple a person as I am."

"Sir," said Beaumains, "I thank you for your good will, but the noble knight Sir Launcelot made me knight."

"Ah," said Sir Persaunt, "of all the knights in the world your sponsor may be called chief, for there are none who can surpass him. God speed you well, young sir, and if you match the red knight you shall be called the fourth knight of the world, after Sir Launcelot, Sir Tristram and Sir Lamorak."

"Sir," said Beaumains, "I wish to be of good fame and of chivalry, and I will tell you that I come of good blood. For my father was a noble man. If you will keep it secret, and you, too, damsel, I will tell you of what kin I am."

"We will not betray you," said they both, "by the faith that we owe unto God."

"Truly," said he, "my name is Sir Gareth of Orkney, and King Lot was my father, and my mother is King Arthur's sister, whose name is Dame Morgawse, and Sir Gawaine and Sir Agravaine and Sir Gaheris are my brothers. I am the youngest of them all, and as yet neither King Arthur nor Sir Gawaine know who I am."

XIV

The lady who was besieged was told by the dwarf of her sister's coming, and how she brought a knight with her, and how he had passed all the perilous passages.

"What manner of man is he?" asked Dame Lyones.

"He is a noble knight, truly, madam," said the dwarf, "and though but young, he is as handsome a man as ever you saw."

"Who is he?" asked the lady. "Of what kin? By whom was he made knight?"

"Madam," said the dwarf, "he is the king's son of Orkney, but his name I will not tell you. But Sir Launcelot du Lake made him a knight, for from no other would he receive the order of chivalry. And Sir Kaye named him Beaumains."

"How escaped he the brothers of Sir Persaunt?"

"Madam, as a noble knight should. First, he slew two brothers at a ford."

"They were good knights," said the lady, "but they were murderers; one was called Sir Gherard le Brewse, and the other Sir Arnold le Brewse."

"Then, madam, he fought with the black knight, and killed him in combat. Then he took his horse and armor and fought with the green knight and defeated him. So did he serve the red knight, and afterward attended to the blue knight and defeated him."

"Then," said the lady, "he has overcome Sir Persaunt of Ind, one of the noblest knights of the world."

"Yet he did more," said the dwarf, "for he overthrew Sir Kaye the seneschal, and left him nearly dead upon the earth. And he did great battle with Sir Launcelot, and Sir Launcelot made him knight."

"Dwarf, I am glad of these tidings," said the lady. "Therefore go to a hermitage of mine near here. Take there two silver flagons of my wine, a quantity of bread, some baked venison, and dainty fowls. And here is a rich and precious cup of gold. Put all these in the hermits' hands.

"And when you have done this, go to my sister, greet her, and commend me to that gentle knight. Pray him to eat and drink and make himself strong. Tell him that I thank him for his courtesy and his kindness in doing all this for me who never did anything for him. Pray him also that he be courageous, for he shall meet a knight of great valor, but one who has no courtesy or gentleness, for he thinks of nothing but murder. And that is why I can neither praise him nor love him."

Then the dwarf left and came to Sir Persaunt, where he found Linet and Sir Beaumains. And there he told them all this. And they took their leave, but Sir Persaunt conveyed them on their way and at last left them commending them to God.

Within a little while they came to the hermitage, and there they drank the wine and ate the venison and the fowls which had been baked. When they had feasted, the dwarf returned to the castle. There the Red Knight of the Red Lands met him, and asked him from whence he came.

"Sir," said the dwarf, "I have been with my lady's sister of this castle. She has been at King Arthur's court and has brought a knight back with her."

"Then I account her travel lost," said the murderer, "for though she had brought with her Sir Launcelot, Sir Tristram, Sir Lamorak, or Sir Gawaine, I should still think myself good enough to deal with such."

"That may well be," said the dwarf, "but this knight has come safely through all the perilous passages, and has slain the black knight and two others, and has defeated the green knight, the red knight, and the blue knight."

"Then he bears one of the four names I have mentioned."

"He is none of those, truly," said the dwarf, "but he is a great king's son."

"What is his name?" asked the Red Knight of Red Lands.

"That I cannot tell you," said the dwarf, "but Sir Kaye in scorn called him Beaumains."

"I care not for him, whoever he is," said the red knight, "for I shall soon fight him. He shall have a shameful death, as many others have had."

"That would be a pity," said the dwarf. "Why do you make such shameful war upon noble knights?"

XV

Sir Beaumains stayed all night in the hermitage. In the morning he and the damsel Linet heard mass and broke their fast. Then they took their horses and rode through a fair forest to a plain where there were many pavilions and tents. There was a fair castle here, with much smoke and great noise.

When they came near the siege, Sir Beaumains saw upon high trees as he rode nearly forty armed knights hanged by the neck, with their shields and their swords about their necks. Then was Sir Beaumains angry.

"What means this?" he asked.

"Fair sir," said the damsel, "do not be sad at this sight, for you must have courage, or you will lose. All these knights came hither to rescue my sister, Dame Lyones. And when the Red Knight of the Red Lands had overcome them, he put them to this shameful death, without mercy or pity. In the same wise will he serve you unless you overcome him."

"Now may heaven defend me," said Sir Beaumains "from such a villainous death! For rather would I be slain in battle than fare like this."

"Do not trust him," said Linet, "for he has no courtesy. All go to death or shameful murder. That is a great pity, for he is a handsome man and a knight of great bravery and a lord of great lands and possessions."

"Truly," said Sir Beaumains, "he may well be a brave knight, but he has shameful customs. It is a marvel that he lives so long and that none of the powerful knights of my lord King Arthur's court has fought with him."

Then they rode to the ditches, and saw them doubly built with full strong walls. And many lords were lodged near the walls. There was loud noise of minstrels, and the sea beat upon one side of the castle, and the many cries of "Hale and ho!" of the mariners could be heard.

Near a sycamore tree hung a horn, the largest that they had ever seen, made of an elephant's bone.

Said Linet, "This knight of the Red Lands has hung it there so that if any errant knight comes by he will blow that horn. And then will the murderous fellow make him ready and come out to the knight to battle with him. But, sir, I pray you," said the damsel, "blow not on the horn until it be high noon, for now it is about dawn. His strength increases now, and men say he has seven men's strength."

"Ah, shame! Do not speak like that to me. For, no matter how good a knight he is, I will never fail him in his greatest power. I will either win worship from him or die right nobly in the field."

Therewith Beaumains spurred his horse to the sycamore tree and blew the horn so eagerly that all the camp of the siege and the castle rang.

Then knights leaped out of their tents and pavilions, and those who were within the castle looked over the walls and out of the windows. Then the Red Knight of the Red Lands armed hastily, and two barons set his spurs upon his heels. All was blood red: his armor, his spear, and his shield. An earl buckled his helmet on his head. Then they brought him a red spear and a steed, and so he rode into a little vale under the castle so that all in the castle and at the siege might behold the battle.

XVI

"Sir," said Linet unto Sir Beaumains, "be merry and light, for yonder is your deadly enemy. And at yonder window is my lady, my sister Dame Lyones."

"Where?" asked Sir Beaumains.

"There," said the damsel, and pointed with her finger.

"She seems from here to be the fairest lady that ever I looked upon," said Sir Beaumains. "Truly, she shall be my lady, and for her will I fight."

And he looked up at the window with glad countenance, and the Lady Lyones curtsied down to the ground. Then the red knight called to him.

"Stop your gazing, sir knight," he said, "and look at me, I advise you. I warn you that she is my lady, and for her sake I have fought many fierce battles."

"If you have done so," said Sir Beaumains, "it seems wasted labor to me. For she does not love your fellowship. To love one who does not love you is great folly. If I thought she was not glad of my coming, I would wait before I did battle for her but I see by the besieging of this castle that she does not desire your company. Therefore, know you well, you Red Knight of the Red Lands, that I love her and will rescue her, or die in the quarrel."

"Say you that?" asked the red knight. "You ought to beware because of the knights that you saw hanging on yonder elms."

"Shame," said Sir Beaumains, "that you should say or do such evil! For by that deed you have put shame upon yourself and upon the order of knighthood. You may be sure that no lady will love you who knows your detestable customs. You thought that the sight of those hanged knights would make me afraid? No, truly not. That shameful sight gives me courage and greater strength against you, more than I would have had if you had been a courteous knight."

"Make ready," said the Red Knight of the Red Lands, "and chatter at me no longer."

Then Sir Beaumains bade the damsel leave him. The knights came together with all the might they had, and each smote the other in the midst of his shield, so that the breastplates, girths, and cruppers broke. Both fell to the earth with the reins of their bridles in their hands, and lay there a great while stunned.

All those who were in the castle and at the siege feared their necks had been broken. Then many a stranger said that the errant knight was a big man and a noble jouster.

"Before now," they said, "we never saw a knight who could match the Red Knight of the Red Lands."

Such were the words spoken both within the castle and without.

Then the two adversaries freed themselves from their horses, put their shields before them, drew their swords, and ran together like two fierce lions. Each gave the other such buffets upon their helmets that they both reeled backward two strides. Then they recovered, and hewed great pieces from each other's harness and from their shields so that a great part fell into the field.

XVII

And thus they fought until it was past noon, and would not stop. At last both lacked wind, and then they stood swaying and staggering, panting, blowing, and bleeding so that all those who beheld them wept for pity. And when the champions had rested a while they went to battle again, thrusting, hacking and hewing like two boars.

Like two wild rams they hurled themselves together so fiercely that they fell to the ground groveling, and often in their madness either took the other's sword instead of his own. Thus they fought until evensong time, and no one who watched them could know which was more likely to win the battle. Their armor was so hewn that men could see their naked sides, and in other places they were bare too. But always they defended the unprotected spots.

The red knight was a wily man of war, and his sly fighting taught Sir Beaumains to be wise. But full sorely the youth bought his teaching before he understood the manner of the red knight's attack. Finally both consented to rest a while, and so they sat down on two molehills beside the fighting place. And both of them unlaced their helmets and took the cold wind on their faces, for their pages were near them.

When Sir Beaumains' helmet was off, he looked toward the window, and there he saw the fair lady Dame Lyones. Her expression made his heart light and joyful. Therewith he started up suddenly and bade the red knight make ready to fight to the uttermost.

"Right willing am I," said the Red Knight of the Red Lands.

Then they laced up their helmets, and their pages stepped aside. The knights advanced and fought fiercely. But the red knight waited for Sir Beaumains, and suddenly struck him in the hand, so that his sword fell. Then he gave him a second buffet on the helmet so that Sir Beaumains fell down groveling to the earth, and the red knight fell over him to hold him down.

Then came a cry from Linet.

"O Sir Beaumains, where is your courage? Alas, the lady, my sister, is watching you, and she sobs and weeps so that it makes my heart sad."

And when the fallen youth heard the maiden say that, he rose up with great might. Lightly he leaped to his sword and caught it in his hand. Then the red knight and Sir Beaumains fought a new battle together.

But Sir Beaumains doubled his strokes and struck so fast that he drove the sword out of the red knight's hand. Thereafter he crashed down upon his helmet so that he fell to the ground. And Sir Beaumains fell upon him like a ferret at a rat, and unlaced his helmet to kill him.

At last the red knight yielded to him and asked for mercy.

"O noble knight," he said with a loud voice, "I yield to you."

Beaumains remembered the knights that had been hanged so shamefully.

"I cannot honorably save your life," he then said, "because of the shameful deaths that you caused so many good knights."

"Sir," said the Red Knight of the Red Lands, "wait until I tell you why I put them to a shameful death."

"Speak, then," said Beaumains.

"Sir, I once loved a lady, a fair damsel, whose brother

was slain. She swore that it was Sir Launcelot du Lake
or Sir Gawaine who had done the deed, and that foully.
She prayed me that, as I loved her, I would promise by
the faith of my knighthood to labor daily in arms until
I had met with one of them, and all I might overcome
she made me promise to put to a villainous death.
This is why, fair sir, I have hanged so many good knights.
I swore to her to all this wickedness to King Arthur's
knights, and that I should take vengeance on them all.
And, sir, now I will tell you that every day my strength
increases until noon, and that all this time I have had
seven men's strength."

XVIII

Many earls came and barons and noble knights who
prayed Sir Beaumains to save the knight's life and
take him prisoner. They fell on their knees and asked
his mercy, begging him to spare the red knight.

"It would be better," they said, "to take homage
of him and let him hold his lands of you than to slay him.
For by his death you shall have no advantage. All the
wrongs that he has done may not be undone. Therefore let him make amends to all parties, and all of us
here will become your men, and do you homage and
fealty."

"Fair lords," said Sir Beaumains, "I am full loath
to kill this knight, although he has done much wrong.
But as he did all at a lady's request, I blame him the less.
For your sakes I will release him, and he shall have his
life upon this covenant: that he go into the castle and

yield there to the lady Dame Lyones. If she will forgive him, so will I also, if he make her amends for all the trespasses he has done against her and her lands. When that is done, he must go to the court of King Arthur, and there beg pardon of Sir Launcelot and Sir Gawaine for the evil will that he has had against them."

"Sir," said the Red Knight of the Red Lands, "all this will I do as you command, and certain assurance and pledges shall you have."

Then the red knight paid his homage and fealty, and so did all the earls and barons with him. Then Linet came to Sir Beaumains and unarmed him, and cared for his wounds and stopped his bleeding. So also did she do to the Red Knight of the Red Lands.

They sojourned ten days in their tents to heal their many wounds. During this time the red knight made his lords and servants serve Beaumains as well as they could. Soon after, the defeated knight went to the castle and yielded to the Lady Lyones. All the damages he had done were paid for so that she did not complain.

Then the red knight departed and went to the court of King Arthur, where he openly offered himself to the mercy of Sir Launcelot and Sir Gawaine. There he told truthfully before everyone how he was overcome and by whom. He told of all the strife from the beginning to the end.

"Mercy upon us all!" said King Arthur and Sir Gawaine. "From what parentage is this young knight come? For he is a noble fighter."

"Do not wonder," said Sir Launcelot, "for you shall

soon know that he is come of proud lineage. As for his might and bravery, there are few living now that are as mighty as he, and as noble."

"It seems," said King Arthur, "that you know his name and of what blood he is."

"I suppose I do," said Launcelot, "or I would not have given him the order of knighthood. But at that time he charged me not to tell it until he asked me to do so."

XIX

Sir Beaumains asked the damsel Linet if he might see her sister, his lady.

"Sir," said she, "I want you to see her."

Then Sir Beaumains armed, took his horse and his spear, and rode straight to the castle. And when he came to the gate he found many armed men, who pulled up the drawbridge and drew the port close. Then he wondered why they would not allow him to enter and he looked up to the window. There he saw the fair lady Dame Lyones, who said, "Go your way, Sir Beaumains, for you shall not wholly have my love until you are called one of the number of the worthy knights. Therefore go and labor in arms worshipfully for twelve months, and then you shall hear new tidings."

"Alas, fair lady," said Sir Beaumains, "I have not deserved this coldness that you show me. I had thought that I should have kindness from you. I have deserved thanks and kindness, and I am sure that I have bought your love with part of the best blood in my body."

"Fair, courteous knight," said Dame Lyones, "be not displeased, nor overhasty. Neither your great labor nor your love shall be lost, for I know your bounty and your goodness. Therefore go on your way, and see that you be ever happy, for all will be for your honor and for the best. A twelve-month will soon be gone. Trust me, fair knight. I shall be true to you, and shall never betray you. Until my death shall I love you and none other."

Then she turned her from the window.

Sir Beaumains rode away from the castle in sorrow. He rode here and there and knew not which way he was going until it was dark night. And then he happened to come to a poor man's house, where he was harbored all night.

But Sir Beaumains could not rest, but suffered for the love of the lady of the castle. And so on the morrow he took his horse and his armor and rode until it was noon. Then he came to a broad water where there was a great lodge. There he alighted and laid his head upon his shield to sleep, leaving his horse with the dwarf and commanding him to watch all night.

Now the lady of the castle thought much about Sir Beaumains. She called Sir Gringamor, her brother, and prayed him as he loved her to ride after her affianced knight.

"And ever wait upon him," she said, "until you find him sleeping. For I am sure that in his grief he will lie down to sleep somewhere. And therefore keep watch over him. And secretly take his dwarf from him, and bring the dwarf here as fast as ever you can before Sir Beaumains awakes. For my sister Linet says that the dwarf can tell of what family my love is, and what his right name is."

"And in the meanwhile, my sister and I will ride to your castle to wait for you. And then I will ask the dwarf what Sir Beaumains' right name is, and of what kindred he is come, for until I know this I shall never be happy."

"Sister," said Sir Gringamor, "all this shall be done as you wish."

So he left and rode all that day and night until he found Sir Beaumains lying asleep by a waterside with his head upon his shield. And when he saw that the young knight was dreaming, Gringamor crept behind the dwarf and took him close under his arm. Then he rode away with him as hard as ever he could unto his castle.

Now Sir Gringamor's armor and all that belonged to him was all black. But as the dwarf rode toward Gringamor's castle the little squire called to his lord and prayed his help. Then Sir Beaumains awoke and leaped up lightly. He saw the direction in which Sir Gringamor rode with the dwarf before they got out of sight.

XX

Then Sir Beaumains put on his helmet and buckled his shield. He took his horse and rode after them as fast as he could ride, through marshes and field sand great dales. Often his horse and he plunged over the head in deep mires. For Beaumains knew not the way, but in his madness he took the next path, so that he was often in danger of death.

At last he happened to come to a fair green way where he met a poor man of the countryside, whom he saluted. He asked him whether he had not met a knight upon a black horse with black harness, and a little dwarf sitting behind him.

"Sir," said the poor man, "a knight who is called Sir Gringamor passed by me here with such a dwarf, mourning. But I counsel that you follow him not, for he is one of the most perilous knights of the world. His castle is near here within these two miles, and therefore I advise you not to ride after him unless you feel good will toward him."

Let us now leave Beaumains riding toward the castle and turn to Sir Gringamor and the dwarf.

When the little squire came to the castle, Dame Lyones and Dame Linet her sister asked him where his master was born and of what lineage he was.

"Unless you tell me the truth," said Dame Lyones, "you will never escape this castle, but forever shall be captive here."

"As for that," said the dwarf, "I do not fear greatly to tell his name or of what kin he comes. He is a king's son, and his mother is sister to King Arthur, and he is a brother of the good knight Sir Gawaine. His name is Sir Gareth of Orkney. Now I pray you, fair lady, let me go to my lord. For he will never leave this country

until I come again.   And if he is angry he will do much
harm before he stops, and will work much unhappiness
in this land."

"As for that threat," said Sir Gringamor, "never
mind.   Let us go to dinner."

So they washed and had food.   They made merry
and were well at ease, for they had great joy because
Dame Lyones, the lady of the castle, was there.

"Truly, madam," said Linet to her sister, "well
may he be a king's son.   For he has many good qualities.
He is courteous and mild and is more long-suffering
than any man that ever I met.   For I dare say there was
never a gentlewoman that reviled a man in so shocking
a manner as I have reviled him.   Yet at all times was he
courteous."

While they sat thus talking Sir Beaumains came to
the gate with an angry countenance, and his sword
drawn in his hand.

"You traitor, Sir Gringamor," he cried aloud, so
that all the castle might hear him, "deliver my dwarf
again, or, by the faith that I owe the order of knighthood, I will do you all the harm that I can."

Then Sir Gringamor looked out of a window and said,
"Sir Gareth of Orkney, leave your boasting words, for
you will not get your dwarf again."

"You coward knight," said Sir Gareth, "bring him
with you, and come and fight with me!   If you win him,
take him."

"That will I do," said Sir Gringamor.   "But for all
your great words you will not get him."

"Ah, fair brother," said Dame Lyones, "I would Sir Beaumains had his dwarf again. I would he were not angry, for now that the dwarf has told me all I wish to know I will no longer keep the little squire. And also, brother, Sir Beaumains has done much for me, and delivered me from the Red Knight of the Red Lands. So I owe him my service before all knights living. And know that I love him more than all others. I should like to speak with him, but he must not know who I am, but think that I am another strange lady."

"Well," said Sir Gringamor, "since I know your will, I will obey him."

Then he went down to Sir Gareth.

"Sir, I ask your pardon," he said. "All that I have misdone against you I will amend as you please. Therefore I pray you that you will alight and take such cheer as I can give you here in the castle."

"Shall I have my dwarf again?" asked Sir Gareth.

"Yes, sir, and all the pleasure that I can give you. For as soon as your dwarf told me who you are and of what blood you come, and of all the noble deeds you have done in this country, then I repented of my acts."

Then Sir Gareth got down from his horse, and his little squire came and took the steed away.

"O my fellow," said Sir Gareth, "I have had many evil adventures for your sake."

So Sir Gringamor took him by the hand and led him into the hall where Sir Gringamor's wife was.

XXI

Then there came into the hall Dame Lyones arrayed
like a princess. And she was courteous to Sir Beaumains
and he to her again. Gareth many times thought,
"Would that my lady of the Castle Perilous were half
as fair as she!"

There were all manner of games and plays, both of
dancing and of leaping. And the more the young
knight looked at the lady, the more he loved her. His
love was so great that he could not understand it.

Toward evening they went to supper, but Sir Gareth
could not eat because of his love. All this Sir Gringamor
saw, and after the meal was done he called his sister
Dame Lyones into a room.

"Fair sister," Sir Gringamor said, "I have watched
you and this knight. I wish you to know that he is a
noble knight, and if you can make him stay here I will
do to him all the pleasure that I can. For were you better than you are your love would still be well bestowed
upon him."

"Fair brother," said Dame Lyones, "I understand
that the knight is good and is come of a noble house.
Nevertheless, I would test him better, although I am
more grateful to him than to any earthly man. For he
has had hard labor for my love and has passed many
a dangerous adventure."

Then Sir Gringamor went to Sir Gareth.

"Sir," said he, "take good cheer, for you shall have
no other cause, since my sister, this lady, is yours at all

times. For she loves you as well as you do her, and better if better may be."

"If I knew that," said Sir Gareth, "no man alive would be gladder than I am."

"Upon my honor," said Sir Gringamor, "trust to my promise. And as long as you like you shall sojourn with me, and this lady shall be with us daily and nightly to make you all the cheer that she can."

"I am willing," said Sir Gareth, "for I have promised to be near this country these twelve months. I am sure that my lord King Arthur and many other noble knights will find me wherever I am within the year. For I shall be greatly sought, and found if I am alive."

Then the noble knight Sir Gareth went to Dame Lyones, whom he much loved, and kissed her. And they were happy. There she promised him her love, faithfully to turn to him and no other, all the days of her life.

Dame Lyones then, by the consent of her brother, told Sir Gareth all the truth; that she was the same lady that he fought for, and that she was lady of the Castle Perilous. Then she told him why she caused her brother to take away his dwarf, so that she might certainly know what was his name. Then was Sir Gareth more glad than he was before.

XXII

When King Arthur at the next Pentecost held his feast, there came the green knight with fifty noble fellows in chivalry who all yielded to him as sovereign. Then

there came the red knight, his brother, who yielded to
Arthur and threescore knights with him. The blue
knight who was brother to the other two, came with a
hundred knights, and they all yielded to King Arthur.
The green knight's name was Sir Pertolope, and the red
knight's name was Sir Perimones, and the blue knight's
name was Sir Persaunt of Ind. These three brothers
told their new liege lord how they were overcome by a
knight called Beaumains whom a damsel had with her.

"By the faith of my body!" said the king. "I
marvel who that knight is, and what his lineage is. He
was with me for twelve months, and poorly and shamefully was he taken care of. And Sir Kaye, who knows
not everything, in scorn named him Beaumains."

Right as King Arthur stood talking thus with these
three brothers, Sir Launcelot du Lake came. He told
his sovereign that a goodly lord was come with five
hundred knights. Then the king went out of Carlion —
for in that place was the feast held — and there came to
him this lord, who saluted in a good manner.

"What is your will?" asked King Arthur. "And
what is your errand?"

"Sir," said the other, "I am called the Red Knight
of the Red Lands, but my name is Sir Ironside. And
you shall know, my lord, that I am sent here by a knight
called Sir Beaumains. For he won me in plain battle,
hand for hand, and no knight has ever done this in thirty
years. He charged and commanded me to yield to your
grace and will."

"You are welcome," said the king, "for you have

long been a great foe to me and to my court. And now
I trust to heaven I shall so treat you that you will be
my friend."

"Sir, both I and these five hundred knights shall
always be at your beck and call, to do you service as
much as lies in our power."

"Truly," said King Arthur, "I am much beholden
to Sir Beaumains who has so imperiled himself to honor
me and my court. You, Ironside, who are called the Red
Knight of the Red Lands, are dubbed a perilous knight.
If you will be loyal to me, I will honor you and give you
a place at the Table Round. But then you must no
more be a murderer."

"Sir, as to that, I have promised Sir Beaumains never
again to use such a custom. For all the villainies I have
performed I did at the request of a lady whom I loved.
And therefore I must go to Sir Launcelot and to Sir
Gawaine, and ask them forgiveness for the evil will that
I had unto them, for all those that I put to death were
for their sake."

"They are here now before you," said the king.
"You may say to them what you wish."

And then Sir Ironside kneeled down to Sir Launcelot
and to Sir Gawaine, and prayed them for forgiveness
of the evil that he had committed against them both.

XXIII

Then they all said at once, "God forgive you as we
do. And now tell us, we pray you, where we may find
this Sir Beaumains."

"Fair lords," said Sir Ironside, "I cannot tell you, for it is full hard to find him, since all such young knights as he, when they are on their adventures, will never stay in one place."

To tell all the fine things that the Red Knight of the Red Lands and Sir Persaunt and his brothers said of Sir Beaumains would take too long.

"Well, my fair lords," said King Arthur, "know you well I shall do you honor for the love of Sir Beaumains. And as soon as ever I meet him I shall make you all on that day knights of the Round Table. And as for you, Sir Persaunt of Ind, you have ever been called a full noble knight, and so have ever been your three brothers. But I marvel that I hear not of the black knight, your brother. He was a noble knight, too."

"Sir," said Sir Pertolope, the green knight, "his name was Sir Percard. Sir Beaumains slew him with his spear."

"That was great pity." said the king.

So said many knights more, for these four brothers were well known by the noble knights in Arthur's court, since for a long time they had warred against the Round Table.

"At the ford of the Mortaise River," said Sir Pertolope to the king, "Sir Beaumains fought with two brothers that guarded the ford. And they were two manly fighters. There he slew the elder brother in the water, and struck him such a buffet on the head that he fell down in the stream and was drowned; and his name was Sir Gherard le Brewse. And soon thereafter Beaumains killed the other brother, Sir Arnold le Brewse."

XXIV

Then the king and all the others went to their food and were served in the best manner. As they sat at their food and drink the Queen of Orkney came in with a great number of ladies and knights.

Sir Gawaine, Sir Agravaine, and Sir Gaheris arose and went to her, and saluted her on their knees, and asked for her blessing. For in the space of fifteen years they had not seen her.

"But where is my young son, Sir Gareth?" she asked her brother, King Arthur. "He was here among you for twelve months, and you made a kitchen knave of him, which is a great shame to you all. Alas! What have you done to my dear son who was my joy?"

"O dear mother," said Sir Gawaine, "I did not know him."

"Nor did I," said the king, "of which I repent now. But thank God he has proved to be as worshipful a knight as any now living of his years, and I shall never be glad until I find him."

"O brother," said the Queen of Orkney to King Arthur, "you dishonored yourself when you kept my son Gareth in the kitchen and fed him like a poor hog."

"Fair sister," said the king, "you know that I did not know him, nor did Sir Gawaine or his brothers. But since he has gone from us all, we must seek to find him. I think, sister, you should have let me know of Gareth's coming. And then if I had not been kind to the lad you might have blamed me. But when he came to this court he came leaning upon two men's shoulders, as though he could hardly walk. Then he asked me for three requests, and the one he asked that same day was that for twelve months I would give him food."

"What were the other two, forsooth?"

"He asked that same day, twelve months after, the other two gifts: that he might have the adventure of the damsel Linet; and the third was that Sir Launcelot might make him knight when he desired. So I granted him all his wishes. And many in this court marveled that the unknown lad wished for his sustenance for twelve months, and therefore many thought that he had not come of a noble house."

"Sir," said the Queen of Orkney to her brother, "know that I sent him to you well armed and horsed and richly clothed. Gold and silver a great plenty had he."

"That may be," said the king, "but we saw none of it, save that on the day he left us knights told me that a dwarf came here suddenly and brought him armor and a good courser with rich trappings. We all marveled greatly where the riches came from, and we all thought he must come of noble lineage."

"Brother, I believe you," said the queen. "Ever since he was grown he has been wonderfully keen, and always faithful to his promises. But I am surprised that Sir Kaye mocked him and gave him the name Beaumains. Yet Sir Kaye perhaps named him better than he intended, for I dare say that Gareth is a fair-handed man and as well disposed as any living."

Then said King Arthur, "By heaven's grace the lad

shall be found if he is within these seven realms. Let us all be merry, for Gareth is proved a man of honor, and that gives me great joy."

XXV

Then said Sir Gawaine and his brothers to King Arthur, "Sir, if you will grant us leave, we will go to seek our kin."

"No," said Sir Launcelot, "you do not need to go." And so said Sir Boudwin of Britain.

"For by our advice the king shall send a messenger to Dame Lyones and ask that she will come to the king's court in all the haste that she may. And I do not doubt but that she will come. She will tell you where you may find him."

"This is excellent advice," said King Arthur.

Letters were written, and in all haste a messenger was sent forth who rode night and day until he came to the Castle Perilous. Then was the Dame Lyones sent for, as she was with Sir Gringamor, her brother, and Sir Gareth.

When she understood the letter, she bade the courier ride on his way to King Arthur, and said she would come after him as quickly as possible.

"You have been sent for because of me," said Sir Gareth.

"Now tell me," said Dame Lyones, "what shall I say and how shall I act?"

"My lady and my love," said Sir Gareth, "I pray you in no manner of wise know where I am, for I know my mother and all my brothers are there and they will try to find me. When the king, madam, questions you about me, tell him that, if it please him, you will proclaim at the Feast of the Assumption of Our Lady that the knight who proves best shall wed you and all your lands. If the victor shall be a man who is wedded already, his wife shall have a white gerfalcon, and a coronal of gold, set with precious stones to the value of one thousand pounds."

Then Dame Lyones left and came to King Arthur, where she was nobly received. There she was asked many questions by King Arthur and the Queen of Orkney. And she answered that she could not tell where Sir Gareth was. But she said to Arthur, "Sir, I will proclaim a tournament that shall be held in front of my castle at the Assumption of Our Lady. And the cry shall be thus: that you, my lord Arthur, will be there with your knights. And I will have my knights against yours, and then I am sure you will hear of Sir Gareth."

"This is good advice," said King Arthur.

And so she left. Then the king and the lady provided for the tournament. When Dame Lyones came to the Isle of Avalon, where her brother Sir Gringamor dwelt, she told him all that she had done, and the promise she had made to King Arthur.

"Alas!" said Sir Gareth. "I have been so wounded that I shall not be able to joust at that tournament as a knight should, for I have never been well since I was hurt."

"Be of good cheer," said Linet, "for I promise within

these fifteen days to make you as well as ever you were."

Then she put an ointment and a salve on him, so that he was never so well.

"Send to Sir Persaunt of Ind," said Linet, "and command him and his knights to be here with you as they have promised. Also send to Sir Ironside, the Red Knight of the Red Lands, and charge him to be ready with you with all his company of knights; then you will be able to match with King Arthur and his knights of the Round Table."

So this was done, and all the knights were sent to the Castle Perilous. The red knight then answered Dame Lyones and Sir Gareth, "Madam, and my lord Sir Gareth, I have been at King Arthur's court with Sir Persaunt of Ind and his brothers. There we have done our homage as you commanded."

Sir Ironside also said, "I have taken upon me with Sir Persaunt of Ind and his brethren to hold a joust against my lord Sir Launcelot and the knights of that court. This have I done for the love of lady Dame Lyones and for you, my lord Sir Gareth."

"You have done well," said the young knight, "but know well that we shall be matched against the noblest men of the world. Therefore we must get brave knights wherever we can."

"That is well said," quoth Sir Persaunt.

So it was proclaimed in all England, Wales, and Scotland, Ireland, and Cornwall and in Britany that at the next Feast of the Assumption of Our Lady men should come to the Castle Perilous near the Isle of Avalon.

There all the knights that came should choose whether they wished to be on the side of the company of the castle or on the other side with King Arthur. Two months from that day the tournament should be held.

Many good knights who held against King Arthur and his fellowship of the Round Table came on the side of the castle.

Sir Epinogris, who was the son of the King of Northumberland, was the first. And Sir Palamides the Saracen was another, with Sir Safere and Sir Sagwarides his brothers, but they were christened in the true faith. Next came Sir Brian de les Isles, a noble knight, and Sir Grummore Grummorsum, a good knight of Scotland. Then Sir Carados of the dolorous tower, and Sir Turquine his brother, and two brothers Sir Arnold and Sir Gauter, good knights of Cornwall, were not far behind. Sir Tristram de Lyones came, and with him Sir Dinadan the seneschal, and Sir Sadoke—Sir Tristram at that time was not a knight of the Round Table.

Noble knights accompanied them, with the lady of the castle and the Red Knight of the Red Lands.

XXVI

With King Arthur came Sir Gawaine and his two brothers Sir Agravaine and Sir Gaheris, and his nephews Sir Ewaine le Blanche Mains, Sir Aglovale, Sir Tor, Sir Percivale de Galis, and Sir Lamorak de Galis. Then rode Sir Launcelot du Lake with his brothers, nephews, and cousins, and Sir Lionel, Sir Ector de Maris, Sir Bors de Ganis, Sir Galihodin, Sir Galihud, and many more of Sir Launcelot's blood. Sir Dinadan's brother, Sir La-Cote-Male-Taile, and Sir Sagramour appeared, good knights both; also most of the knights of the Round Table.

There came too with King Arthur these knights: the King of Ireland, Agwisaunce, and the King of Scotland, Carados, and King Urience of the land of Gore, and King Bagdemagus and his son Sir Maliagaunce, and Sir Galahault, the noble prince; Sir Brandiles, and Sir Ewaine les Avoutres, and Sir Kaye, Sir Bedivere, Sir Meliot de Logurs, Sir Petipace of Winchelsea, and Sir Godelake.

The lady Dame Lyones made great preparations for the noble knights; all manner of lodging and food of every sort came by land and by water. None of her following lacked anything, and there was plenty to be had for gold and silver for King Arthur and his knights. Then came the harbingers for the visiting sovereign to arrange lodging for him and his kings, dukes, earls, barons, and knights.

Sir Gareth asked his lady Dame Lyones, and Sir Ironside the Red Knight of the Red Lands, and Sir Persaunt of Ind and his brother, and Sir Gringamor that none of them should tell his name, and that they should show him no more attention than the other knights.

Then Dame Lyones said to Sir Gareth, "Sir, I will give you a ring, but I pray you if you love me well let me have it again when the tournament is done. For that ring increases my beauty. It is a talisman; it will turn green to red, and red to green. Blue the ring will turn to white, and white to blue. Whosoever wears my ring shall lose no blood, and because of my great love I will give you this magic ring."

"Gramercy," said Sir Gareth. "For this ring will aid me greatly, my own lady, since it will change my appearance and I shall not be known."

Then Sir Gringamor gave Sir Gareth a bay courser that was a good horse. He presented him also with good armor, and a noble sword that Sir Gringamor's father had won from a heathen tyrant long before.

Every knight made him ready for the tournament. King Arthur came two days before the Assumption of Our Lady. And there was all manner of royalty and all kinds of minstrels. Queen Guenever came, too, and the Queen of Orkney, Sir Gareth's mother.

On the day of the Assumption, when mass and matins were said, heralds with trumpets announced the opening on the field. Then Sir Epinogris, the king's son from Northumberland, came from the castle and encountered Sir Sagramour le Desirous. Both of them broke their spears to their hands. Then Sir Palamides came out of the castle and fought Sir Gawaine. Each smote the other so hard that both knights and their horses fell to the earth. And then their fellows on each side rescued their knights.

Sir Safere and Sir Sagwarides, brothers of Sir Palamides, then entered. With the first of these Sir Agravaine fought, and Sir Gaheris encountered the other. Sir Safere smote down Sir Agravaine, brother of Sir Gawaine; and Sir Sagwarides smote down Sir Gaheris.

Then Sir Ewaine le Blanche Mains fought with Sir Malgrine, a knight of the castle, and gave him a fall so great that he almost broke his neck.

XXVII

Then Sir Brian de les Isles and Sir Grummore Grummorsum, both knights of the castle, fought with Sir Aglovale and Sir Tor and were struck to the ground. Sir Carados of the dolorous tower and Sir Turquine, knights of the castle, came in and fought with Sir Percivale de Galis and Sir Lamorak de Galis, who were overthrown. Throughout the day many knights on both sides fought mightily and broke spears in their hands. All this was announced by noble heralds, with the names of those who bore themselves best. Knightly battles were waged with equal fortune for both sides.

Then came in the Red Knight of the Red Lands and Sir Gareth from the castle. With these two Sir Bors de Ganis and Sir Bleoberis fought. There the red knight and Sir Bors struck each other so hard that their spears broke and their horses fell groveling to the earth. Then Sir Bleoberis broke his spear upon Sir Gareth, but with that great stroke fell to the earth.

When Sir Galihodin saw that, he bade Sir Gareth wait, but Sir Galihodin was struck to the ground. Then Sir Galihud got a spear to revenge his brother's defeat, and was served in the same way by Sir Gareth. Four other great fighters the knight bore down with a single spear: Sir Dinadan and his brother, La-Cote-Male-Taile, Sir Sagramour le Desirous, and Dodinas le Savage.

When King Agwisaunce of Ireland saw Gareth fighting thus, he wondered who the knight was that at one
time seemed green and another time shone blue. With
every course the man so changed color that neither king
nor knight could recognize him. Then Agwisaunce
fought Gareth, and the young man struck the Irish
king from his horse, saddle and all. Then rode in King
Carados of Scotland, and Sir Gareth smote him down,
horse and man, and a few moments after in the same
way he served King Urience of the land of Gore, and then
King Bagdemagus, whose son Maliagaunce broke a vain
spear upon Sir Gareth.

"Knight of many colors," then cried the noble prince
Sir Galahault, "well have you jousted. Now make ready
that I may fight with you."

When Sir Gareth heard that summons he took a great
spear, and they encountered. The prince broke his spear,
but Sir Gareth smote him on the left side of the helmet
so that he reeled and would have fallen down had not
his men helped him.

"Truly," said King Arthur, "that knight with the
many colors is a good fighter."

Then the king called Sir Launcelot du Lake to him
and asked him to encounter this hardy antagonist.

"Sir," said Sir Launcelot, "I think it would be kind
to put it off, for he has fought enough today. And
when a good knight fights so well on one day, no other
knight should take the honor from him. Perhaps this
is his quarrel today, and maybe he is best beloved by
this lady of all who are here. For I notice he is striving

hard to do great deeds. Therefore, sir, as for me, this day he shall have the honor. If it were in my power to keep him from it, I would not do it."

XXVIII

When this was over, there was drawing of swords and a great tournament began. Here Sir Launcelot did marvelous feats of arms. And between Sir Lamorak and Sir Ironside, the Red Knight of the Red Lands, there was a great battle, and there was fierce fighting between Sir Palamides and Sir Bleoberis. And Sir Gawaine and Sir Tristram met, and there the first knight had the worst of the fight, for he was pulled from his horse and was long on foot.

Then came Sir Launcelot, who smote Sir Turquine, and he him again. Sir Carados, the brother of Turquine, rushed in and both attacked the pride of Arthur's court. This knight, the most noble of the world, fought with them both right worshipfully, so that all men wondered at the power of Sir Launcelot when he engaged with those two perilous knights. Then Sir Gareth rode in with his good horse and separated the adversaries, but he would not strike at Sir Launcelot. When this knight saw that, he thought his rescuer must be the good knight Sir Gareth.

Then the young conqueror rode here and there, striking on the right hand an on the left, so that everyone watched him as he rode. And by fortune he met his brother Sir Gawaine and put him to the worst, for he put off his helmet. He served five or six knights of the

Round Table in the same way, so that all men said he was the greatest in combat. When Sir Tristram saw how he first jousted and thereafter fought so well with a sword, he rode to Sir Ironside and to Sir Persaunt of Ind.

"By your faith," he said to them, "who is yonder knight who seems to wear so many colors? He is making a great effort, for he never ceases."

"Do you not know who he is?" asked Sir Ironside.

"No, in all truth," said Sir Tristram.

"Then you must know that this is he who loves the lady of the castle, and she loves him greatly. This is the knight who defeated me when I besieged Dame Lyones, and this is he who won Sir Persaunt of Ind and his three brothers."

"What is his name?" Sir Tristram asked. "And of what blood is he sprung?"

"He was called in King Arthur's court Beaumains, but his name is Sir Gareth of Orkney, brother unto Sir Gawaine."

"By my head," said Sir Tristram, "he is a good knight and a big man of arms. If he is young, he shall prove to be a full great knight."

"He is but a child," said they all. "And Sir Launcelot brought him to the order of chivalry."

"For that he is much better," said Sir Tristram gallantly.

Then four of them, Sir Tristram, Sir Ironside, Sir Persaunt, and his brother, rode together to help Sir Gareth in the fray, where many hard strokes were given.

Once Sir Gareth rode aside to mend his helmet.

Then said his dwarf, "Give me your ring so that you do not lose it while you drink."

When the youth had his drink he put on his helmet again and eagerly took his horse and rode into the field. But he forgot his ring and left it with his little squire. The dwarf was glad that at the last the ring was not with his knight, for then he knew well that his master would be known.

When Sir Gareth came into the field, all the people saw plainly that he was in yellow colors. There he struck off helmets and pulled down knights so that King Arthur wondered what knight he was, for the king now saw by his hair that it was the same knight, who was in so many colors before.

XXIX

"Now go," said King Arthur unto divers heralds, "and ride about him and see what manner of knight he is, for I have asked many today who are of his party, and all have said they do not know him."

Then a herald rode as near Sir Gareth as he could, and there he saw written about his helmet in gold, "This is Sir Gareth of Orkney."

Then the herald cried aloud as if he were mad, and many heralds with him, "This is Sir Gareth of Orkney in the yellow arms."

Then all the kings and knights on King Arthur's side waited for him, and then they advanced eagerly to behold him, while the heralds were calling, "This is Sir Gareth of Orkney, King Lot's son."

When the youth knew that he was discovered, he began to double his strokes, and he smote down Sir Sagramour and Sir Gawaine.

"O brother," said Sir Gawaine, "I should not have thought that you would strike me."

And when Sir Gareth heard him say so, he got out of the press with great difficulty and met his dwarf.

"O boy," said the young knight, "you have beguiled me evilly today by keeping my ring. Give it me again that I may hide my body withal."

And so he took the ring, and then they all knew not what had become of him. When Sir Gawaine saw where Sir Gareth rode, he rode after with all his might. But the young knight stole lightly into the forest so that Gawaine might lose him from sight. When Sir Gareth knew that Sir Gawaine had passed, he asked the dwarf for his counsel.

"Sir," said the little squire, "I think you should send my lady Dame Lyones her ring now that you no longer need it."

"That is well advised," said Sir Gareth. "Now take it to her, and say that I commend myself to her good grace. Tell her I will come when I may and that I pray her to be true and faithful to me as I will be to her."

"Sir," said the dwarf, "it shall be done as you have commanded."

And so he rode on his way and performed his errand. Then the lady asked, "Where is my lord Sir Gareth?"

"Madam," said the dwarf, "he bade me say that he would not be long from you."

Quickly the little squire came again to Sir Gareth, who wished for a lodging, as he needed rest. Then a storm arose with thunder and rain, as if heaven and earth would come together. Sir Gareth was full weary, for all that day he had rested little, and his horse was as tired as he. They rode so long in that forest that night came, and ever it lightened and thundered so that it was a wonder to see. Finally by good fortune he came to a castle and there Sir Gareth heard the watchman on the walls.

XXX

Then Sir Gareth rode straight to the gate of the castle, and prayed the porter to let him come in. The porter answered him most uncivilly.

"You get no lodging here," he said.

"Fair sir," said Sir Gareth, "do not say that. For I am a knight of King Arthur, and I pray the lord or lady of this stronghold to give me lodging for the king's love."

Then the porter went to the duchess of the castle and told her that a knight of King Arthur wished shelter.

"Let him in," said the duchess, "for I will see that gentleman. And for King Arthur's sake he shall not be without shelter."

And then the duchess went up to a tower over the gate with a great torchlight. When Sir Gareth saw the torchlight, he cried, "Whether you be lord or lady, giant or champion, give me shelter and rest tonight. And if

I must fight, do not spare me tomorrow when I have rested, for tonight both I and my horse are weary."

"Sir knight," said the duchess, "you speak mightily and boldly, but I must tell you that the lord of this castle loves not King Arthur or any of his court. For my lord has always been against him. Therefore it would be better for you if you did not come into this castle. But if you do enter tonight, you must agree that wheresoever you meet my Lord, in the street or on the road, you will yield to him as prisoner."

"Madam," Sir Gareth asked, "who is your lord, and what is his name?"

"Sir, he is called the Duke de la Rowse."

"Well, madam," said Sir Gareth, "I shall promise you wherever I meet your lord I will yield me to his good grace, so that I may know he will do me no harm. And if I may understand what he wishes, then I will get my release as I can with my spear and with my sword."

"You are right," said the duchess.

And then she let the drawbridge down, and he rode into the hall and alighted there. While his horse was brought to a stable he unarmed.

"Madam," he said, "I will not leave your hall tonight. But when it is daylight, if a knight wishes to fight me, he will find me ready."

Then was food given to him and he had many good dishes and was eager to eat. There were many fair ladies near him, and some of them said they never had seen a more handsome man nor one with such fine manners. Then they made him good cheer, and shortly after supper his bed was made there in the hall, and there he rested all night.

On the next day he heard mass and, after breakfast, took his leave of the kind duchess and of them all, thanking her for her lodging and her entertainment. Then she asked him for his name.

"Madam," he said, "truly my name is Sir Gareth of Orkney, and some men call me Beaumains."

Then she knew well that it was the knight who fought for Dame Lyones.

So Sir Gareth departed, and he rode up a mountain, where a knight met him whose name was Sir Bendelaine.

"You shall not pass this way," he said to Gareth, "unless you joust with me or be my prisoner."

"Then will I joust with you," said Sir Gareth.

So they let their horses run, and Sir Gareth struck him through the body, and Sir Bendelaine rode to his castle near there, where he died. Sir Gareth wished to rest, but as he came riding toward Sir Bendelaine's castle the knight's men and his servants saw that it was the man who had slain their lord. Then twenty good men armed and came out and fought Sir Gareth. He had no spear, but only his sword. Nevertheless, he put his shield before him, and they all broke their spears upon it there and attacked him. But Sir Gareth defended himself like a noble knight.

When they saw that they could not overcome him, they rode away from him and, after discussion, decided to kill his horse. Then came they again upon Sir Gareth and with spears killed his horse, after which they fought him passing hard. When he was on foot there was none that he caught without giving him such a buffet that he never recovered afterward.

So he killed them one after another until there were only four, and these fled. Then Sir Gareth took one of their good horses and rode his way. He rode quickly until he came to a castle where he heard many ladies and gentlewomen mourning. A page came by him then.

"What is that noise I hear within this castle?" asked Sir Gareth.

"Sir knight," said the page, "here within these walls are thirty ladies, and all of them are widows. For a knight waits daily near this castle, and his name is the Brown Knight without Pity, and he is the most dangerous man alive. Therefore, sir, I bid you escape."

"No," said Sir Gareth, "I will not fly though you are afraid of them."

And then the page saw the brown knight coming.

"Lo," said the trembling youth, "yonder he comes now."

"Let me deal with him," said Sir Gareth.

And when they saw each other they let their horses run. The brown knight broke his spear, and there Sir Gareth struck him through the body so that he fell to the ground stark dead. Then Gareth rode on into the castle and asked the ladies if he might rest there.

"Alas!" said the ladies. "You may not stay here."

"Greet him heartily," said the page, "for this knight has slain your enemy."

Then they entertained him as well as they could, for they were but poor gentlewomen. On the next morning he went to mass, and there he saw the thirty ladies kneel and lie groveling upon different tombs, moaning sorrowfully. Then Sir Gareth knew that in those tombs their lords were laid.

"Fair ladies," he said, "you must come to the next Feast of Pentecost at the court of King Arthur and say that I, Sir Gareth, sent you there."

"We shall do as you command," said the poor women.

So he left, and by chance he came to a mountain where he found a good knight who said, "Wait, fair sir, and joust with me."

"Who are you?" asked Sir Gareth.

Said the other, "My name is the Duke de la Rowse."

"Ah, sir, you are the same knight at whose castle I once lodged, and there I promised your lady that I would yield to you."

"Faith," said the duke, "then you are the proud knight who promised to fight with my knights. Therefore make ready, for I will fight with you."

When they let their horses run, Sir Gareth struck the duke down from his courser. But the noble lord got lightly off his horse, set his shield before him, drew his sword, and bade Sir Gareth alight and fight with him. The youth, nothing loath, alighted, and they fought for more than an hour, and each hurt the other cruelly. At last Sir Gareth got the duke to the earth and would have killed him. Then his adversary yielded.

"Now must you go," said Sir Gareth, " to my lord

King Arthur at the next Feast of Pentecost and say that I, Sir Gareth of Orkney, sent you to him."

"It shall be done," said the duke, "and I will give you my homage and fealty with a hundred knights with me, and all the days of my life will I do you service wherever you will command me."

XXXI

So the duke left, and Sir Gareth stood there alone. Before long he saw an armed knight spurring toward him.

Then Sir Gareth took the duke's shield and mounted on horseback. Straight without waiting the two ran together with a noise like thunder, and there that knight hurt Sir Gareth under the side with his spear. Then they alighted and drew their swords, and gave each other great strokes, so that the blood flowed to the ground on every side. Thus they fought for two hours.

At last the damsel Linet, whom some men call the "damsel savage," came riding upon an ambling mule. Then she cried, "Sir Gawaine, Sir Gawaine, stop fighting with your brother Sir Gareth!"

And when he heard what the maiden said, he threw away his shield and sword, and ran to Sir Gareth. Then he took him in his arms, and knelt down and asked his mercy.

"Who are you," asked Sir Gareth, "that right now were so strong and so mighty, and now so suddenly yield to me?"

"O Gareth, I am your brother Gawaine, who for your sake have had great sorrow and trouble."

Then the younger knight unlaced his helm and knelt down to his brother, and asked his mercy. Then they both rose and embraced each other, weeping, and each of them gave the other the prize of battle with many kind words.

"Alas, my fair brother," said Sir Gawaine, "by my faith, I ought to honor you even if you were not my kin, for you have honored King Arthur and all his court by sending him more noble knights these twelve months than six of the best of the Round Table have done, except Sir Launcelot."

Then came the damsel savage, who was the lady Linet who had made the long journey with Sir Gareth. She cared for the young knight's wounds and those of Sir Gawaine.

"Now what will you do?" said the damsel Linet. "I think King Arthur ought to know about both of you, for your horses are so bruised that they cannot carry you."

"Well, fair damsel," said Sir Gawaine, "I pray you to ride to my uncle King Arthur and tell him what adventure has happened to us here, and I suppose he will not delay long."

Then she took her mule and came to King Arthur, who was only two miles away from that place. And when she had told him the news the king bade them give him a palfrey, and when he was upon horseback he bade the lords and ladies who wished to come after him.

Then was there saddling and bridling of queens' horses and princes' horses, and all hurried to get ready. So, when the king came where they were, he saw Sir

Gawaine and Sir Gareth sitting on a little hillside. The king alighted from his palfrey then, and when he came near Sir Gareth he tried to speak but could not, and therewith fell down in a happy swoon.

The brothers went to their uncle then, entreating him to be of good cheer. The king was passing joyous and wept like a child. When the youth's mother, the Queen of Orkney, Dame Morgawse, came and she saw that her son Sir Gareth was really there, she could not weep, but suddenly swooned and lay there a great while as if she were dead. When she recovered, Sir Gareth comforted his mother and made her happy.

Then the king commanded that all the knights under his protection should make their lodgings there for the love of his nephews. So it was done, and all manner of provisions were brought, so that they lacked nothing which might be bought for gold or silver. By the help of Linet, Sir Gawaine and Sir Gareth were healed of their wounds, and they sojourned there eight days.

Then said King Arthur to Linet, "I am surprised that your sister Dame Lyones does not come here to me and to visit her knight, my nephew Sir Gareth, who has had so much labor for her love."

"My lord," said the damsel Linet, "you must excuse her, for she knows not that my lord Sir Gareth is here."

"Then go for her," said King Arthur, "that we may do what is best as my nephew pleases."

"Sir," said the damsel Linet, "that shall be done."

So she rode to her sister, and as soon as she could get ready Dame Lyones came, with her brother Sir

Gringamor and with her forty knights. And when she had come King Arthur and many other kings and queens greeted her and honored her.

XXXII

Among all these ladies Dame Lyones was called the fairest and the peerless. When Sir Gareth saw her, both were so happy that all the knights were pleased to see their meeting.

In the presence of all the kings, and of Queen Guenever and the Queen of Orkney, King Arthur asked his nephew whether he would have the lady as his wife.

"My lord," said Sir Gareth, "know that I love her above all other ladies living."

"Now, fair lady," said the king, "what do you say?"

"Most noble sovereign," said Dame Lyones, "know that I would rather have my lord Sir Gareth as my husband than any king or prince christened. If I may not have him, I promise you that I will never have any one. He is my first love and he shall be my last, and if you will allow him to have his will and free choice, I dare say he will choose me."

"That is true," said Sir Gareth, "and if I cannot wed you as my wife, no lady or gentlewoman will ever make me happy."

"What, nephew," cried the king, "is the wind that way? I would not for my crown cause you to be unhappy. And I wish to increase your happiness instead of distressing you. You shall have my love and anything that lies in my power."

And so said Gareth's mother.

Then was the day of marriage provided for, and by the king's advice it was ordained to be at Michaelmas next following, at Kinkenadon by the seaside, for that was a beautiful country. So the wedding was proclaimed throughout the realm.

Then Sir Gareth sent his messengers to all those knights and ladies that he had won in battle, inviting them to be at his marriage at Kinkenadon by the sands. Then Dame Lyones and the damsel Linet, with Sir Gringamor, rode to their castle. And a goodly and rich ring Lyones gave to Gareth and he gave her another, and King Arthur gave her a rich necklace of beads of gold. Then she left, while the king and his knights rode toward Kinkenadon. Sir Gareth took his lady on her way, then came to the king again and rode with him.

The great cheer that Sir Launcelot du Lake made for his ward Sir Gareth was marvelous to see. For there was never a knight that Gareth loved so well as he did his sponsor Sir Launcelot, and always he wished to be in the famous knight's company. For, to tell the truth, after Sir Gareth knew Sir Gawaine well, he withdrew himself from his brother's company, for Sir Gawaine was revengeful and unmerciful, and whenever he hated he would be revenged by murder and treason, and that Sir Gareth hated.

XXXIII

When it drew toward Michaelmas, to Kinkenadon rode Dame Lyones and her sister Dame Linet, with

Sir Gringamor their brother with them, for he had promised to conduct those ladies there. And there were they lodged as King Arthur commanded.

And on Michaelmas Day the Archbishop of Canterbury wedded Sir Gareth and the Lady Lyones with great solemnity. And King Arthur arranged that Sir Gaheris married Dame Linet. Sir Agravaine wedded Dame Lyones' niece, a fair lady whose name was Dame Laurel.

When the service was over, the green knight called Sir Pertolope came in with thirty knights to do homage and fealty to Sir Gareth forevermore. Also Sir Pertolope said, "I pray that at this feast I may be your chamberlain."

"With a right good will," answered Sir Gareth, "since you are pleased to take so simple an office."

Then the red knight with threescore knights with him entered and gave to Sir Gareth homage and fealty, to hold all those knights of him forevermore. And then Sir Perimones said, "I pray you allow me to be chief butler at your high feast."

"I am willing," said Sir Gareth, "that you should have this office, but wish it were a better service."

Then came Sir Persaunt of Ind with a hundred knights. His homage and fealty he offered to the bridegroom, and swore that all his knights should serve Gareth and hold their lands of him forevermore. Then Sir Persaunt asked to be chief server at the feast, and his request was granted.

The Duke de la Rowse, with a hundred knights, and Sir Ironside, the Red Knight of the Red Lands, who brought three hundred knights, also gave Gareth their homage. At their request they were allowed to serve that day as his carver and as the carrier of his wine cup.

Then thirty ladies appeared at court; widows they were, and they brought with them many fair gentle-women. All of them kneeled down at once to King Arthur and to Sir Gareth. Then all those ladies there told the sovereign how the young knight had delivered them from the dolorous tower, and how he had killed the Brown Knight without Pity.

"And therefore," they said, "we and our heirs for-evermore will do homage unto Sir Gareth of Orkney."

Then all the kings and queens, princes, earls, and barons, and bold knights feasted. There was all manner of provision, and all manner of revels and games, with sweet music.

For three days there was great jousting. But the king would not suffer Sir Gareth to joust, for at the request of the bride, Dame Lyones, none of those recently wedded should joust at this feast.

On the first day Sir Lamorak de Galis overthrew thirty knights and did great and marvelous deeds of arms. Then King Arthur made Sir Persant of Ind and his two brothers knights of the Round Table, and gave them great lands. On the second day Sir Tristram jousted best, for he overthrew forty knights. King Arthur made Sir Ironsides, the Red Knight of the Red Lands, a knight of the Round Table that day.

The third day Sir Launcelot du Lake jousted, and he overthrew fifty knights and did most valiantly of all, so that men wondered at his noble deeds. King Arthur gave rich possessions to the Duke de la Rowse and made him a knight of the Round Table all his life.

When these jousts were over, Sir Lamorak and Sir Tristram left suddenly and King Arthur and all the court were sore displeased and so they held the feast with great solemnity for forty days.

This Sir Gareth was always a noble knight, courteous in speech, and brave and just in all his deeds.

Book the Eighth

LA-COTE-MALE-TAILE AND
SIR TRISTRAM DE LYONES

I

One day there came into the court of King Arthur a tall, well-built young man. He was richly clothed but his overgarment did not fit well, although it was good and of rich cloth of gold. This young man desired to be made a knight of King Arthur.

"Sir," said the young man, "my name is Brewnor le Noyre, and within a short time you shall know that I come of good kin."

"That may well be," said Sir Kaye the seneschal, "but in mockery you shall be called La-Cote-Male-Taile, or the Evil-shapen Coat."

"You ask a great boon," said the king. "Why do you wear that rich coat? Tell me, for it must be for a good reason."

"Sir," said the youth, "I had a father, a noble knight, and one day as he rode out hunting he happened to lie down to sleep. There came a knight who had long been his enemy, and when he saw my father was fast asleep he cut him to pieces. And this coat my father wore at that time. The coat fits me poorly, for it is as I found it, and it shall never be mended for me. To keep my father's death in remembrance until I am revenged, I wear this coat. And because you are called the most noble king of the world I came to you to ask you to make me a knight."

"Sir," said Sir Lamorak and Sir Gaheris, "it would be well to make him a knight, for in person and in bearing he shall prove to be a good man, and a good and mighty knight. For, sir, if you will remember, Sir Launcelot du Lake, when he came first to this court, was such a person and very few of us knew whence he came. And now he has proved to be the man of most worship in the world. All your court and all your Round Table are made more worthy by Sir Launcelot than by any knight now living."

"That is true," said King Arthur, "and tomorrow at your request I will make this youth a knight."

On the morrow a hart was found, and King Arthur with a company of knights rode forth to slay the hart. This young man that Sir Kaye had named La-Cote-Male-Taile was left behind with Queen Guenever at the court. Suddenly a mighty lion, which was kept in a strong tower of stone, broke loose and came after the queen and her knights.

When the queen saw the lion, she cried and fled, and prayed her knights to rescue her, but all fled except twelve.

Then said La-Cote-Male-Taile, "Now I see well that all coward knights are not dead."

Thereupon he drew out his sword and advanced to the lion. That king of beasts came upon him with wide-open jaws, eager to devour him. Then La-Cote-Male-Taile struck the wild animal on the middle of the head with such a mighty blow that he cut it in two, and it fell down dead.

The queen was told that the lion had been slain by the young man that Sir Kaye dubbed La-Cote-Male-Taile. When King Arthur came home and Guenever told him of that adventure, he was well pleased.

"Upon my life," he said, "he shall prove to be a noble man and a faithful knight, and true to his promises."

Then the king made him knight.

"And now, sir," said the knight Sir Brewnor le Noyre, "of your good grace I pray you and all the knights of your court to call me no other name but La-Cote-Male-Taile, as Sir Kaye has named me."

"I consent to that," said the king.

On that same day a damsel came to the king's court, and she brought with her a great black shield, with a white hand on it holding a sword. There was no other picture on that shield. When King Arthur saw her he asked her whence she came and what she wished to have in his court.

"Sir," said the damsel, "I have gone for many a day with this black shield, and for this reason I come to your court. And he that owned this shield was a right good knight, but this knight had undertaken to achieve a great deed of arms. Then it happened that another good fighter encountered him suddenly. Each wounded the other grievously. They fought long and were so weary that they left the battle even. So this knight to whom this shield belonged saw that there was no other way but that he must die. Then he commanded me to bear this shield to the court of King Arthur, praying that some good knight take this shield and fulfill the quest that he was in."

"Now what do you say to the quest?" said King Arthur. "Is there a knight here who will dare to wield this black shield?"

Then no one spoke a word. Sir Kaye took the black shield in his hand.

"Sir knight," asked the damsel, "what is your name?"

"Know," said he, "that my name is Sir Kaye the seneschal, who is known well in many places."

"Sir," said the maiden, "lay down that shield, for know that it will not fall to you. He must be a better knight than you who shall wield this shield."

"Damsel," said Sir Kaye, "I took this buckler in my hands by your leave to look at it, not for the purpose you suggest. Go wherever you will, for I will not go with you."

Then the maiden stood still a long while and looked at many of those knights. Suddenly then the youth known as La-Cote-Male-Taile spoke: "Fair damsel, I will take upon me that black shield and that adventure, if I may know in which direction my journey should be. Because I was made knight today, I would take this adventure upon me."

"What is your name, fair young sir?" said the damsel.

Said he, "My name is La-Cote-Male-Taile."

"Well may you be called so," said the damsel, "the knight with the evil-shapen coat. But if you are rash enough to undertake to carry that black shield, and follow me, know that your skin will be as well hewn as your coat."

"As for that," said La-Cote-Male-Taile, "I will ask no salve from you to heal me, if I am so hewn."

Thereupon two squires came into the court and brought him a great horse, his armor, and his spear. Soon he was armed and ready to take his leave.

"I would not willingly have you take that hard adventure upon you," said the king.

"Sir," said the young knight, "this adventure is mine, and the first that ever I took upon me. I will follow, whatever comes."

Then the damsel left, and La-Cote-Male-Taile followed fast after her. In a short while he overtook the damsel, and she rebuked him in the most uncivil manner.

II

Sir Kaye then ordered Sir Dagonet, King Arthur's court fool, to follow the pair. In all haste Sir Kaye armed and horsed this poor puppet, and bade him pursue Sir La-Cote-Male-Taile and offer to joust with him. Then the young knight, when the court fool cried out to him and bade him make ready to joust, struck Sir Dagonet over his horse's croup. The damsel then mocked La-Cote-Male-Taile.

"Shamed are you now," said she, "in King Arthur's court, if they send a fool to joust with you, especially at your first jousts."

Thus she rode along, chiding him. And soon Sir Bleoberis the good knight came and jousted there with

Sir La-Cote-Male-Taile and smote him so hard that horse and all fell to the earth. Then the youth rose, dressed his shield, and drew his sword. He wished to fight to the uttermost, for he was mad with wrath.

"Not so," said Sir Bleoberis. "At this time I will not fight on foot."

Then the damsel Maledisaunt rebuked La-Cote-Male-Taile cruelly and bade him, "Turn again, coward!"

"O damsel," said he, "I pray you taunt me no more. My grief is enough though you do not speak. I consider myself never the worse knight because the court fool followed me. And also I am never the worse fighter because of a fall from Sir Bleoberis."

For two days he rode with her and then Sir Palamides happened to meet them. The knight fought with La-Cote-Male-Taile and served him as Sir Bleoberis had done before.

"What are you doing here in my company?" asked the damsel Maledisaunt. "You cannot fight a knight or withstand a blow except from the fool Sir Dagonet."

"Ah, fair damsel, I am not the worse for a fall from Sir Palamides. Great dishonor have I none yet, for neither Bleoberis nor yet Palamides would battle with me on foot."

"As for that," said the maiden, "you know well that they scorn to alight from their horses to fight such a poor knight as you."

In the meanwhile Sir Mordred, Sir Gawaine's brother, came and fell into the company of the damsel Maledisaunt. Soon they came before the Castle Orgulus, and there was a custom that no knight might pass that castle without jousting or becoming a prisoner, or at least losing his horse and his harness.

Out of that stronghold came two knights against them. Sir Mordred jousted with the foremost, and the knight of the castle smote him down off his horse. Then Sir La-Cote-Male-Taile jousted with that other knight, and each of them smote the other down, horse and man, to the ground. Then they got off their horses, and each took the other's horse. Sir La-Cote-Male-Taile rode to the knight, who smote down Sir Mordred and jousted with him. There our young knight hurt and wounded that knight sorely, and threw him from his horse to the earth as though he were dead. Then he turned to the knight that had met him before but the knight fled and Sir La-Cote-Male-Taile rode after him into the castle, and there he killed him.

III

Thereafter a hundred knights came about Sir La-Cote-Male-Taile and attacked him. And when he saw that his horse would be slain, he alighted, put the bridle under his horse's feet, and so put him out of the gate.

Then he hurled in among them all and dressed his back to the wall of a lady's chamber, thinking that he would rather die there with honor than endure the rebukes of the damsel Maledisaunt.

While he stood and fought, that lady whose room it was went slyly out at a postern and outside the gates she found La-Cote-Male-Taile's horse. Then she got the animal by the bridle and tied him to the postern. After that she returned to her room quietly, to watch how that one knight fought against a hundred. When she had watched for a long time, she went to a window behind his back.

"Knight, you fight wondrous well," she said, "but for all that at last you must die unless you can through your great strength get to that postern yonder. There have I fastened your horse to await you. Think not of dying, but remember your honor, for to get as far as that posterr you must fight powerfully and nobly."

When La-Cote-Male-Taile heard her say that, he took his sword, put his shield before him, and hurled through the thickest of the press. There, at the postern, he found four knights ready. With two strokes he killed two of them, and the other two fled. So he got on his horse and rode from them.

And all this just as it happened was told in King Arthur's court—how he slew twelve knights within the Castle Orgulus and then rode on his way.

"I think my foolish knight must be either slain or taken prisoner," the damsel said to Sir Mordred. But just then they saw him come riding toward them.

Then he told them how he had fared, and had escaped in spite of them all.

"And some of the best of them will tell no tales of the encounter." he said.

"You lie," said the damsel, "I dare say. As a fool and a dastard to all knighthood they have let you pass."

"You may prove it," said Sir La-Cote-Male-Taile.

Then she sent a courier of hers, who always rode with her, to learn the truth of this adventure. The messenger rode there quickly and asked how and in what manner Sir La-Cote-Male-Taile had escaped out of the castle. Then all the knights there cursed him.

"He is a fiend and no man," they said, "for he has slain here twelve of our best knights, and we know that that would have been too much for Sir Launcelot du Lake or for Sir Tristram de Lyones. In spite of us all he escaped from us."

With this answer the courier took leave and, coming again unto his lady, the damsel Maledisaunt, told her how Sir La-Cote-Male-Taile had succeeded at the Castle Orgulus. Then she bowed her head, but said little.

"By my faith," said Sir Mordred to the maiden, "you are greatly to blame to taunt him. For I warn you plainly that he is a good knight and I am sure he will prove to be a noble champion. But as yet he does not sit surely on horseback. He that would be a good horseman must learn it by practice and exercise.

"But when it comes to strokes of his sword he is powerful. Sir Bleoberis and Sir Palamides saw that well enough. They are sly men of arms and when they see a young knight, they know by his riding whether they should give him a fall from his horse or a great blow.

"Yet for the most part they will not fight on foot with young knights, since they are powerful and strongly armed.

"Sir Launcelot du Lake, when he was first made

knight, was often put to the worse on horseback, but ever he recovered his renown when he fought on foot, for he defeated and killed many knights of the Round Table. Therefore the lesson that Sir Launcelot taught to many knights caused men of prowess to be careful. I have often seen old and proved knights rebuked and slain by those who were beginners."

Thus they rode, talking together along the way.

IV

When Launcelot came to the court of King Arthur he heard of the young knight Sir La-Cote-Male-Taile, how he slew the lion, and also how he took upon him the adventure of the black shield, which was called at that time the most dreadful adventure in the world.

"So God help me," said Sir Launcelot unto many of his fellows, "it is a shame to all you noble knights that you suffered so young a knight to take such an adventure upon him to his own destruction. For I want you to know that the damsel Maledisaunt has borne that shield many a day, to seek out the most proved knights. Breus Sans Pitié took that shield away from her, but Sir Tristram de Lyones rescued it and gave it to her again. Shortly before that time Sir Tristram fought with my nephew Sir Blamor de Galis for a quarrel that was between the King of Ireland and him."

Then many knights were sorry that Sir La-Cote-Male-Taile had gone on that adventure.

"Truly," said Sir Launcelot, "I will ride after him."

And within seven days this pride of knighthood

overtook La-Cote-Male-Taile, and then saluted him and the damsel Maledisaunt. And when Sir Mordred saw Sir Launcelot he left their company. So Launcelot rode with them all that day, and the damsel Maledisaunt continued taunting Sir La-Cote-Male-Taile uncourteously. When the older knight answered for him, the maiden stopped chiding her knight and taunted Sir Launcelot.

In the meantime Sir Tristram de Lyones sent a letter by a damsel to Sir Launcelot.

Sir Tristram had been told that Sir Launcelot had spoken great shame of him since he had been a false knight to his lady La Beale Isoude. He had been told that Sir Launcelot would be his mortal enemy in every place where they might meet. Sir Tristram was sore grieved and ashamed that noble knights should speak slightingly of him for his lady's sake. And of all knights he had most loved to be in Sir Launcelot's company.

In the meantime La Beale Isoude had written to Queen Guenever, complaining of Sir Tristram's unfaithfulness and telling her that he was wedding the king's daughter of Brittany. Then Queen Guenever answered La Beale Isoude, bidding her to be of good cheer, for she should have joy after sorrow, for Sir Tristram was a noble and honorable knight. By the crafts of sorcery, such ladies would make honorable men wed them.

"But in the end," Guenever had said, "he will hate her and love you better than ever before."

So it happened that Sir Tristram, dreading Sir Launcelot's disapproval of him, sent this letter in excuse for his wedding the fair damsel Isoude la Blanche Mains.

Courtsously and gently Sir Tristram wrote to his former friend, asking him always to be a good friend to him and to La Beale Isoude of Cornwall, and requesting Sir Launcelot to excuse him if he saw her. In a short time, said Sir Tristram, by the grace of heaven, he would speak with La Beale Isoude and with Launcelot.

Then Sir Launcelot left the damsel Maledisaunt and Sir La-Cote-Male-Taile to write an answer to Sir Tristram de Lyones.

In the meantime Sir La-Cote-Male-Taile rode with the damsel until they came to a castle called Pendragon, and there they saw six knights standing before them. One of the knights offered to joust with the young knight.

And there Sir La-Cote-Male-Taile struck him over his horse's croup. Then the five knights set upon him all at once with their spears. They struck down the knight, horse and man, then alighted suddenly and all together took him prisoner. They led him to the castle and kept him as captive there.

Now on the next day Sir Launcelot arose and delivered letters to the damsel for Sir Tristram. He then rode after La-Cote-Male-Taile. As he came upon a bridge a knight offered to joust with Sir Launcelot, and was straightway smitten down by him. Then they fought on foot a noble and mighty battle together.

At last Sir Launcelot smote down his adversary so that he groveled upon his hands and knees; then that knight yielded and Sir Launcelot answered him courteously.

"Sir," said the other, "I require you to tell me your name, for I feel much good will for you.

"No," said Sir Launcelot, "I will not tell you who I am unless you tell me your name."

"Certainly I will," said the knight; "my name is Sir Neroveus, who was made knight by my lord Sir Launcelot du Lake."

"Ah, Neroveus de Lyle, I am right glad that you have proved a good knight, for know now that I am Sir Launcelot du Lake."

"Alas!" said Sir Neroveus de Lyle. "What have I done?"

Therewith he fell to Sir Launcelot's feet and would have kissed them, but his sponsor would not allow him. And then they rejoiced in each other. Sir Neroveus told Sir Launcelot that he should not go to the castle Pendragon.

"For there is a knight, a mighty lord, who has many knights with him. And this night I heard them say that yesterday they took prisoner a knight who rode with a damsel, and they say he is a knight of the Round Table."

V

"In good faith," said Sir Launcelot, "that knight is my fellow, and I will rescue him or lose my life for him."

Therewith he rode forth until he came to the Castle of Pendragon. There six knights came, and all of them made ready to attack Sir Launcelot at once. Then our hero took his spear and smote at the foremost so that he broke his back in sunder. And then Sir Launcelot passed through them, lightly turned again, and struck another knight through the body and through the horse. Therewith his spear broke.

Then the four knights drew their swords and full eagerly they lashed at Sir Launcelot. At every stroke that he gave they were hurt so that they got off their saddles, sorely wounded. Forthwith he rode into the castle. The lord of the castle at that time was called Sir Brian de les Isles, a noble man and a great enemy of King Arthur. In a short time he was armed and on horseback. Then they hurled themselves together so fiercely that both their horses fell to the earth.

Quickly they got their horses, dressed their shields, and drew their swords. They fought together as madmen, and there were many strokes given in a short time. At last Sir Launcelot gave Sir Brian such a blow that he fell upon his knees. Thereupon Sir Launcelot leaped upon him and with great force pulled off his helm.

And when Sir Brian saw that he would be slain he yielded and asked for mercy. Sir Launcelot made him deliver all the prisoners that he had within his castle (among them thirty knights of King Arthur's court, and forty ladies). Launcelot delivered them and rode away.

And when Sir La-Cote-Male-Taile was delivered he got his horse and his harness and his damsel Maledisaunt. In the meantime Sir Neroveus, whom Sir Launcelot had fought at the bridge, sent a damsel after Sir Launcelot to know how he had sped at the Castle of Pendragon. Those who were within the castle wondered what knight it was, to whom Sir Brian and his knights delivered all these prisoners.

"Do not wonder," said the damsel, "for he is the best knight in the world. Know that it was Sir Launcelot du Lake."

Then was Sir Brian glad, and so was his lady, and all his knights, that such a noble man should conquer them. And when the damsel and Sir La-Cote-Male-Taile understood that it was Sir Launcelot who had ridden with them in company, Maledisaunt remembered how she had taunted him and called him coward. Then was she sorrowful and unhappy.

VI

They took their horses then and rode after Sir Launcelot. And within two miles they overtook him and saluted him. They thanked him greatly, and the damsel asked mercy because of her evil speech and said, "Now I know the flower of all true and loyal knighthood is divided between Sir Tristram and you. For heaven knows that I have sought you two long, and now I thank God I have met you. Once at Camelot I met Sir Tristram, and there he rescued this black shield with the white hand holding the naked sword, which Sir Breus Sans Pitié had taken away from me."

"Now, fair damsel," said Sir Launcelot, "who told you my name?"

"Sir," said she, "there came a damsel from a knight that you fought with at the bridge, and she told me who you were."

"She should be blamed," said Sir Launcelot, "unless her lord Sir Neroveus told her.   But, fair maid, upon this agreement I will ride with you, if you will not taunt this knight Sir La-Cote-Male-Taile any more.   For he is a right good knight, and I know that he will prove to be a noble champion.   For his sake, so that he will not be destroyed, I follow him to help him in his great need."

"God reward you!" said the damsel.   "For now I will tell you and him both that I taunted him, not because I hated him, but for the great love that I had for him. I thought he was too young to try these adventures, therefore I wanted to drive him back because of the jealousy I had of his life.   No young knight could pursue this quest to the end."

"By my faith," said Sir Launcelot, "that is well spoken.   Instead of the damsel 'Maledisaunt,' I will call you the maiden Bienpensaunt."

Then they rode forth a long while until they came to the borders of the country of Surluse.   There they found a fair village with a strong bridge like a fortress.   And when they arrived at the bridge many gentlemen and yeomen came toward them.

"Fair lords," they said "you may pass neither this bridge nor this fortress, because of the black shield that we see one of you bear.   Only one of you shall pass at a time.   Therefore choose which of you shall enter this bridge first."

Then Sir Launcelot offered to enter it first.

"Sir," said La-Cote-Male-Taile, "I beseech you to

let me enter first within this fortress. And if I speed
well, I will send for you. If it happens that I am slain,
well and good. But if I am taken prisoner, then you may
come and rescue me."

"I am loath," said Sir Launcelot, "to let you try
this passage."

"Sir," said La-Cote-Male-Taile, "I pray you let me
put my body in this adventure."

"Then go your way, and God be your speed!"

So La-Cote-Male-Taile entered, and there met him
two brethren, one called Sir Plaine de Force and the
other Sir Plaine de Amours. La-Cote-Male-Taile smote
down Sir Plaine de Force first and soon after smote
down the other. Then they dressed them to their shields
and swords.

When they bade Sir La-Cote-Male-Taile alight, he
did so. Then there was much slashing and thrusting
with swords. They began full hard to test the venture-
some young knight. They gave him many great wounds
upon his head and breast and upon his shoulders. And
in return he gave them sad strokes again. Then the two
brothers circled about in order to be on both sides of Sir
La-Cote-Male-Taile but by fine force and knightly
prowess he kept them in front of him.

When he knew that he was sorely wounded, he
doubled his strokes and gave the brothers so many
wounds that he felled them to the earth, and would have
killed them if they had not yielded. So La-Cote-Male-
Taile took the best horse of the three, and rode forth on
his way to the other fortress and bridge. There he met

with the third brother, whose name was Sir Plenorius, a noble knight. They jousted together there, and each struck the other down, horse and man, to the earth.

Then both alighted from their horses and dressed their shields. They drew their swords and delivered many sad blows. Sometimes one knight was on the bridge, and sometimes the other. Thus they fought two hours and more and never rested, and Sir Launcelot and the damsel watched them always.

"Alas," said the maiden, "my knight fights hard and overlong."

"Now may you see that he is a noble knight," said Sir Launcelot. "Since this is his first battle and he has grievous wounds it is a great marvel that he can endure this long battle with that great knight."

VII

In the meantime Sir La-Cote-Male-Taile sank down on the earth, for from loss of blood and his grievous wounds he could not longer stand. Then the other knight had pity on him.

"Fair young sir," he said, "be not dismayed. For if you had been fresh when you met me, I know well I could not have endured as long as you have. Therefore, because of your noble deeds and valor, I will show you great kindness and gentleness in all that I can."

Then the noble knight Sir Plenorius took him up in his arms and led him into his tower. And he commanded that wine be given the youth, and had his wounds dressed.

"Sir," said La-Cote-Male-Taile, "leave me, and go to yonder bridge again. For there you will meet a better knight than I am."

"Why," said Sir Plenorius, "is there another knight in your company?"

"Yes, truly," said the young knight. "There is a much better knight than I am."

"What is his name'" asked Sir Plenorius.

"You shall not learn it from me at this time."

"Well, he shall be met, whosoever he be."

At that moment Sir Plenorius heard a knight call to him.

"Where are you, Sir Plenorius?" said the voice. "Either deliver to me the prisoner that you have led into your tower, or come and fight with me."

Then Sir Plenorius got his horse and came with a great spear in his hand, galloping toward Sir Launcelot as if the whirlwind had carried him. Then they came together like thunder and struck each other so hard that their horses fell down under them. Then they got off their horses and drew out their swords. Like two bulls they lashed together with great strokes, but Sir Launcelot always gained ground, and when Sir Plenorius tried to go around him, he would not allow it, but bore him back and farther back until he came near the tower gate.

"I know you well for a good knight," said Sir Launcelot then, "but know you that your life or death is in my hands. Therefore yield to me, and give up your prisoners."

The other answered not a word, but struck mightily

upon Sir Launcelot's helmet, so that fire sprang out of his eyes. Then Sir Launcelot doubled his strokes so thick and smote at him so mightily that he made the other fall on his knees. Then he leaped upon him and pulled him down groveling.

Thereupon Sir Plenorius yielded himself and his tower and all his prisoners. Then Sir Launcelot took the knight's oath and rode to the other bridge, where he jousted with three other brothers, the one called Sir Pellogris, another Sir Pillounes, and the third Sir Pellandris. On horseback Sir Launcelot beat them down, and then smote them on foot and made them yield to him.

Then he returned to Sir Plenorius and found in his prison King Carados of Scotland and many other knights, and they all were delivered. Then Sir Launcelot would have given to Sir La-Cote-Male-Taile all these fortresses and these bridges.

"No," said the youth, "I will not take Sir Plenorius' livelihood. If he will promise you, my lord Sir Launcelot, to come to King Arthur' scourt and be his knight, with all his brothers, I will pray you to let him have his livelihood."

"I am willing," said Launcelot, "if he will come with his five brothers to King Arthur's court and become his knight. And, Sir Plenorius, I will try at the next feast coming, if there is a vacant place, to have you join the fellowship of the Round Table."

"Sir," said Sir Plenorius, "at the next Feast of Pentecost I will be at King Arthur's court. And at that time I will be guided and ruled as King Arthur and you will have me."

Then Sir Launcelot and Sir La-Cote-Male-Taile rested there until the younger knight had recovered from his wounds. And they had great cheer and good rest and many games, for at the castle there were many fair ladies.

VIII

In the meantime Sir Kaye the seneschal and Sir Brandiles came and stayed with them. Then within ten days the knights of King Arthur's court left all these fortresses. And as Sir Launcelot came by the castle of Pendragon he took it from Sir Brian de les Isles, because that knight would never agree with King Arthur. And all that castle of Pendragon, with all the lands thereof, Sir Launcelot gave to Sir La-Cote-Male-Taile.

And then Sir Launcelot sent for Sir Neroveus, whom he had once made knight, and he made him have all the rule of that castle and of the country roundabout under La-Cote-Male-Taile. And together they all rode to King Arthur's court.

At the Pentecost following, Sir Plenorius and also Sir La-Cote-Male-Taile, otherwise called Sir Brewnor le Noyre, were made knights of the Round Table, and King Arthur assigned great lands to them. And there Sir Brewnor le Noyre wedded the damsel Maledisaunt, and after that she was called Beauvivant.

But Sir Brewnor le Noyre was generally called Sir La-Cote-Male-Taile and proved to be a brave and mighty knight. He did many worshipful deeds after this time. Sir Plenorius, too, proved to be a knight full of prowess, and all the days of his life waited upon Sir Launcelot. The brothers of Sir Plenorius were always knights of King Arthur. And Sir La-Cote-Male-Taile later avenged his father's death.

IX

Now when Sir Tristram's love and lady, La Beale Isoude, King Mark's wife, understood that Tristram was married, she sent by her maid Bragwaine as piteous letters to him as could be thought of. She said that if it pleased him he could come to her court and bring with him his bride, Isoude la Blanche Mains. There they should be kept as well as she herself.

Then Sir Tristram called Sir Kay Hedius to him and asked him whether he would go with him into Cornwall secretly. This knight said he was ready at all times; so they secretly prepared a little ship, in which Sir Tristram, Kay Hedius, Dame Bragwaine, and Governale, Sir Tristram's squire, went. When they were on the sea, a contrary wind blew them onto the coast of North Wales near the Castle Perilous.

"Here must you wait ten days," then said Sir Tristram, "and Governale, my squire, with you. And if I do not come back by that day, take the nearest way into Cornwall. For within this forest are many strange adventures, as I have heard people say, and some of them will I prove before I depart. And when I may, I will hasten after you."

Then Sir Tristram and Sir Kay Hedius took their horses and left the company. They rode in that forest for a mile and more. At last Sir Tristram saw before him a handsome knight, all armed, sitting by a clear fountain or well. And near him, tied to a great oak, was a strong, mighty horse. And a man near him led a horse that was laden with spears.

The knight that was near the fountain seemed by his face to be passing sad. Then Sir Tristram rode up to him.

"Fair knight," he said, "why sit you here so sad? You seem to be a knight errant by your arms and your harness. Therefore prepare to joust with one or both of us."

The knight made no answer, but took his shield and buckled it about his neck. Quickly he took his horse and leaped upon him. Then he received a great spear from his squire and drew off his distance. Sir Kay Hedius asked Sir Tristram to let him joust first.

"Do your best," said Sir Tristram.

So they met, and there Sir Kay Hedius had a fall and was wounded in the breast.

"Knight," then said Sir Tristram, "you have jousted well; now make ready for me."

"I am ready enough," said the knight.

So he took another great spear in his hand and fought with Sir Tristram. There by great force the knight smote down Sir Tristram from his horse and gave him a great fall. Then Sir Tristram felt great shame, and got off his horse. He put his shield before him and drew out his sword. Then he asked that strange knight to alight and fight with him upon foot.

"I am willing," said the knight.

So he alighted from his horse. He put his shield on his shoulder and drew out his sword. They fought a long battle together there for nearly two hours.

Then Sir Tristram said, "Fair knight, cease fighting, and tell me your name and whence you come."

"As for that," said the knight, "if you will tell me who you are, perhaps I will tell you my name."

"Know, fair knight," said the first, "my name is Sir Tristram de Lyones."

"Sir," said the other noble, "my name is Sir Lamorak de Galis."

"Ah, Sir Lamorak, we are well met. Remember now the shame that you caused me by sending the horn to King Mark's court, with the intention of killing or dishonoring my lady the queen, La Beale Isoude. And therefore know that one of us will die before we leave."

"Sir," said Sir Lamorak, "remember that we were together in the isle of Savage. At that time you promised me great friendship."

Then Sir Tristram would not delay longer, but lashed at his adversary. And they fought for a long time until each was weary of the other.

"In all my life," said Sir Tristram to Sir Lamorak, "I never met a knight that was so big and so well breathed as you. Therefore it would be a pity that either of us should be killed."

"Sir," said Sir Lamorak, "for your renown I wish

you to have the best of this battle, and therefore I will yield to you."

Therewith he took hold of his sword to yield it to Sir Tristram.

"No," said Sir Tristram, "you shall not do so, for I know well that your proffers are from gentleness rather than from any fear you have of me."

Therewith Sir Tristram proffered his sword to him, saying, "Sir Lamorak, as an overcome knight I yield to you, as to a man of the most noble prowess that ever I met."

"No," said Sir Lamorak, "I will treat you with gentleness. Let us be sworn that neither of us shall after this day fight against the other."

Then Sir Tristram and Sir Lamorak swore that neither of them would ever fight the other.

XI

In the meantime the good knight Sir Palamides came, following a questing beast that had a serpent's head and a body like a leopard, haunches like a lion, and hoofs like a hart. In the beast's body there was a noise like thirty couple of hounds questing. This sound the beast made wheresoever he went.

Sir Palamides followed this monster everywhere, for it was called his quest. And as he followed this beast it came by Sir Tristram and Sir Lamorak. And, to shorten the tale, Sir Palamides struck down both knights with a single spear, and followed after his beast "Glatisaunt," as it was called.

Now no man was ever made who could be victorious always. Sometimes by evil fortune the worse knight puts the better knight to shame.

Then Sir Tristram and Sir Lamorak got Sir Kay Hedius upon a shield between them both and led him to a forester's lodge. And there they charged the forester to keep him, and with him they stayed three days and more. Then the two knights took their horses and at a cross they separated.

And then said Sir Tristram unto Sir Lamorak, "I require you, if you happen to meet Sir Palamides, to say to him that he will find me at the well where I met him. There shall I prove whether he or I be the better knight."

And so they took leave of each other and rode different paths. Sir Tristram rode near where Sir Kay Hedius was, and Sir Lamorak rode until he came to a chapel, where he put his horse to pasture.

And soon Sir Maliagaunce, who was King Bademagus' son, came. There he too put his horse to graze and did not see Sir Lamorak. When this king's son made moan of the love that he had for Queen Guenever, and made a most lamentable complaint, Sir Lamorak heard all. On the next morning Sir Lamorak took his horse and rode into the forest, where he met two knights lingering in a grove.

"Fair knights," said Sir Lamorak, "what are you doing watching there? If you are knights errant who will joust, why then, lo! I am ready."

"No, sir knight," said they, "not so. We are not

waiting here to joust with you. We lie here in wait
for the knight who slew our brother."

"What knight would you fain meet withal?"

"Sir," they said, "it was Sir Launcelot du Lake who
slew our brother. And if ever we meet him, he shall
not escape."

"You take upon yourselves a great charge, fair
knights. For Sir Launcelot is a proved knight."

"We do not doubt that," said they. "None is good
enough for him but ourselves."

"I will not believe that," said Sir Lamorak, "for I
never yet in all the days of my life heard of any knight
for whom Sir Launcelot was not too big."

XII

As they stood talking thus, Sir Lamorak saw Sir
Launcelot come riding straight toward them. Then each
saluted the other and Sir Lamorak asked Launcelot if there
were anything that he might do for him in that country.

"No," said Sir Launcelot, "not at this time, I thank
you."

And so each left the other, and Sir Lamorak rode
again where he had left the two knights, and he found
them hid in the leafy woods.

"Fie on you, false cowards," said he. "Great pity
and shame it is that any of you should take the high order
of knighthood."

So Sir Lamorak left them, and within a short time
met Sir Maliagaunce. He then asked the king's son
why he loved Queen Guenever as he did.

"For I was not far from you," he said to him, "when you made your complaint near the chapel."

"Did you hear me?" said Sir Maliagaunce. "Then I will abide by it: I love Queen Guenever. What will you do about it? I will prove it and make it good that she is the fairest and most beautiful lady in the world."

"As to that," said Sir Lamorak, "I say no thereto. For Queen Morgawse of Orkney, mother of Sir Gawaine, is the fairest lady that is alive."

"That is not so," said the other, "and that will I prove with my hands upon your body."

"Will you so?" said Sir Lamorak. "In a better quarrel I could not fight."

And then they left each other in great wrath and came running together like thunder. Each struck the other so hard that their horses fell backward to the earth. Then they leaped from their horses, dressed their shields, and drew their swords. And then they fought together like two wild boars.

Thus they fought for a great while, for Sir Maliagaunce was a good knight and a man of great prowess, but Sir Lamorak was too strong for him, and ever forced him back. But each had sore wounded the other, and as they stood thus fighting, by fortune there came riding along Sir Launcelot and Sir Bleoberis. Then Sir Launcelot rode between the fighters and asked them why they were fighting each other.

"For you are both knights of King Arthur's court," said he.

XIII

"Sir," said Maliagaunce, "I will tell you why we fight this battle. I praised my lady Queen Guenever and said she was the fairest gentlewoman of the world. But Sir Lamorak said no; he said that Queen Morgawse of Orkney was fairer than she and more beautiful."

"Ah, Sir Lamorak," cried Launcelot, "why do you say so? It is not your place to dispraise the princess that you and all of us serve."

Therewith he alighted.

"For this quarrel make you ready, sir," he said. "For I will prove to you that Queen Guenever is the fairest lady and most beautiful in the world."

"Sir," said Sir Lamorak, "I am loath to fight with you in this quarrel, since every man thinks his own lady the fairest. And, though I praise the lady that I love most, you should not therefore be angry. For, though my lady Queen Guenever is the fairest in your eye, Queen Morgawse of Orkney is the most beautiful to me. And so thinks every knight of his own lady. Know, sir, you are the man in the world (except Sir Tristram) that I am most loath to fight with. But if you must fight with me, I shall endure as long as I can."

"My lord, Sir Launcelot," then said Sir Bleoberis, "I never knew you as unreasonable as you are now, for Sir Lamorak speaks in reason and rightly. Here I warn you that I have a lady, and I think she is the fairest alive. Were this a great reason that you should be angry with me for such language? And you know well that Sir Lamorak is a noble knight, and he has always felt for you and us good will.   Therefor I pray you be good friends."

Then said Sir Launcelot, "I pray you forgive me all my ill will, and if I was unreasonable I will amend it."

"Sir," said Sir Lamorak, "the amends are soon made between you and me."

Then the four knights left one another.   And in a short while King Arthur came and met Sir Lamorak and jousted with him.   And there he was struck down by the king and wounded with a spear.   Then the king rode away.   Therefore Sir Lamorak was angry because he would not fight with him on foot, for the knight did not recognize King Arthur.

XIV

Now let us speak of Sir Tristram de Lyones, who, as he rode, met Sir Kaye the seneschal.   Sir Kaye asked Sir Tristram of what country he was come.   Then Sir Tristram answered that he was of the country of Cornwall.

"That may well be," said the seneschal, "for I never yet heard that ever any good knights came out of Cornwall."

"That is evilly spoken," said Sir Tristram.   "But tell me your name I pray."

"Sir, I would have you know that my right name is Sir Kaye the seneschal."

"Is that your name truly?   Now, know well that you are called the most shameful knight with the tongue that now is living in the world.   Nevertheless it is said you are a good knight, though unfortunate with your tongue."

And thus they rode together until they came to a bridge. And there was a knight who would not let them pass until one of them had jousted with him.

And so that knight jousted with Sir Kaye and gave him a fall from his horse. And that knight's name was Sir Tor, the half brother of Sir Lamorak. And then both rode to their lodging, where they found Sir Brandiles. And Sir Tor came after them later.

As these four knights sat at their supper three of them spoke shamefully of Cornish knights. Sir Tristram heard all that they said, and answered but little, but he thought the more. At that time he did not tell his name.

In the morning he took his horse and accompanied them on their way. And there Sir Brandiles offered to joust with Sir Tristram and was by him struck down, horse and all, to the earth. Thereafter Sir Tor le Fils de Vasher fought Sir Tristram and by him was struck from his horse. Then the Cornish knight rode his way, and Sir Kaye followed him, but he would not allow him company.

Then came Sir Brandiles to Sir Kaye and said, "I would that I knew what that knight's name is."

"Come on your way with me," said the seneschal, "and we shall ask him to tell us his name."

So they rode together until they came near Sir Tristram. They saw him sitting by a well, where he had put off his helmet to drink. And when he saw them come he laced on his helmet, took his horse, and proffered to joust.

"No," said Sir Brandiles, "we jousted late enough
with you, so we come not with that intent. We come to
ask you by your knighthood to tell us your name."

"Fair knights, since it is your desire, you shall know
that my name is Sir Tristram de Lyones, nephew to
King Mark of Cornwall."

"In good time and well are you found," said Sir
Brandiles. "And know that we are right glad that we
have discovered you. And we are of a fellowship that
would be right glad of your company, for you are the
knight of the world that the company of the Round
Table desires most to have of its number."

"I thank them," said Sir Tristram, "for their great
goodness. But, as yet I feel well that I am unable to
be of their fellowship, for I have never done deeds
worthy to be one of that company."

"Ah," said Sir Kaye, "if you are Sir Tristram de
Lyones, you are the man now called greatest in prowess
except for Sir Launcelot du Lake. No Christian or
heathen can find such another knight, to speak of his
prowess and of his hands and of his truth withal. No
creature could ever say anything dishonorable about
him and prove it."

And thus they talked a great while, and then they
left one another and went in such directions as seemed
best to them.

XV

Now shall you hear why King Arthur came to the
Forest Perilous that was in North Wales. A lady, named

Annowre, came to King Arthur at Cardiff, and by fair
promises and fair requests made the king ride with her
to that forest perilous.

She was a great sorceress. For many days she had
loved King Arthur, and because she wished to win his
love she came into that country.

When the king had gone with her, many of his
knights missed him and followed after— Sir Launcelot,
Sir Brandiles, and many others. And when Annowre
had brought him to her tower, she desired the king
through her magic to forget he was wedded to Queen
Guenever and to be her husband and lord. But the
king remembered his real lady, and would have nothing
to do with Annowre in spite of all her magic.

Then was she passing angry, though she did not show
it. Every day she would make Arthur ride into that
forest with her own knights, intending to kill him. For
when this lady Annowre saw that she might not have
the king, she tried to destroy him.

And then the Lady of the Lake, who had always
been friendly to King Arthur, understood by her subtle
crafts that he was in danger of death. Therefore this
Lady of the Lake, called Nimue, came into that magic
wood to seek Sir Launcelot du Lake or Sir Tristram to
help King Arthur, for this Lady of the Lake knew that
the sovereign would be killed unless he had the aid of
one of those two knights. And thus she rode up hill
and down dale until she met Sir Tristram. As soon as
she saw him she knew him.

"O my lord Sir Tristram," said she, "well be you

met, and blessed be the time that I have found you! For today, within two hours, shall the foulest deed be done that ever was done in this great country."

"Fair damsel," said Sir Tristram, "show me the way straight so that I may right the wrong."

"Come with me," she said, "and that in all the haste you can. For you shall see the most worshipful knight in all the world hard bested."

"Then am I ready to help such a noble man, fair damsel."

"He is neither better nor worse than the noble King Arthur himself," said the Lady of the Lake.

"God defend," said Sir Tristram, "that ever he should be in such distress!"

Then they rode together at full speed until they came to a turret or castle. And underneath the wall of it they saw a knight standing on his feet, fighting with two others. And at last the two fighters smote down the one knight, and the one of them unlaced his helmet to kill him. And the lady Annowre got King Arthur's sword in her hand to cut off his head. Then came Sir Tristram with his sword drawn in his hand, crying, "Foul traitress, cease!"

Then Sir Tristram struck one of the two knights through the body so that he fell down dead. And then he rushed to the other knight, smiting him so hard that he fell from his horse and broke his back in sunder.

In the meantime the Lady of the Lake cried to King Arthur, "Let not that false lady escape you!"

So King Arthur overtook the sorceress, and with the same sword he struck off her head. This the Lady of the Lake took up and hung at her saddle bow by its hair. Then Sir Tristram horsed King Arthur and rode on his way with him. But he charged the Lady of the Lake not to discover his name at that time.

So when King Arthur was horsed he heartily thanked Sir Tristram and desired to know his name. But the knight would not tell his name, saying only that he was a poor knight seeking adventure. Thus he bore King Arthur company until Arthur met with some of his own knights.

Within a mile he met Sir Ector de Maris, and this one knew not King Arthur nor Sir Tristram and so desired to joust with one of them. Then the Cornish knight rode unto Sir Ector and smote him down from his horse. And when he had so done he came again unto the sovereign and said, "My lord, yonder is one of your men who may bear you company. On another day, by the deed which I have done for you, I trust you will understand that I would do you service."

"Alas," said the king, "let me know who you are."

"Not at this time," said Sir Tristram.

So he departed and left King Arthur and Sir Ector together.

XVI

And then on a day that they had set Sir Tristram and Sir Lamorak met at the well. Then they took Sir Kay Hedius from the forester's lodge and rode with him to the ship where they had left Dame Bragwaine and Governale the squire.

Then all sailed into Cornwall together. According to directions given by Dame Bragwaine, when they were landed they rode to Sir Dinas the seneschal, a good and trusted friend of Sir Tristram. Then Dame Bragwaine and Sir Dinas went to King Mark's court and told the queen, La Beale Isoude, that Sir Tristram was near her in that country. Then for very joy La Beale Isoude swooned.

"Gentle knight seneschal," she said when she could speak, "let me speak with Sir Tristram or my heart will break."

Then Sir Dinas and Dame Bragwaine brought Sir Tristram and Sir Kay Hedius secretly into a room to which La Beale Isoude had directed them. And no tongue could tell the joy that was between the queen and Sir Tristram, nor heart think it, nor pen write it.

The first time that ever Sir Kay Hedius saw La Beale Isoude he loved her so that he could never change his love—indeed, at the last, Sir Kay Hedius died for the love of La Beale Isoude. And then privily he wrote letters to her, and poems—the best that were written in those days. And when the queen understood his letters she had great pity for him, and unadvisedly wrote a letter to comfort him. Sir Tristram was all this time in a turret at the command of La Beale Isoude, and whenever she might she came to him.

But one day King Mark played at chess under a chamber window, and at that time Sir Tristram and

Sir Kay Hedius were in the room directly above where the king sat. It mishappened that Sir Tristram found that letter that his friend had sent to La Beale Isoude, and the one she had written back to him. And at that very time the queen came into the room where they were.

Then Sir Tristram said to her, "Madam, here is a letter that was sent to you, and here is the letter that you sent to him who wrote that letter. Alas, madam, for the great love that I have had for you! Many lands and great riches have I forsaken for your love! Now you are a traitress to me, which causes me great pain.

"But, as for you, Sir Kay Hedius, I brought you out of Britain into this country. And I won the lands of your father, King Howel, and I wedded your own sister Isoude la Blanche Mains for the kindness she gave me. But know, Sir Kay Hedius, that the falsehood and treason that you have shown me I will revenge upon you."

Then Sir Tristram drew out his sword and said, "Take care, Sir Kay Hedius!"

Then La Beale Isoude swooned. And when Sir Kay Hedius saw Sir Tristram come toward him, he leaped out of the window even over the head of King Mark, who was playing chess. The king fell back when he saw some one come leaping over his head.

"Fellow," he cried, "who are you, and why do you come leaping out of that window?"

"My lord the king," said the young knight, "I happened to be asleep in the window above your head, and as I slept I fell."

And so Sir Kay Hedius excused himself.

XVII

Then Sir Tristram feared that his presence had been discovered by the king, so he armed him in such armor as he had to fight with them who would oppose him.

But when Sir Tristram saw that no resistance was planned against him, he sent Governale for his horse and his spear, and he rode forth openly out of the castle of Tintagil. At the gate he met Sir Gingalin, the son of Sir Gawaine.

And then Sir Gingalin put his spear in the rest and ran against Sir Tristram and broke his spear. And the Cornish knight had at that time only a sword, but he gave Gawaine's son such a buffet upon the helmet that he fell down from the saddle to the earth. And his sword slipped down and carved asunder his horse's neck. And then Sir Tristram rode forth on his way into the forest.

And all this King Mark saw. Then he sent a squire to the hurt knight and commanded him to come to him. When King Mark knew that it was Sir Gingalin, he welcomed him and gave him a horse, and asked him what knight it was who had fought with him.

"Sir," said Gingalin, "I do not know what knight it was, but well I know that he sighed and mourned."

Sir Tristram in a short while met a knight of his own called Sir Fergus. And when he had met him he made great sorrow, so that he fell down off his horse in a swoon which lasted for three days and three nights. Then at the last Sir Tristram sent to the court by Sir Fergus to know what news there was. And as the courier rode by the way he met a damsel who came from Sir Palamides to know and see how Sir Tristram did. And Sir Fergus told her that his master was almost out of his mind.

"Alas," said the damsel, "where shall I find him?"

Then Fergus directed her so that she could find him.

Sir Fergus found that Queen Isoude was ill in her bed from grief.

When the damsel from Sir Palamides came to Sir Tristram, she was sore distressed because she could not help him, for the more she did for him, the greater was his pain.

At last Sir Tristram took his horse and rode away from her. She could not find him again to bring him meat and drink for three days and three nights, and then he would take none. When Sir Tristram escaped from the fostering damsel, he happened to pass by the same castle where once he had fought with Sir Palamides when La Beale Isoude separated them. There by fortune the damsel found Sir Tristram again, sorrowing bitterly. And the damsel went to the lady of the castle and told her of the unhappiness of Sir Tristram.

"Alas! Where is my lord Sir Tristram?" asked the lady.

"There by your castle," said the damsel.

"In good time," said the lady, "if he be near me, he shall have meat and drink of the best, and a harp I have of his on which he taught me to play. For as a goodly harper he bears the prize of the world."

So this lady and the damsel brought him meat and

drink, but he ate little of it. At night he would put his horse from him and unlace his armor and go into the wilderness. There would he break down trees and boughs. When he found the harp that the lady sent him, he would play upon it and weep.

And at other times, when Sir Tristram was in the wood and the lady knew not where he was, she would sit down and play upon the harp. Then would Sir Tristram come to where she played and listen to the harp. Thus lived he there a quarter of a year, then at the last he ran away, and the lady knew not what had become of him.

Sir Tristram became lean and weak, and he fell into the company of herdsmen and shepherds, and daily they gave him of their meat and drink. When he did anything foolish, they would beat him with rods, and they clipped him with shears and made him look like a fool.

One day Sir Dagonet, King Arthur's fool, came into Cornwall with two squires. As the three rode through the forest they came to a fair well where Sir Tristram often stayed. Because the weather was hot they alighted to drink of the fountain. In the meantime their horses broke loose.

Just then Sir Tristram came to them, and first he soused Sir Dagonet in the well and after that his squires. Then the shepherds laughed, and Tristram ran after the three horses and brought them again one by one. And right wet as Sir Dagonet and the squires were, he made them leap on the horses and ride away.

Thus Sir Tristram stayed there for half a year and

would never come to a town or a village. In the meantime the damsel sent by Sir Palamides to seek Sir Tristram returned to her master and told him all the trouble of the demented knight.

"Ah, me!" said Sir Palamides. "It is great pity that ever so noble a knight should go mad for the love of a lady. But nevertheless I will go seek him and comfort him if I can."

A little before this time La Beale Isoude had commanded Sir Kay Hedius to leave the country of Cornwall. So he departed with a sad heart. By adventure that knight met Sir Palamides, and they journeyed together. And both complained to each other of the deep love they felt for La Beale Isoude.

"Now let us seek Sir Tristram," said Sir Palamides, "who loves her as well as we do, and let us see if we can help him to recover."

They rode into the forest then, and for three days and three nights they did not rest, but sought tirelessly after the lost knight.

By chance they met King Mark, who had ridden off, away from his men. When they saw him, Sir Palamides recognized him, but Sir Kay Hedius did not.

"Ah, false king!" said Sir Palamides, "it is great pity that you are alive. For you are a destroyer of worshipful knights and by your vengeance you have caused the downfall of that most noble lord, Sir Tristram de Lyones. Therefore defend yourself, for you will die today."

"That would be shameful," said King Mark, "for you are both armed and I am without a suitable weapon."

"As for that," said Sir Palamides, "I will find a remedy for that. Here is a knight with me, and you shall have his harness."

"No," said King Mark, "I will not fight with you, for cause you have none. All the unhappiness that Sir Tristram had was because of a letter he found. As for me, I did him no harm, and I am sore grieved because of his malady."

So, when King Mark had excused himself, they were good friends, and King Mark wanted them to return with him to Tintagil. But Sir Palamides would not, and turned to the realm of Logris. And Sir Kay Hedius said he would go into Britain.

Now when Sir Dagonet and his squires were on horseback they thought that the fool had been sent to treat them so because they had laughed at the shepherds. Then they rode to the keepers of beasts to beat them.

When Sir Tristram saw those beaten who were wont to give him meat and drink, he ran there and got Sir Dagonet by the head and gave him such a fall that he lay still. Then he took his sword out of his hand and with it ran to one of the squires and smote off his head. The other fled, and so Sir Tristram went on his way with that sword in his hand, running as if he were mad. Then Sir Dagonet rode to King Mark and told him how he had fared in the forest.

"Therefore," said Sir Dagonet, "beware, King Mark, that you do not come near that well in the forest. For there is a naked fool near there, and that fool and I met, and he almost killed me."

"Ah, that is Sir Matto le Breune," said King Mark, "who went mad because he lost his lady. For after Sir Gaheris smote down Sir Matto, and won his lady from him, he was never in his mind afterward. And that was a pity, for he was a good knight."

XVIII

Then Sir Andret, a cousin to Sir Tristram, made a lady who loved him report to everyone that she had been with Sir Tristram before he died. This tale she brought to King Mark's court—how she had buried Sir Tristram by a well, and that before he died he prayed King Mark to make his cousin Andret king of the country of Lyones, of which Sir Tristram was lord. All this Sir Andret did because he wanted Sir Tristram's lands.

And when King Mark heard that Sir Tristram, his nephew, was dead he wept sorrowfully. But when the queen La Beale Isoude heard the news she almost went out of her mind. And so one day she decided to kill herself, for she did not care to live after Sir Tristram's death.

La Beale Isoude got a sword secretly and took it into her garden. There she put the blade into a plum tree up to the hilt, so that it stuck fast and stood breast high. Then she kneeled down and said, "Sweet Lord, have mercy upon me! For I may not live after the death of my love, Sir Tristram de Lyones. For he was my first love and he shall be my last."

All this King Mark heard and, as she began to run

toward the sword to kill herself, he came and took her in his arms. Then he drew away the sword and took her with him into a strong tower, where he kept and watched her. After that she lay long sick at the point of death.

Meanwhile Sir Tristram ran about in the forest with a sword in his hand. When he came to a hermitage, he laid him down to sleep there, and while he slept the hermit stole the weapon away and put food near him. He was kept there for ten days, then he left and went to the herdsmen again.

Now there was a giant called Tauleas in that country, and for fear of Sir Tristram for more than seven years he had not dared go at large, but stayed in a sure castle of his own. When Sir Tauleas heard that Sir Tristram was dead, he again went at large daily. It happened one day that he came among the shepherds and sat down to rest among them.

Along came a knight of Cornwall whose name was Sir Dinaunt, leading a lady with him. When the giant saw him, he left the herdsmen and hid him under a tree. When the knight came to the well and alighted to rest, the giant Sir Tauleas came between the knight and his steed and leaped upon the horse. Forthwith he rode to Sir Dinaunt, took him by the collar, drew him before him on the horse, and started to cut off his head.

Then the herdsmen said to Sir Tristram, "Help yonder knight."

"Help you him," said Sir Tristram.

"We dare not," said the herdsmen.

Then Sir Tristram saw the sword of the knight where

it lay forgotten on the ground. And he ran there, took up the weapon, and struck off Sir Tauleas' head. Then he went back to the herdsmen again.

XIX

Then the knight took up the giant's head and bore it with him to King Mark. He told the king what an adventure had happened to him in the forest, and how a madman rescued him from the fierce giant Tauleas.

"Where did this adventure happen?" asked the king.

"Forsooth," said Sir Dinaunt, "at the fair fountain in your forest where many adventurous knights meet. There the madman stays."

"Well," said King Mark, "I will see that witless knave."

So within a day or two King Mark commanded his knights and his hunters to take that madman kindly and bring him to the royal castle. So they did very quietly, and put clothing upon Sir Tristram. They led him to Tintagil, where they bathed him and washed him and gave him good hot broths until they had brought back his memory.

In all this time there was no creature who knew Sir Tristram. But one day the queen La Beale Isoude heard of the man who ran mad in the forest, and how the king had brought him home to the court. Then La Beale Isoude called to her Dame Bragwaine.

"Come with me," she said, "for we will go and see this fellow that my lord has lately brought from the forest."

So they asked where the sick man was, and the squire told the queen that he was in the garden resting. When the queen looked at Sir Tristram she did not recognize him, but said to Dame Bragwaine, "It seems to me that I have seen this man before in many places."

But as soon as Sir Tristram saw her he knew her well enough, and then he turned away his face and wept. Now La Beale Isoude always had a little brachet with her that Sir Tristram had given her the first time she came into Cornwall. And that brachet would never leave her unless his old master was where La Beale Isoude was. This brachet had been sent from the king's daughter of France to Sir Tristram for the great love she had for him.

As soon as this little brachet went near Sir Tristram she leaped upon him and licked his cheeks and his ears, whined, and smelled at his feet and his hands.

"Ah, my lady," said Dame Bragwaine to her mistress, "I see that it is my own lord Sir Tristram."

Then La Beale Isoude fell down in a swoon, and so lay for a great while.

"My lord Sir Tristram," she said, when she could speak, "blessed be God you are alive! And now I am sure you will be discovered because of this little brachet, for she will never leave you. I am sure that as soon as my lord King Mark recognizes you he will banish you out of the country of Cornwall, or else will destroy you. Therefore, my own lord, grant King Mark his will and then go to the court of King Arthur, for there you are beloved. And whenever I may I will send for you. And if you wish you may come to me. At all times, early and late, will I be at your command, to live as poor a life as ever queen or lady lived."

"O madam," said Sir Tristram, "leave me, for much anger and danger have I suffered for your love."

XX

Then La Beale Isoude left, but the brachet would not leave Sir Tristram. Then King Mark came, and the brachet sat upon her master's knee and bayed at them all. Then Sir Andret spoke.

"Sir, this is Sir Tristram," he said, "I see by the brachet!"

"No," said the king, "I cannot think that it is he."

So the king asked the madman who he was and what was his name, upon his honor.

"Truly," said he, "my name is Sir Tristram de Lyones and now you may do with me as you wish."

"Ah," said King Mark, "I am sorry for your recovery."

And then he called his barons to judge Sir Tristram to death. But many of his barons would not consent, especially Sir Dinas the seneschal and Sir Fergus. By their advice Sir Tristram was banished out of the country of Cornwall for ten years, and so he took his oath upon a book before the king and the barons.

Thus he was made to leave the country of Cornwall. And many barons brought him to his ship, some of whom were his friends and some his foes.

In the meanwhile came a knight of King Arthur whose name was Sir Dinadan, and his errand was to seek Sir Tristram. Then they showed him where he was, armed at all points, going to the ship.

"Now fair knight," said Sir Dinadan, "before you pass this court, you must joust with me."

"With a right good will," said Sir Tristram, "if these lords will grant me leave."

So these barons granted it, and then the two knights ran together. And there Sir Tristram gave the other a fall, and Sir Dinadan prayed his adversary to give him leave to go in his company.

"You shall be right welcome," said Sir Tristram.

So they took their horses and rode to their ships together.

"Greet King Mark and all my enemies well," said Sir Tristram when he was in the ship, "and tell them that I will come again when I can. Well have I been rewarded for fighting with Sir Marhaus and for delivering all the country from servitude. And well have I been rewarded for bringing La Beale Isoude out of Ireland and for all the danger that I have been in first and last. Well indeed have I been rewarded for fighting with Sir Bleoberis for Sir Sagwarides' wife; and for fighting with Sir Blamor de Ganis for King Anguish, father unto La Beale Isoude, and for smiting down the good knight Sir Lamorak de Galis at King Mark's request, and for fighting with the King with the Hundred Knights and the King of Northgales, both of whom would have put this land in servitude. Well have I been rewarded for slaying Tauleas, the mighty giant, and for fighting with the good knight Sir Palamides and rescuing Queen Isoude from him. Many more deeds have I done for King Mark—and now have I my reward. Do not forget to say to King Mark that many noble knights of the Round Table have spared the barons of this country for my sake!"

Then Sir Tristram sailed away.

XXI

At the next landing fast by the sea Sir Tristram and Sir Dinadan encountered the two gallant knights Sir Ector de Maris and Sir Bors de Ganis. There Sir Ector fought with Sir Dinadan and smote him and his horse down all in a heap on the ground. Then Sir Tristram wished to joust with Sir Bors de Ganis, but that knight said he would not joust with any Cornish fighters, for they were not considered knights of honor. All this happened upon a bridge.

Just then Sir Bleoberis and Sir Driaunt came, and the first of these offered to joust with Sir Tristram, who thereupon smote him down.

"I never knew a Cornish knight of such valor," then said Sir Bors de Ganis, "as that noble whose horse's trappings are embroidered with crowns."

Then Sir Tristram and Sir Dinadan left them and rode into a forest. There came a damsel who met them for love of Sir Launcelot, seeking for some noble knights of King Arthur's court to rescue him. For Queen Morgan le Fay had ordered thirty knights to lie in wait for that knight. The damsel had learned of this treason, and so had come to seek for help, since either that night or the day after Sir Launcelot would come where these thirty knights were. The maiden had met Sir Bors, Sir Bleoberis, Sir Ector, and Sir Driaunt. When she told them of the craft of Queen Morgan le Fay they all had promised her that they would be near where Sir Launcelot should neet the thirty knights, and that if he were set upon they would rescue him as well as they could.

Then the damsel departed, and it happened she met Sir Tristram and Sir Dinadan, whom she told of all the treachery that was prepared for Sir Launcelot.

"Fair damsel," said Sir Tristram, "bring me to the place where they shall meet with him."

"What will you do?" then said Sir Dinadan. "We cannot fight thirty knights. To match one knight against two or three is enough. But to match fifteen knights, that will I never allow you to do."

"Shame!" said Sir Tristram. "Do your part."

"No," said Sir Dinadan, "I will not do it, unless you will lend me your shield. For you bear a shield of Cornwall, and the knights of Cornwall are considered cowards."

"No," said Sir Tristram, "I will not give up my shield, for the sake of the lady who gave it to me. But one thing I promise you, Sir Dinadan. If you will not promise to stay with me, I will kill you, for I desire only that you should fight one knight. If you are afraid, stand by and look upon them and me."

"Sir," said Sir Dinadan, "I promise you to look on and do what I can to save myself, but I would I had never met you."

Then these thirty knights came fast by the four knights, and each saw the other. These thirty knights did not wish to anger the four knights, because they thought perhaps the four knights would also fight Sir Launcelot. Now the four knights let them pass because they wished to see what the thirty knights would do with Sir Launcelot. So the thirty knights passed on their way and came near Sir Tristram and Sir Dinadan.

"Lo," cried Sir Tristram, "here is a knight who rides against you for the love of Sir Launcelot!"

And then he slew two with one spear, and ten with his sword. Sir Dinadan came in then and he did passing well. Of the thirty knights but ten rode away, and they fled madly.

This battle Sir Bors de Ganis and his three fellows saw. And they noticed that it was the same knight who had jousted with them at the bridge. Then they took their horses and rode to Sir Tristram, praised him, and thanked him for his good deeds. Then all desired him to go with them to their lodging.

"No, I will go to no lodging," he said.

"We pray you then to tell us your name," said all four knights.

"Fair lords," said Sir Tristram, "at this time I will not tell you my name."

XXII

Then Sir Tristram and Sir Dinadan rode on their way until they came to the shepherds and herdsmen.

They asked them if they knew any lodging or shelter near there.

"Forsooth, fair lords," said the herdsmen, "near here is a good lodging in a castle, but the custom is that no knight shall be lodged there unless he first joust with two knights. When you are within, you soon will be matched."

"That is an evil lodging," said Sir Dinadan. "Find shelter where you will, for I will not lodge there."

"Shame!" said Sir Tristram. "Are you not a knight of the Round Table? Therefore you may not with honor refuse this lodging."

"Not so," said the herdsmen, "for if you are beaten you shall not be lodged there. But if you beat them you shall be well lodged."

"Ah!" said Sir Dinadan, "they are two noble knights!"

Then Sir Dinadan would not be lodged there but Sir Tristram required it of his knighthood. So they rode there, and Sir Tristram and Sir Dinadan smote down both the guardians and entered into the castle. There they had as good cheer as could well be devised.

But when they were unarmed, and were ready to rest, in at the gate came Sir Palamides and Sir Gaheris, requiring the custom of the castle.

"What is this?" asked Sir Dinadan. "I would have my rest."

"That may not be," said Sir Tristram. "Now must we defend the custom of the castle, because we have had the better of the lord of it. Therefore you must make ready."

"In the devil's name, I wish I had never come into your company!" said Sir Dinadan.

So they made them ready. Sir Gaheris encountered Sir Tristram and was struck down by him. And Sir Palamides rushed together with Sir Dinadan and struck him to the earth. Then they had to fight on foot but Sir Dinadan would not, for he was sore bruised and hurt from the fall that his adversary had given him. Then Sir Tristram unlaced Sir Dinadan's helmet and prayed him to help him.

"I will not," said the surly knight, "for I am sore wounded from the battle we had with the thirty knights. You go about like a madman, and like a fool who is out of his mind and would cast himself away. I may curse the time that ever I saw you. For in all the world there are not two such knights as Sir Launcelot and you. Once I came into the company of Sir Launcelot, and he set me so to work that for a quarter of a year and more afterward I kept to my bed. Heaven defend me from two such knights, and especially from you!"

"Then will I fight with them both," said Sir Tristram.

So he bade them both come forth. Then Sir Palamides and Sir Gaheris dressed them and struck at them both. Sir Dinadan aimed at Sir Gaheris a stroke or two, then turned from him.

"No," said Sir Palamides, "it is shameful for two knights of us to fight with one."

Then he bade Sir Gaheris stand aside with the knight that had no wish to fight. Sir Palamides and Sir Tristram rode together and fought for a long while, and at last

Sir Tristram doubled his strokes and drove Sir Palamides back more than three great strides. And then Sir Gaheris and Sir Dinadan went between them and separated them. Sir Tristram then said they would lodge together.

But Sir Dinadan would not seek lodging in that castle, and cursed the time that ever he came into their company. And so he took his horse and his harness and rode away. Sir Tristram then asked the lords of the castle to send him a man who would bring him to a lodging. This they did and overtook Sir Dinadan, and rode two miles from there to a lodging with a good man in a priory, where they were well at ease. That same night Sir Bors, Sir Bleoberis, Sir Ector, and Sir Driaunt stayed in the same place where Sir Tristram had fought with the thirty knights. There they met Sir Launcelot that night, and promised to lodge with Sir Colgrevance.

XXIII

But as soon as the most noble knight Sir Launcelot heard of the shield of Cornwall, then he knew well that it was Sir Tristram who had fought with his enemies. Then Sir Launcelot praised the noble Cornish knight and called him the man of most worship in the world.

There was a knight in that priory called Sir Pellinore who desired to know the name of Sir Tristram, but in no wise could find out. And so Sir Tristram departed and left behind him Sir Dinadan in the priory, for he was so weary and so bruised that he could not ride. Then this Sir Pellinore said to Sir Dinadan after Tristram left, "Since you will not tell me this knight's name, I will ride after him and make him tell me who he is, or he shall die."

"Beware, sir knight," said Sir Dinadan. "If you follow him, you will repent it."

But Sir Pellinore rode after Sir Tristram and required him to joust with him. Then the Cornish knight struck his adversary down and wounded him through the shoulder, then passed on his way. On the next day following, Sir Tristram met with heralds who told him that a great tournament was proclaimed between King Carados of Scotland and the King of Northgales, who would joust against each other at the Castle of Maidens. Sir Tristram thought to be at these jousts and tournaments, for these heralds sought through all the country for good knights. Especially King Carados was seeking Sir Launcelot, and the King of Northgales, Sir Tristram.

By chance they met Sir Kaye the seneschal and Sir Sagramour le Desirous, and Sir Kaye asked Sir Tristram to joust. He refused because he did not wish to be hurt or bruised at the great jousts that would be at the Castle of Maidens. He wished to keep fresh and rest himself, but always Sir Kaye cried out, "Sir knight of Cornwall, joust with me, or else yield to me as overcome."

When Sir Tristram heard him say that he turned toward him to joust. But when Sir Kaye saw him coming, then he refused and turned his back.

Then said Tristram, "As I find you, so shall I take you."

Sir Kaye turned back then, with an evil will. And

Sir Tristram struck him down and rode on his way. Then Sir Sagramour le Desirous rode fast after Sir Tristram and persuaded him to joust. Then the Cornish knight smote Sir Sagramour le Desirous down from his horse and rode on his way.

On that same day Tristram met a damsel who told him that he should win great honor because of a knight adventurous who did much harm in the country. When Sir Tristram heard her say so, he was glad to go with her to win such honor. So he rode with that damsel for six miles, and then met Sir Gawaine. Sir Gawaine knew that the damsel was a messenger of Queen Morgan le Fay, and understood that she led the knight into mischief.

"Fair sir," Gawaine asked, "where are you riding with that maiden?"

"I know not where I shall ride," said Sir Tristram, "but as the damsel leads me."

"Sir," said Gawaine, "you shall not ride with her, for she and her lady never do good, but evil."

At that Sir Gawaine drew out his sword and said, "Damsel, unless you tell me why you lead this knight with you, you shall die for it straightway. I know all your lady's treason and yours."

"Mercy, Sir Gawaine," said the maiden. "If you will save my life I will tell you all."

"Speak, and you shall have your life."

"Sir, my lady Morgan le Fay, King Arthur's sister, has ordered thirty ladies to seek after Sir Launcelot or Sir Tristram. These ladies, if they may meet either of

these two knights, must turn them with their wiles to
Queen Morgan le Fay's castle, saying that the knights
might do deeds of worship there. But if either of those
two knights came there, there are thirty knights watching
from a tower to wait upon him."

"Shame," said Sir Gawaine, "that ever such false
treason should be wrought by a queen and a king's sister,
and a king's and a queen's daughter!"

XXIV

"Sir," said Sir Gawaine, "will you stand with me,
and we will see the malice of these thirty knights?"

"Fair knight," said Sir Tristram, "go you to them
if it please you, and you shall see that I will not fail you.
For it is not long since that I and a fellow met thirty
knights of that queen's fellowship. God so speed us
that we may win worship!"

So then Sir Gawaine and Sir Tristram rode toward
the castle where Morgan le Fay was, and Sir Gawaine
knew well that his companion was Sir Tristram de
Lyones, because he had heard of the two knights who
had slain and beaten thirty fighters. At last they came
before the castle which they sought.

"Queen Morgan le Fay," spoke Sir Gawaine, "send
out your knights whom you have commanded to watch
for Sir Launcelot or for Sir Tristram. Now I know
your false treason and through all places where I ride
men shall know of your devilish plots. And now let see
whether you dare come out of your castle, you thirty
knights."

Then spoke Morgan le Fay, "Sir Gawaine, all that you do and say you speak because of that good knight that is there beside you. For there are some of us here who know full well the hands of that knight. It is more for his sake, by my faith, than for your own that we do not venture forth from our stronghold, Sir Gawaine. That knight who bears the arms of Cornwall—we know full well who he is."

Then the two knights left and rode on their way for a day or two together. By chance they met Sir Kaye and Sir Sagramour le Desirous, who were very glad to see Sir Gawaine and he them, but they did not know who the knight with the shield of Cornwall was. And thus all four rode together for a day or two. Then they saw Sir Breus Sans Pitié chasing a lady to kill her, for he had just killed her lover.

"Hold you all still," said Sir Gawaine, "and do not come forth. You shall see me reward that false knight. If he sees you, he is so well horsed that he will escape."

And then Sir Gawaine rode between Breus Sans Pitié and the lady.

"False knight," he said, "leave that lady and fight with me."

When Sir Breus saw only Sir Gawaine, he rode toward him, and Sir Gawaine against him. There the false knight overthrew the lady's champion, and then he rode over and over him about twenty times, to destroy him. When Sir Tristram saw him do so villainous a deed, he rushed out against him.

And when Sir Breus saw him with the shield of

Cornwall, he knew well that it was Sir Tristram. Then he fled, and the Cornish knight followed after him. But Sir Breus Sans Pitié was so well horsed that he got away. Sir Tristram followed him a long time, for he wished to be revenged on him. When he had chased him long he came to a fair well. There he rode to rest him, and tied his horse to a tree.

XXV

Then he pulled off his helmet and washed his face and his hands and fell asleep.

A damsel came then who had sought Sir Tristram for many days and through many paths. When she came to the well and looked at the sleeping knight, she did not remember Sir Tristram, but she knew him by his horse, Passe-Brewell, which had been Sir Tristram's courser for many years. For while Tristram was mad in the forest Sir Fergus had kept the horse.

The damsel Bragwaine waited there until the Cornish knight awoke. And when she saw that he was wide awake again she saluted him and he her, for they were old friends. Then she told him how she had sought him long and far, and that she had letters from La Beale Isoude. When Sir Tristram read them, he was glad and happy, for there were many pitiful words from his love, the queen.

"Lady Bragwaine," then said Sir Tristram, "ride with me until the tournament at the Castle of Maidens is over, and then shall you bear letters and tidings back with you."

Then Sir Tristram took his horse and sought lodging. Soon he met an ancient knight who prayed him to lodge with him, and to Sir Tristram came Governale, his squire, who was glad to see Dame Bragwaine again.

Now this old knight's name was Sir Pellounes, and he told of the great tournament that should be held at the Castle of Maidens. There Sir Launcelot and thirty-two knights of his blood would fight.

Thereupon one came to Sir Pellounes and told him that Sir Persides de Bloise had come home. Then did that ancient knight hold up his hands and thank God, for, as he told Sir Tristram, in two years he had not seen his son Persides.

"Sir," said the Cornish knight, "I know your son well as a noble and valorous fighter."

Sir Tristram and Sir Persides, when they came to their lodging, welcomed each other. They unarmed and dressed in the clothes of peace. Sir Persides had learned that Sir Tristram was a knight of Cornwall, but did not know who he was.

"I was once in that kingdom," he said, "and jousted before King Mark. And by chance at that time I over-threw ten knights. And then came Sir Tristram de Lyones and overthrew me and took my lady from me. That shall I never forget. But I shall remember if ever I meet him."

"Ah," said Sir Tristram, "now I understand that you hate this Sir Tristram. Do you think that Sir Tristram will not be able to withstand your anger?"

"Yes," said Sir Persides, "I know well that Sir

Tristram is a noble knight, and a much better fighter than I am, but I shall not feel any good will to him."

As they stood thus talking at a bay window of the castle, they saw many knights riding to and fro toward the tournament. And then Sir Tristram saw a likely knight riding upon a mighty black horse, with a black-covered shield.

"What knight is that with the black horse and shield?" asked Sir Tristram. "He seems to be a good knight."

"I know him well," said Sir Persides. He is one of the strongest knights of the world."

"Then is it Sir Launcelot?" asked Sir Tristram.

"No," said the other, "it is Sir Palamides, who is yet unchristened."

XXVI

Then they saw many country people salute Sir Palamides. And within a short time after that there came a squire of the castle who told Sir Pellounes, the lord of the castle, that a knight with a black shield had struck down thirteen knights.

"Fair brother," said Sir Tristram to Sir Persides, "let us put our cloaks on and go and see the play."

"Not so," said Sir Persides; "we will not go thither like knaves. Let us ride like men and knights to withstand our enemies."

So they armed, and took their horses and spears and went where many knights jousted before the tournament. Soon Sir Palamides saw Sir Persides, and sent

a squire to him saying, "Go to yonder knight with the
green shield and a lion of gold thereon and say to him
that I require him to joust with me. Tell him that
my name is Sir Palamides."

When Sir Persides understood this request, he made
ready. Soon they met together there, but Sir Persides
had a fall. Then Sir Tristram got ready to revenge the
fall of Persides upon Sir Palamides. And the knight,
who was ready, saw that Sir Tristram was not prepared.
Sir Palamides thus took him at advantage and smote
him over the horse's tail when he had no spear in his
rest. Then Sir Tristram started up, and was angry
out of measure and sore ashamed of that fall. He sent
to Sir Palamides by Governale, his squire, and prayed
him to joust with him once again at his request.

"No," said Sir Palamides, "at this time I will not
joust with that knight, for I know him better than he
thinks. And if he is angry he may have his revenge
tomorrow at the Castle of Maidens, where he will see
me and many other knights."

With that came Sir Dinadan, and when he saw Sir
Tristram angry he did not dare to jest.

"Lo," said he, "here may a man see that no matter
how strong he is, yet may he have a fall. And be he
ever so wise, he may be fooled. He rides well that
never falls."

Sir Tristram was passing wroth, and said to Sir
Persides and to Sir Dinadan, "I will be revenged upon
that fellow."

As they stood talking, there came by Sir Tristram a

likely knight, riding soberly and heavily, with a black shield.

"Who is that?" asked the Cornish knight.

"I know him well," said Sir Persides. "His name is Sir Briaunt of North Wales."

That knight passed on among the other knights of North Wales, and Sir Launcelot du Lake came with a shield of Cornwall. He sent a squire to Sir Briaunt and required him to joust.

"I will do what I can," said Sir Briaunt.

There Sir Launcelot smote down Sir Briaunt from his horse, and he had a great fall. Then Sir Tristram wondered what knight he was who bore the shield of Cornwall.

"Whoever he is," said Sir Dinadan, "I warrant you he is of King Ban's blood, which produces knights of the greatest prowess in the world."

And then there came two knights of North Wales, one called Sir Hugh de la Mountaine, and the other Sir Madocke de la Mountaine. They challenged Sir Launcelot, who did not refuse them, but made ready and with one spear smote them both down over their horse's croups. Then Sir Launcelot rode on his way.

"By my faith," said Sir Tristram, "he is a good knight that bears the shield of Cornwall. And I think he rides better than ever I saw a knight ride."

Then the King of Northgales hastily rode to Sir Palamides and prayed him for his love to joust with that knight who had shamed them of Northgales.

"Sir," said Sir Palamides, "I am loath to fight with

that knight. For tomorrow the great tournament will be, and therefore I wish to keep fresh."

"No," said the king again, "I pray you joust with him."

"Sir," said Sir Palamides, "I will joust at your request, and require that knight to fight with me. Often have I seen a man have a fall at his own request."

XXVII

Then Sir Palamides sent a squire to Sir Launcelot and required him to joust.

"Fair fellow," said Sir Launcelot, "tell me your lord's name and who he is?"

"Sir," said the squire, "my lord's name is Sir Palamides."

"Why, this is a very blessing of heaven!" said Sir Launcelot. "For, by the faith of my body, there is no knight in the world that I have seen this seven years that I would rather joust with than with Sir Palamides."

And then both knights made them ready with two huge spears.

"You will see that Sir Palamides will acquit him right well," said Sir Dinadan.

"That may well be," said Sir Tristram, "but I wager that the knight with the shield of Cornwall will give him a fall."

"That I do not believe," said Sir Dinadan.

Then the knights spurred their horses, charged, and hit each other with their spears. Sir Palamides broke a spear upon Sir Launcelot, who sat still and did not move. But Sir Launcelot struck his adversary, thrusting him from his saddle. The stroke broke his shield and his hauberk, and if he had not fallen he would have been slain.

"How now?" said Sir Tristram. "I knew well by the manner of their riding that Sir Palamides would have a fall."

Then Sir Launcelot rode away to a well to drink and rest. They of Northgales saw where he went. And twelve knights followed him to injure him, so that on the morrow at the tournament of this Castle of Maidens he should not win the victory.

They came suddenly upon Sir Launcelot, so that he could scarcely put on his helmet or take his horse. Then Sir Launcelot got his spear and rode through them, and killed a knight and broke a spear in his body. Then he drew his sword and smote to the right and to the left, so that in a few strokes he had killed three other knights, and the others he wounded grievously.

Thus Sir Launcelot escaped from his enemies of Northgales. And he rode forth on his way to lodge with a friend until the morrow, for he would not appear the first day in the tournament because he was tired from fighting. On the first day he sat with King Arthur on a scaffold to see who was most worthy. So Sir Launcelot jousted not the first day.

XXVIII

Sir Tristram de Lyones commanded Governale, his servant, to get him a black shield with no inscription on it.

Then Sir Persides and Sir Tristram left their host,

Sir Pellounes, and they rode early toward the tournament. They went on the side of King Carados of Scotland. Knights began to fill the field, some for the King of Northgales' part and some for King Carados' part. There was the confusion and rushing of a great tournament.

When Sir Persides and Sir Tristram came into the fighting, the King of Northgales was put back. Then Sir Bleoberis de Ganis and Sir Gaheris entered for Northgales. Sir Persides was struck down and almost slain, for more than forty horsemen went over him. Sir Bleoberis did great feats of arms, and Sir Gaheris failed him not.

When Sir Tristram saw them do such deeds of arms, he wondered who they were. And Sir Tristram thought it shame that Sir Persides was so done to. So he took a huge spear in his hand, rode to Sir Gaheris, and smote him down from his horse. Then was Sir Bleoberis angry, and rode against Sir Tristram in high rage. But the Cornish knight met him there and smote Sir Bleoberis from his horse.

So then the King with the Hundred Knights was angry, and he horsed Sir Bleoberis again, and Sir Gaheris also. A great affray began. But always Sir Tristram held them, and ever Sir Bleoberis was busy with Sir Tristram. Then Sir Dinadan came against the Cornish knight, who gave him such a buffet that he swooned in the saddle. Sir Dinadan came then to Sir Tristram.

"Sir, I know you better than you think," he said. "But here I promise you that I will never come against you again, and I take oath that sword of yours will never touch my helmet."

Sir Bleoberis came, and Sir Tristram gave him such a buffet that he laid down his head. Then Tristram caught him by the helmet and pulled him under his horse's feet. King Arthur blew the signal then to end the fighting.

Sir Tristram went to his pavilion, and Sir Dinadan rode with him. Sir Persides, King Arthur, and the kings on both sides wondered what knight that was with the black shield. Many guessed, and some knew him to be Sir Tristram, but held their peace and would say nothing.

So on the first day King Arthur and all the kings and lords that were judges gave Sir Tristram the prize, although they knew him not but called him the Knight with the Black Shield.

XXIX

On the morrow Sir Palamides turned from the party of the King of Northgales and rode to King Arthur's side, where were King Carados, the King of Ireland, and Sir Launcelot's kin, and Sir Gawaine's kin. So Sir Palamides sent to Sir Tristram the damsel who had been sent to seek him in the wood when he was out of his mind. The damsel asked Sir Tristram for his right name.

"As for that," said Sir Tristram, "tell Sir Palamides he shall not know at this time, until I have broken two spears upon him. But let him know this, that I am the same knight whom he smote down the evening before the tournament. And tell him plainly that on whatever side Sir Palamides will be, I will be on the opposite side."

"Sir," said the damsel, "understand that Sir Palamides will be on King Arthur's side, where the most noble knights of the world are."

"By my faith," said Sir Tristram, "then will I be with the King of Northgales because Sir Palamides will be on King Arthur's side. Otherwise I, too, would be on King Arthur's side."

When King Arthur had come, they blew the signal for the field. Then a great running and smiting upon helmets began. And King Carados jousted against the King with the Hundred Knights, and the Scotch king had a fall. King Arthur's knights came then, and they bore back the knights of the King of Northgales. Thereupon Sir Tristram entered, and he began so roughly and so valorously that no one could withstand him. Thus the Cornish knight fought for a long while.

At last Sir Tristram came among the company of King Ban, and there fell upon him Sir Bors de Ganis, Sir Ector de Maris, and Sir Blamor de Ganis, with a great many other knights. Then Sir Tristram smote down on the right hand and on the left, so that all the lords and ladies spoke of his noble deeds. But at last Sir Tristram would have had the worst of it had not the King with the Hundred Knights proved to be his good friend. For he came with his knights and rescued the Cornish knight, and brought him away with the knights that bore the shields of Cornwall.

And then Sir Tristram saw another company by

themselves, about forty knights together, with Sir Kaye the seneschal as their leader. He rode in among them all, smote down Sir Kaye from his horse, and fared among those knights like a greyhound among rabbits. Then Sir Launcelot found a knight who was sore wounded upon the head.

"Sir," said Sir Launcelot, "who wounded you so?"

"Sir," said the other, "a champion who bears a black shield, and I may curse the time that ever I met him, for he is a devil and no man."

So Sir Launcelot departed from him and thought to meet the Knight with the Black Shield and rode with his sword drawn in his hand to seek the Cornish knight. Then he saw how he dashed here and there, and at every stroke struck down a knight.

"As heaven is my witness," said King Arthur, "since the time I bore arms evner saw I a knight do such marvelous deeds of arms!"

"If I should set upon this knight," said Sir Launcelot to himself, "I should shame myself." And so he put up his sword.

Then the King with the Hundred Knights and a hundred more of Northgales set upon twenty knights of Launcelot's kin, who always held together like wild swine and none would fail the other. And when Sir Tristram beheld the valor of those twenty knights, he marveled at their noble deeds. For he saw well that they would rather die than avoid the field.

"By my faith!" said Sir Tristram. "Well may he be valiant and full of prowess that has a score of such

noble knights as his kin. He must be a noble knight
who is their leader and governor." (He meant by this,
Sir Launcelot du Lake.)

When Sir Tristram had watched them a long time,
he thought it a shame to see two hundred knights batter-
ing upon twenty. Then Sir Tristram rode to the King
with the Hundred Knights.

"Sir," he said to him, "I pray you leave your fighting
with those twenty knights, for you will win no worship
of them, since you are too many and they too few. They
will not leave the field, I see by their faces and you will
get no honor if you kill them. Therefore leave off
fighting with them or I will ride with the twenty knights
to help them with all my might and power."

"No," said the King with the Hundred Knights,
"you shall not do so. For I see your courage and
courtesy, and I will withdraw my knights. Always one
good knight will favor another, and like will draw to
like."

XXX

Then the King with the Hundred Knights withdrew
his company. And all this time Sir Launcelot had
watched Sir Tristram, desiring his fellowship.

Suddenly Sir Tristram, Sir Dinadan, and Governale
his squire rode into the forest, so that no man saw
where they went. Then King Arthur blew the signal
for closing the day and gave the King of Northgales the
prize because Sir Tristram had been on his side.

Sir Launcelot then rode here and there as angry as

a hungry lion, because he had lost sight of Sir Tristram. He returned to King Arthur, and through all the field there was a great shout which might be heard two miles off, as the lords and ladies cried, "The Knight with the Black Shield has won the field!"

"Alas," said King Arthur, "where has that knight gone? It is a shame to all those in the field to let him so escape from you. With gentleness and courtesy you might have brought him to me to the Castle of Maidens."

Then the noble king went to his knights and comforted them in the best manner that he could.

"My fair fellows," he said, "be not dismayed that you have lost the field this day. Many are hurt and sore wounded, it is true. But many are whole — so look that you be of good cheer. Tomorrow will I be in the field with you and revenge you on your enemies."

So that night King Arthur and his knights rested.

The damsel that came from La Beale Isoude to Sir Tristram stayed during the tournament with Queen Guenever, and ever that queen asked her why she had come to that place.

"Madam," said she, "I come for no other cause but that my lady La Beale Isoude would know how you fare."

For she would not tell Guenever that she came for Sir Tristram's sake. Then this lady, Dame Bragwaine, took her leave of Queen Guenever and rode after the Cornish knight. And as she rode through the forest she heard a great cry. She then commanded her squire to go into the wood to learn what that noise was.

The squire came to a well, and there found a knight bound to a tree, crying as if he were out of his mind. His horse and his harness were standing by him. When he saw the squire, he started and broke himself loose, took his sword in his hands, and ran to kill that squire. But the servant took the knight's horse and fled as fast as ever he could to Dame Bragwaine again, and told her of his adventure. Then she rode to Sir Tristram's pavilion and let him know what adventure she had found in the forest.

"Alas!" said Sir Tristram. "Upon my head, some good knight is in misfortune!"

Then he took his horse and his sword and rode into the forest. And he heard how the knight complained.

"Woeful knight that I am!" he cried. "What misfortune has befallen me, Sir Palamides, who am shamed by the falsehood and treason of Sir Bors and Sir Ector! Alas, why do I live so long?"

Then he took his sword in his hand and made many strange signs and tokens. In his raging he cast his sword into that fountain, then wailed and wrung his hands. At last he sorrowfully ran into that fountain above his waist and sought for his weapon. When Sir Tristram saw that, he ran upon Sir Palamides, and held him fast in his arms.

"Who are you," said the raging knight, "that holds me so?"

"I am a man of this forest," said Sir Tristram, "who would do you no harm."

"Alas!" said Sir Palamides, "I may never win worship

where Sir Tristram is. For ever where he is, if I am there, then get I no honor. If he is away, I have the advantage unless Sir Launcelot du Lake is there, or Sir Lamorak."

"Are Cornish knights, then, better men?"

"Yes, fair sir," said Sir Palamides. "Once in Ireland Sir Tristram put me to the worse, and another time in Cornwall, and in other places."

"What would you do if you had Sir Tristram here?"

"I would fight with him," said Sir Palamides, "and ease my heart upon him. And yet, to say the truth, Sir Tristram is the gentlest knight living in the world."

"What will you do?" said the Cornish knight. "Will you go with me to my lodging?"

"No," said the other, "I will go to the King with the Hundred Knights, for he rescued me from Sir Bors de Ganis and Sir Ector or I should have been slain traitorously."

Thereafter Sir Tristram spoke so kindly to Sir Palamides that he went with him to his lodging. Then Governale went before to charge Dame Bragwaine to go to her lodging, and to bid Sir Persides to make no quarrel with Sir Palamides.

And so they rode together until they came to Sir Tristram's pavilion, and there Sir Palamides had all the cheer that he might have that night. But Sir Palamides could not find out who Sir Tristram was. After supper they went to rest, and the Cornish knight, because of his great labor, slept until it was day. But in his anguish Sir Palamides could not sleep.

And at dawn he took his horse secretly and rode to Sir Gaheris and to Sir Sagramour le Desirous where they were in their pavilion. For they three were fellows at the beginning of this tournament. On the morrow the king blew the signal for the opening of the third day of the tournament.

XXXI

The King of Northgales and the King with the Hundred Knights fought with King Carados and with the King of Ireland and struck down these two knights.

Then in came Sir Palamides, and when he appeared he did great deeds, for he was well known by his indented shield. King Arthur came in, too, and did great deeds of arms and put the King of Northgales and the King with the Hundred Knights to the worse.

Then Sir Tristram came with his black shield, and jousted with Sir Palamides and by fine force smote that unhappy knight over his horse's tail. Then cried King Arthur, "Knight with the Black Shield, make ready for me!"

And in the same wise Sir Tristram smote down King Arthur. And then by force of the king's knights Arthur and Sir Palamides were remounted. King Arthur with great eagerness got a spear in his hand, and smote Sir Tristram over his horse. Full fast Sir Palamides came upon the Cornish knight as he was on foot, and would have overridden him.

But Sir Tristram saw and stepped aside. With great anger he took him by the arm and pulled him down from his horse. Sir Palamides arose, and then they dashed together mightily with their swords. Many kings, queens, and lords stood to watch them.

At last Sir Tristram struck Sir Palamides upon the helm with three mighty strokes, and at every stroke he gave him he said, "Have this for Sir Tristram's sake!"

Then Sir Palamides fell to the earth groveling. The King with the Hundred Knights came and brought Sir Tristram a horse. Sir Palamides was horsed again, and with great anger he jousted at the Cornish knight with his spear, and gave him a great thrust with the weapon. But Sir Tristram got away from his spear's thrust and took Sir Palamides by the neck with both his hands, and pulled him clean out of his saddle. He bore his adversary before him for the length of ten spears, and then in the presence of them all let him fall.

Then Sir Tristram saw King Arthur with a naked sword in his hand. With his spear the knight ran on the sovereign. But Arthur boldly awaited his coming and with his sword smote in two the spear. This astonished Sir Tristram so that King Arthur gave him three or four great strokes before he could get out his sword.

But at last Sir Tristram drew his sword and attacked the king passing hard. Then the great press separated and the Cornish knight rode here and there and did great feats. Eleven of the good knights of the blood of King Ban, Sir Launcelot's kin, Sir Tristram smote down, so all the people marveled at his great deeds, and cried out at the Knight with the Black Shield.

XXXII

This cry was so great that Sir Launcelot heard it, and he took his great spear in his hand and came toward the tumult.

"Knight with the Black Shield," he then cried, "make ready to joust with me!"

When Sir Tristram heard him say so, he took his spear in his hand, and both put down their heads as they came together like thunder. Sir Tristram's spear broke in pieces, and Sir Launcelot by chance gave Sir Tristram a deep wound on the side that almost killed him, but yet he was not thrown from his saddle. And so the spear broke. Though wounded sore, Sir Tristram took out his sword, rushed to his adversary and gave him three great strokes upon the helm so that sparks sprang from it and Sir Launcelot stooped low his head toward his saddlebow. Then Sir Tristram left the field, for he felt himself so wounded that he thought he must soon die.

And Sir Dinadan saw him, and followed him into the forest. But Sir Launcelot stayed and did many marvelous deeds.

When Sir Tristram was in the forest, he alighted and unlaced his harness and cared for his wound. Then Sir Dinadan deemed he would surely die.

"Nay, Dinadan," said Tristram, "never fear! For I am heart whole, and of this wound I shall soon be healed by heaven's grace."

Then his companion saw where Sir Palamides came riding straight upon them, and Sir Tristram knew that

Sir Palamides came to destroy him. Sir Dinadan warned him, saying, "My lord, you are sore wounded so that you may not fight him. Therefore I will ride against him and do what I may. If I am killed, pray for my soul. In the meanwhile withdraw and go into the castle or into the forest, so that he shall not meet you."

Sir Tristram smiled and said, "I thank you, Sir Dinadan, for your good will, but know you that I am able to handle him."

Hastily he armed and took his horse. With a great spear in his hand he said adieu to Sir Dinadan and rode toward Sir Palamides.

When Sir Palamides saw that, he pretended to fix his horse, but he did it to await Sir Gaheris who came after him. When this knight came, he rode to meet Sir Tristram.

Then the Cornish knight sent to Sir Palamides and required him to joust with him. If he smote down Sir Palamides, he promised he would do no more to him, but if it should so happen that his adversary struck him down, then he might do his uttermost.

They met together then, and Sir Tristram struck down his enemy so that he had a grievous fall and lay still as though dead. Then Sir Tristram ran upon Sir Gaheris, though he would not have jousted. But whether he would or not, Sir Tristram struck him over his horse's croup, so that he too lay still as if life had left his body. Then Sir Tristram rode his way and left Sir Persides' squire within the pavilion, while he and Sir Dinadan fared to an old knight's place to lodge there.

And after Sir Tristram departed to go into the forest, Sir Launcelot held the tourney as a man enraged who took no heed of himself. Many a noble knight rode against him, and when King Arthur saw Sir Launcelot do such marvelous deeds of arms, he armed, took his horse, and rode into the field to help Sir Launcelot.

Then the King of Northgales and the King with the Hundred Knights were put to the worse. And because Sir Launcelot stayed and was the last in the field the prize was given to him. But this gentle knight neither for king, queen, nor knight would accept the prize. When the cry came through the field, "Sir Launcelot hath won the field today!" he proclaimed, "Sir Tristram won the field, for he began first, and last endured. So did he the first day, the second, and the third!"

XXXIII

Then those of all the estates and degrees, high and low, praised Sir Launcelot for the honor he did to the Cornish knight. For favoring Sir Tristram he was more praised and renowned than if he had overthrown five hundred knights. And all the people, the high and low and the common people, cried at once, "Sir Launcelot has won the field, no one may say no!"

"Alas!" said the king. "We are all sorry that Sir Tristram has left us. Truly, he is one of the noblest knights ever I saw hold spear or sword in hand, and the most courteous knight in his fighting. For I saw him as he smote Sir Palamides upon his helmet three times."

Sir Launcelot was angry and ashamed at the people's outcry. He rode up to Arthur and these two, with Sir Dodinas le Savage, took their horses to seek Sir Tristram. When they came at last to his pavilion, they found that he and Sir Dinadan had gone. Then were they sad in spirit and returned again to the Castle of Maidens, grieving for the hurt done to Sir Tristram and for his sudden departure.

"May heaven witness," said King Arthur, "I am more sad that I cannot find him than for all the hurts that all my knights have had at the tournament."

Then Sir Gaheris came and told how Sir Tristram had smitten down Sir Palamides at that knight's own request.

"Ah, me!" said King Arthur. "That was great dishonor to Sir Palamides, for Sir Tristram was sorely wounded. And now may we all — kings and knights and men of worship — say that Sir Tristram may be called a noble knight, and one of the best knights that ever I saw in all my life. For never did I see a knight fight so marvelously as he these three days. He was the first to begin and the longest to hold on, save this last day. And, though he was hurt, it was a manly adventure of two noble knights. When two noble men encounter, one must have the worse, as heaven decides at that time."

"As for me," said Sir Launcelot, "for all the lands that ever my father left me, I would not have hurt Sir Tristram if I had known him at that time. When I hurt him, I did not see his shield. For if I had seen his black shield, I would not have meddled with him for any cause, since late he did as much for me as ever a knight did. For he fought with thirty knights for me, with no help save Sir Dinadan. One thing I promise: Sir Palamides shall repent his unkind dealing in following that wounded knight."

Then King Arthur made a great feast for all who would come to it.

After his fall Sir Palamides was enraged and almost out of his wits in anger at his enemy. He followed him, and, as he came near a river, in his madness he would have made his horse leap over it. His horse missed his footing and fell into the river, and Sir Palamides feared that he should be drowned, so he got off his horse and swam to the land, and let his horse drown.

XXXIV

When he came to the land, he took his harness and sat roaring and crying like a man out of his mind. Then came a damsel who was sent from Sir Gawaine and his brother to Sir Mordred, who lay sick in the same place with the old knight where Sir Tristram was. For Sir Persides had wounded Sir Mordred ten days before, and, if it had not been for the love of Sir Gawaine and his brother, Sir Persides would have killed Mordred.

When this damsel came near Sir Palamides, they talked together. Then the damsel rode until she came to the old knight's place, and there she told her host that she had talked with the maddest knight that she had ever met.

"What shield did he have?" asked Sir Tristram.

"It was indented, with white and black," said the maiden.

"Ah," said Sir Tristram, "that was the good knight Sir Palamides. Well I know him to be one of the best knights living in this realm."

Then the old knight took a little hackney and rode for Sir Palamides, and brought him to his house. The Cornish knight recognized his adversary, but he said little, for at that time Sir Tristram was walking and well healed of his hurts. Whenever Sir Palamides saw Sir Tristram, he would look at him strangely, and it always seemed to him that he had seen him somewhere before.

"And if ever I can meet Sir Tristram," he would then say to Sir Dinadan, "he shall not escape me."

"I marvel," said Sir Dinadan, "that you boast about Sir Tristram, since it is but late that he was in your hands. Why would you not hold him when you had him? For twice or thrice I myself saw that you got small honor of Sir Tristram."

Then was Sir Palamides ashamed.

King Arthur said to Sir Launcelot, "If it had not been for you, we should not have lost Sir Tristram, for he was here daily until the time you met him. At an evil time you met him."

"My lord Arthur," said Sir Launcelot, "you blame me as the cause of his leaving. God knows it was against my will. But when men are eager in deeds of arms, often they hurt their friends as well as their foes.

Understand that Sir Tristram is a man I am loath to offend, since he has done for me more than I ever did for him."

Then Sir Launcelot made them bring a book.

"Here we are ten knights," he said, "who will swear upon a book never to rest one night where we rest another for twelve months until we find Sir Tristram. As for me, I promise you upon this book that, if I may meet him either by fair means or by foul I shall bring him with me to this court, or else I shall die therefor."

And the names of the ten knights who undertook this quest were Sir Launcelot, Sir Ector de Maris, Sir Bors de Ganis, Sir Bleoberis, Sir Blamor de Ganis, Sir Lucas the butler, Sir Ewaine, Sir Galihud, Sir Lionel, and Sir Galihodin.

These ten noble knights left the court of King Arthur and rode upon their quest all together until they came to a cross that stood between four highways. There the company divided into four parts to seek Sir Tristram.

And as Sir Launcelot rode, by chance he met Dame Bragwaine, who was sent into that country to seek Sir Tristram. She fled as fast as her palfrey might run, but Sir Launcelot caught up with her and asked her why she fled.

"Ah, fair knight," she said, "I flee for dread of my life, since here follows Sir Breus Sans Pitié to kill me."

"Stay near me," said Sir Launcelot.

And when he saw the caitiff knight, Sir Breus, he called to him, "False wretch, destroyer of ladies and damsels, now your last days are come."

When Sir Breus Sans Pitié saw Sir Launcelot's shield, he knew it well, for at that time he bore not the arms of Cornwall but his own shield. Then the craven knight fled and Sir Launcelot followed after him. But Sir Breus was so well horsed that he escaped Sir Launcelot, who returned to Dame Bragwaine, and she thanked him for his great labor.

XXV

Sir Lucas the butler by chance came riding to the place where Sir Tristram was and he came to ask for shelter. Then the porter asked what his name was.

"Tell your lord that my name is Sir Lucas the butler," he said, "I am a knight of the Round Table."

So the porter went unto Sir Darras, lord of the place, and told him who was there to ask shelter.

"No, no," said Sir Daname, a nephew of Sir Darras, "tell him that he shall not lodge here. But let him know that I will meet with him soon, and bid him make ready."

So Sir Daname came on horseback, and there they met together with spears and Sir Lucas smote down Sir Daname over his horse's croup. Then he fled into the place, and Sir Lucas rode after him and asked for him many times.

"It is a shame to see the lord's cousin of this place defeated," then said Sir Dinadan to Sir Tristram.

"Wait," said Sir Tristram, "and I will revenge it."

In the meantime Sir Dinadan was on horseback and jousted with Sir Lucas the butler. Then Lucas struck

Sir Dinadan through the thick of the thigh and so rode on his way. But Sir Tristram was angry because his friend was hurt, and followed after the fleeing knight to revenge him.

Soon he overtook the butler and bade him turn. When they met together, Sir Tristram hurt Sir Lucas grievously and gave him a fall. Then Sir Ewaine, a gentle knight, came, and when he saw the butler so hurt he called Sir Tristram to joust with him.

"Fair knight," said Sir Tristram, "tell me who you are, I require you."

"Sir, know that my name is Sir Ewaine, and I am son to King Urience."

"Ah," said the Cornish knight, "by my will I would not joust with you ever."

Said Sir Ewaine, "You must fight with me."

When Sir Tristram saw that he must joust, he rode against Sir Ewaine and overthrew him, and hurt him in the side, and so he departed to his lodging. Now when Sir Dinadan understood that Sir Tristram had hurt Sir Lucas he would have gone after the butler to kill him, but Sir Tristram would not suffer him to do it.

Then Sir Ewaine had a horse litter prepared and brought Sir Lucas to the abbey of Ganis. And the castle near there was the Castle of Ganis of which Sir Bleoberis was lord. It was at that castle that Sir Launcelot promised to meet all his fellows in the quest of Sir Tristram.

When Sir Tristram came to his lodging, a damsel appeared who told Sir Darras that three of his sons had been slain at the tournament and that two had been so grievously wounded that they were helpless. All this had been done, she said, by a noble knight who bore a black shield. Then came one who told Sir Darras that that same knight who bore the black shield was he who was with him. Then Sir Darras went to the room of Sir Tristram, where he found his shield and showed it to the damsel.

"Ah, sir," said the damsel, "that shield belongs to the knight who killed your three sons in the tournament."

Without delay Sir Darras put Sir Tristram, Sir Palamides, and Sir Dinadan in a strong prison. There the Cornish knight had a great sickness and almost died, and Sir Palamides would every day reprove him with the old hate that had been between them. Always Sir Tristram spoke kindly to him and said but little.

But when Sir Palamides saw that Sir Tristram was almost dead, he was sorry for him and comforted him as well as he could. Then came forty knights who were kin to Sir Darras and would have slain Sir Tristram and his two fellows. But Sir Darras would not allow it, and kept the three knights in their prison, where they had meat and drink enough. Sir Tristram was in great pain there, for sickness had come to him, and that is the greatest suffering that a prisoner may have. For if a captive may keep the health of his body, he may endure under the mercy of God in the hope of deliverance. But when sickness touches a prisoner's body, then has he cause to wail and to weep.

XXXVI

Now, of the knights who sought Sir Tristram in many parts of this land, some went into Cornwall.

Now it chanced that Sir Gaheris, the nephew of King Arthur, came to King Mark. And there was he well received and sat at King Mark's own table and ate of his own meat.

"Fair knight," said the king to Sir Gaheris, "what news have you for me from the realm of Logris?"

"Sir," said Sir Gaheris, "there the king reigns as a noble knight. And but lately there was a great tournament and jousts such as I never saw before in the realm of Logris. And the most noble knights were at those jousts. But there was one knight who did marvelously for three days there. He bore a black shield, and of all knights that ever I saw he proved the best."

"Then," said King Mark, "that was Sir Launcelot or Sir Palamides the Paynim."

"Not so, good host," said Sir Gaheris, "for both those knights were on the contrary side against this champion with the black shield."

"Then it was Sir Tristram de Lyones," said the king.

"Yes, truly," said Sir Gaheris.

Then the king hung his head, and in his heart he feared that Sir Tristram should get such honor in the realm of Logris that he himself should not be able to withstand him. Thus Sir Gaheris had great cheer with King Mark, and with the queen La Beale Isoude, who was glad of Sir Gaheris' words. For well she knew by

his deeds and his manners that the knight he spoke of
was Sir Tristram.

And then the king made a royal feast, to which came
Sir Ewaine the son of King Urience, whom some called
Sir Ewaine le Blanche Mains. Sir Ewaine challenged
all the knights of Cornwall, and King Mark was mad
with wrath that he had no knights to answer the challenge. Then Sir Andret, nephew of King Mark, leaped up.

"I will fight with Sir Ewaine, "he said.

Then he went and armed and horsed himself as best
he could. And so Sir Ewaine met Sir Andret and struck
him down so that he swooned on the earth. Then was
King Mark sorry and angry out of measure, because he
had no knight to avenge his nephew, Sir Andret.

Then he called to Sir Dinas the seneschal and prayed
him for his sake to joust with Sir Ewaine.

"Sir," said Sir Dinas, "I am full loath to fight with
any knight of the Round Table."

"Yet," said the king, "for my love joust with him."

So Sir Dinas made ready, and anon they met with
great spears. But Sir Dinas was overthrown, horse and
man, and had a great fall to the earth. Who then was
angry but King Mark?

"Alas," said he, "have I no knight that will fight
with yonder champion?"

"Sir," said Sir Gaheris, "for your sake I will joust."

Then Sir Gaheris made ready, and when he was
armed he rode forth into the field. And when Sir
Ewaine saw his shield he rode to him and said, "Sir,
you are not doing your part, for when you were made

knight of the Round Table you swore that you would not fight with your comrades if you knew it. And by my faith, Sir Gaheris, you know my shield well enough, and so do I know yours. Though you are willing to break your oath, I will not break mine. For there is no one here—not even you—who will think I am afraid of you. But I dare fight with you, and yet we are sisters' sons."

Then was Sir Gaheris ashamed. And every knight went his way, and Sir Ewaine went into the country.

Thereupon King Mark armed, took his horse and spear, and with a squire rode after Sir Ewaine. Suddenly at a gap he rode upon him as if he had not seen him. He smote him almost through the body there and left him lying on the ground. Soon Sir Kaye came and found Sir Ewaine, and asked him how he got his wound.

"I do not know," said Sir Ewaine, "why nor wherefore. By treason, I am sure, for there came a knight suddenly upon me before I was aware, and wounded me."

At that time Sir Andret came to seek King Mark.

"You traitor knight," said Sir Kaye, "if I knew it was you that thus traitorously wounded this noble comrade of mine, you would never pass my hands."

"Sir," said Sir Andret, "it was not I that struck him."

"Shame on you, false knights!" said Sir Kaye. "For all you of Cornwall are unworthy."

Then Sir Kaye had Sir Ewaine carried to the abbey of the black cross, where he was healed of his wounds.

Then Sir Gaheris took his leave of King Mark. But before he left he said, "Sir king, you dishonored yourself and your court when you banished Sir Tristram out of his country. For you need not have feared any knight if he had been here."

XXXVII

Sir Kaye the seneschal went to King Mark, where he was entertained well.

"Now, fair lords," said King Mark, "will you go for adventures in the forest of Maris? In this wood I know there are difficult quests."

"Sir," said Sir Kaye, "I am willing."

But Sir Gaheris warned him to be careful, for King Mark was full of treason. Then Sir Gaheris left and rode his way. He lay down to rest, and charged his squire to wait upon Sir Kaye and to warn him of his approach. Soon Sir Kaye came faring down that road. Then Sir Gaheris mounted and met him. "Sir Kaye," he said, "you are not wise to ride at the request of King Mark, for he is not to be trusted."

"Still I ask you to let us prove this adventure," said the seneschal.

"I will not fail you," said Sir Gaheris.

Then they rode to a lake that was called the Perilous Lake, where they waited under the shadow of a wood. In the meantime King Mark, in the Castle of Tintagil, sent out all his barons, except such as were in his secret counsel. Then he called his nephew Sir Andret and bade him arm himself quickly.

By this time it was midnight and King Mark was in black, horse and all. Out of a secret postern both of them went, with their varlets, and rode until they came to the lake.

Sir Kaye saw them first, and proffered to joust, but King Mark rode against him so that they hit each other full hard, for the moon shone as fair as day. Sir Kaye's horse fell down, for his steed was not so big as the king's. Then was Sir Gaheris angry because his comrade had a fall.

"Sir knight," he then cried, "sit fast in your saddle, for I will avenge my friend if I can."

King Mark was much afraid of Sir Gaheris and rode against him with an evil will. Sir Gaheris then gave him such a blow that he fell down. The victorious knight immediately hurtled into Sir Andret and smote him from his horse a spear's length. His helmet smote in the earth half a foot deep, and Sir Andret's neck was almost broken.

Then Sir Gaheris alighted and helped up Sir Kaye. Both went on foot then to the fallen knights and bade them yield and tell their names, or they should die. With great pain Sir Andret spoke first.

"This knight who struck down Sir Kaye," he said, "is King Mark of Cornwall. Therefore beware what you do. And I am Sir Andret, his nephew."

"Shame on you both!" said Sir Gaheris. "You are false traitors. Wicked treason have both of you wrought under feigned courtesy. It would be great pity to let you live any longer."

"Save my life," said King Mark, "and I will make amends. Remember that I am a king anointed."

"The more shame it would be to spare you!" said Sir Gaheris. "You are a king, and therefore you should have honor. For this you are worthy of death."

Then, without saying further, he lashed at King Mark, who covered him with his shield and defended himself as he might. Then Sir Kaye lashed at the false companion. King Mark yielded to Sir Gaheris, and knelt down to make an oath upon the cross of the sword that never while he lived would he fight against errant knights. And he swore to be a good friend to Sir Tristram if ever that knight came again into Cornwall. By that time Sir Andret was on the earth, and Sir Kaye would have slain him.

"I pray you," said Sir Gaheris, "slay him not."

"It would be a pity," said Sir Kaye, "for him to live any longer, for he is a near cousin to Sir Tristram, and has ever been a traitor to him. By him was that noble knight exiled out of Cornwall, so I will kill him."

"You shall not," said Sir Gaheris. "Since I have given the king his life, I pray you do the same for him."

So Sir Kaye let Sir Andret go. Then he and his fellow rode forth on their way to Sir Dinas the seneschal; because they had heard him say that he loved Sir Tristram well, they trusted him. Soon afterward they rode to the realm of Logris.

There they met Sir Launcelot, who had Dame Bragwaine always with him, for in that way he thought he would meet Sir Tristram sooner. And Sir Launcelot asked them whether they had heard of the Cornish knight or not. Sir Kaye and Sir Gaheris answered that they had not heard of him.   Then they told Sir Launcelot, word by word, of their adventure.   He smiled and said, "Hard it is to take out of the flesh what is bred in the bone."

And all of them were merry together.

XVIII

Now Sir Launcelot was sore grieved that he could hear no news of Sir Tristram.   For all this while the Cornish knight was in the prison of Sir Darras, with Sir Palamides and Sir Dinadan.

Then Dame Bragwaine took her leave to go into Cornwall, and her companions rode to seek Sir Tristram in the country of Surluse.

Every day in the prison Sir Palamides brawled and taunted the Cornish knight.

"I marvel at you, Sir Palamides," said Sir Dinadan. "If you had Sir Tristram here, you would do him no harm.   For if a wolf and a sheep were in prison together, the wolf would suffer the sheep to be in peace.   Know that this is Sir Tristram.   Now must you do your best with him, and let us see how you can shift with your hands."

Then was Sir Palamides afraid and said little.

"Sir Palamides," said Sir Tristram, "I have heard much of your spite against me.   But I will not meddle with you at this time by my will, because I fear the lord of this place who has us in charge.   For if I did not fear him more than I do you, it would soon be settled."

Then a damsel came to them.

"Gentle knights," she said, "be glad, for you are sure of your lives. I heard my lord Darras say so."

Then all three were glad, for they had thought every day that they would be put to death. But Sir Tristram was so ill that he was in danger of his life and Sir Dinadan wept, and so did Sir Palamides. When the damsel came she found them mourning. Then she went to Sir Darras and told him that the mighty knight that bore the black shield was going to die.

"That shall not be," said Sir Darras, "for God forbid that when any knights come to me for help I should suffer them to die in my prison. Bring that knight to me, therefore, and both of his comrades."

When Sir Darras saw Sir Tristram before him, "Sir knight," he said, "I am sorry for your sickness, for you are considered a very noble knight, and so it would appear. Know well that it shall never be said that Sir Darras destroyed in prison a knight of such honor as you are, although you killed three of my sons, and I was greatly grieved.

"But now you shall go away with your comrades. Your horses and your harness have been kept clean. You shall go wheresoever you please, upon this oath: that you, sir knight, promise to be a good friend to me and my two living sons as long as you live, and also that you tell me your name."

"Sir, my name is Sir Tristram de Lyones, and in Cornwall was I born. King Meliodas was my father, and I am a nephew of King Mark. As for the death of your sons, I could not do otherwise, for if they had been my next in kin I should have fought with them under the same circumstances.   If I had slain them by treason or by treachery, then I should have deserved death."

"I know," said Sir Darras, "that all that you did was by force of knighthood.   For that reason I would not put you to death.   But, since you are the good knight Sir Tristram, I pray you heartily to be a good friend to me and to my sons."

"Sir," said Sir Tristram, "I promise you, by the faith of my body, that while I live I will do you service. For you have done to us only what a knight would naturally do."

When Tristram was well and strong they took their leave.   Every knight took his horse and so departed. They rode together until they came to a crossway.

"Now, comrades," said Sir Tristram, "here shall we part."

XXXIX

As Sir Dinadan rode by a well he found a lady who sorrowed greatly.

"What is the matter?" asked Sir Dinadan.

"Sir knight," said the lady, "I am the most woeful lady in the world.   Within the last five days a knight called Sir Breus Sans Pitié came and killed my brother. Since that time he has kept me with him, and of all the men in the world I hate him most.   Therefore I ask you of your knighthood to avenge me, for he will be here soon."

"Let him come," said Sir Dinadan.   "And because

of the honor in which I hold all women, I will do my part."

Then Sir Breus Sans Pitié appeared, and when he saw a knight with his lady he was right angry.

"Sir knight," he said to Sir Dinadan, "keep away from me."

So they hurled themselves together, and each smote the other grievously. But Sir Dinadan struck Sir Breus through the shoulder, giving him a terrible wound, and before he could turn to face Sir Breus again the caitiff had fled. Then the lady prayed him to take her to a castle about four miles away from that place. So Sir Dinadan took her there, where she was most welcome, for the lord of the castle was her uncle. Then Sir Dinadan rode away upon his adventure.

Now it happened that Sir Tristram came to ask for lodging at a castle where Queen Morgan le Fay was. When the Cornish knight was admitted there, he had good cheer all that night. On the next day, when he wished to leave, the queen said, "You shall not leave here easily, for you are here as a prisoner."

"Heaven preserve me!" said Sir Tristram. "For I was but late a captive."

"Fair knight," said the queen, "you shall stay with me until I know who you are and where you come from."

So the wicked queen would set Sir Tristram on one side, and her lover and lord on the other side. And ever Morgan le Fay would keep looking at Sir Tristram, and the knight was jealous and wished to kill Sir Tristram with a sword.

"Tell me your name," said the queen, "and I will let you depart when you wish."

"Upon that convenant I will tell you that my name is Sir Tristram de Lyones."

"Ah," said Morgan le Fay, "if I had known that, you should not have soon left. But since I have made a promise I will hold it, if you promise me to bear a shield, which I shall give you, to the Castle of the Hard Rock, where King Arthur has proclaimed a great tournament. I pray you that you will be there and that you will do for me such deeds of arms as you can."

"Why do you ask that?" said the Cornish knight.

"Because at the Castle of Maidens, Sir Tristram, you performed as marvelous deeds of arms as ever I heard of a knight doing."

"Madam," said Sir Tristram, "let me see the shield that I shall bear."

So the shield was brought forth, and it was of gold, with a king and a queen painted thereon, and a knight was standing above them, with one foot upon the king's head, and the other upon the queen's head.

"Madam," said Sir Tristram, "this is a fair and mighty shield. But what does this royal couple signify, and that knight standing upon both their heads?"

"I shall tell you," said Morgan le Fay. "It shows King Arthur and Queen Guenever, and a knight who holds them both in bondage."

"Who is that knight?" asked Sir Tristram.

"That shall you not know at this time," said the queen.

But Queen Morgan le Fay loved Sir Launcelot best, and ever she desired him.   But he would never love her, nor do anything at her request.   Therefore she kept many knights together to take him by strength.   Now because she thought in her evil mind that Sir Launcelot loved Queen Guenever, and she him again, Morgan le Fay had ordered that shield to put Sir Launcelot to shame, to the intent that King Arthur might understand the love between them.

So Sir Tristram took the shield and promised her to bear it at the tournament at the Castle of Hard Rock. But Sir Tristram knew not that shield was intended to shame Sir Launcelot, although he knew it well enough afterward.

XL

So then Sir Tristram took his leave of the queen and carried the shield with him.   And then came the knight that held Queen Morgan le Fay as lady, and his name was Sir Hemison.   He made ready to follow Sir Tristram.

"My fair friend," said Morgan le Fay, "ride not after that knight, for certainly you shall win no worship of him."

"Shame on the coward!" said Sir Hemison.   "For I never yet knew a good knight who came out of Cornwall, except Sir Tristram de Lyones."

"And if that be he?" said Morgan le Fay.

"No, no," said he, "the Cornish knight is with La Beale Isoude.   This is but a simple, foolish fellow."

"Alas, my fair friend, you shall find him the best

knight that ever you met. For I know him better than you do."

"And for your sake," said Sir Hemison, "I shall kill him."

"Ah, fair friend," said Morgan le Fay, "I am sorry that you will follow that knight, for I fear you will never come again."

Then this knight rode his way in a rage. And he pursued Sir Tristram as fast as he could. When Sir Tristram heard horse's hoofs coming behind him so fast, he turned about and saw who it was. When the pursuer came near Sir Tristram, he cried, "Sir knight, keep from me!"

Then they rushed together fiercely, and Sir Hemison broke his spear on Sir Tristram, but Sir Tristram's harness was so good that the jealous knight could not hurt him. And so Sir Tristram smote him harder and bore Sir Hemison through the body so that he fell over his horse's croup. And then Sir Tristram turned to do more with his sword, but he saw so much blood go from the other knight that it seemed he was likely to die. Then he departed from him and came to a fair manor belonging to an old knight, and there Sir Tristram lodged.

XLI

The knight, Sir Hemison, was wounded to death. His varlet alighted and took off his helmet. Then he asked his master if there was any life left in him.

"There is life in me," said the knight, "but it is very little. Therefore leap up behind me, and when you have helped me up then hold me fast so that I cannot fall. Bring me to Queen Morgan le Fay, for deep draughts of death draw near my heart. I wish to speak with her before I die, or my soul will be in great peril."

With great pain his varlet brought him to the castle, and there Sir Hemison fell down dead. And when Queen Morgan le Fay saw him dead she was very sorrowful. Then she took off his blood-stained clothes and had him put in a tomb. On the tomb she wrote:

"Here lies Sir Hemison, slain by the hands of Sir Tristram de Lyones."

Sir Tristram asked the old knight, his host, if he had seen any knights lately.

"Sir," said he, "the last knight who lodged with me here was Sir Ector de Maris, who came with a damsel. The maiden told me that he was one of the best knights of the world."

"It is not so," said Sir Tristram, "for I know four better knights of his own blood: and the first is Sir Launcelot du Lake, then Sir Bors de Ganis, Sir Bleoberis, Sir Blamor de Ganis, and Sir Gaheris."

"Nay," said his host, "Sir Gawaine is a better knight than he."

"Far from it," said Sir Tristram, "for I have met with them both, and Gaheris was the better knight. And Sir Lamorak—I call him as good as any of them, except Sir Launcelot."

"Why do you not name Sir Tristram?" said his host. "For I account him as good as any of them."

"I know him not," said the Cornish knight.

Thus they talked, and then they went to rest. On the next day Sir Tristram departed and took his leave of his host. He rode toward the Castle of the Hard Rock, but had no adventure on the way. And he rested not until he came to the castle where he saw five hundred tents.

XLII

Here the King of Scotland and the King of Ireland held against King Arthur's knights.

So then Sir Tristram came rushing in and did marvelous deeds of arms, for he struck down many knights, and always he was before King Arthur with that shield. And when the sovereign saw the shield he marveled why it was so designed.

But Queen Guenever knew what it meant, and therefore was she sad.

Now there was a damsel of Queen Morgan in a chamber next the King, and when she heard King Arthur speak of the shield, she addressed him openly.

"Sir King, know you well, this shield was intended for you to warn you of the shame and dishonor that belong to you and your queen."

Straightway, the damsel fled away secretly, so that no man knew where she had gone. At that King Arthur was angry and asked whence the damsel came. But there was not one who knew her or what had become of her.

Then Queen Guenever called to her Sir Ector de Maris and made complaint: "I know well that this shield was made by Morgan le Fay out of spite for me and Sir Launcelot; wherefore I dread lest I be destroyed."

And ever the King watched Sir Tristram, who did such marvelous deeds of arms that Arthur sorely wondered what knight he could be. Well he knew it was not Sir Launcelot.

Now it had been told Arthur that Sir Tristram was in Britain with Isoude la Blanche Mains. For the King deemed that if Sir Tristram had been in the realm of Logris Sir Launcelot or some of his fellows would have found him before that time. And so King Arthur marveled what knight he might be, and ever his eyes were on that shield.

The queen espied all this, and was sore afraid. And ever Sir Tristram smote down knights upon the right hand and upon the left so that it was a marvel to behold him, and no knight could withstand him. And the King of the Scots and the King of Ireland began to withdraw.

When Arthur saw that, he determined that the knight with the strange shield should not escape him. He summoned Sir Uwaine la Blanche Mains and bade him arm and make ready.

Straightway King Arthur and Sir Uwaine approached Sir Tristram and required him to tell them whence he had won that shield.

"If so be you can describe what you bear, you are worthy to bear the arms," they said.

"As for that," said Sir Tristram, "I will answer you. This shield was given me, unasked for, by Queen

Morgan le Fay. And as for me, I cannot describe these arms, for it is no point of my charge; yet I trust to bear them with honor."

"Truly," said King Arthur, "you should bear no arms unless you know what you bear. But I pray you, tell me your name, for I would know it."

"Sir," replied Sir Tristram, "you shall not know it at this time."

"Then shall you and I do battle together," said King Arthur.

Therewithal King Arthur dressed his shield and his spear, and likewise did Sir Tristram. They came together eagerly. And there King Arthur broke his spear to pieces upon Sir Tristram's shield. But Sir Tristram hit King Arthur again so that horse and man fell to the earth. Arthur was wounded on the left side with a great and perilous wound.

When Sir Uwaine saw his lord Arthur lying on the ground sorely wounded, he was heavy of heart. Then he dressed his shield and spear, and cried aloud to Sir Tristram, "Knight, defend thee!"

They came together like thunder and Sir Uwaine broke his spear to pieces upon Sir Tristram's shield. And Sir Tristram smote him harder and sorer, with such might that he bore him clean out of his saddle to the earth.

Then King Arthur and Sir Uwaine arose and said to Sir Tristram, "We have had as we deserved; for through our pride we demanded battle of you, and yet we knew not your name!"

Then Sir Tristram departed and rode into a forest.

Nor did any of the knights of the Round Table find him until he came to the tomb set in the meadow by the river of Camelot to fight Sir Palamides, and there fought with a strange knight, as Merlin had foretold.

XLIII

Now shall you hear how after many adventures Sir Tristram came to the tomb that Merlin had made where Sir Lanceor, the king's son of Ireland, was slain tofore. And there his love, the fair Columbe, when he was dead took his sword and thrust it through her body. By the craft of Merlin this knight and lady were buried under one stone. And Merlin prophesied that in this place should fight the two best knights that ever were in Arthur's days and the two best lovers.

So when Sir Tristram came to the tomb of Sir Lanceor and his lady he looked about him for Sir Palamides. Then he was aware that a knight in white with a covered shield, was riding toward him.

When the knight came near, Sir Tristram called aloud, "You are welcome, Sir Knight, and well and truly have you kept your promise."

The two made ready their shields and spears and came together with all their horses' might. And they met so fiercely that both horses and knights fell to the earth. As fast as they could get clear of their horses, the two knights placed their shields before them and thrust at each other with swords. They were men of might, and each wounded the other sorely, so that the blood ran out upon the grass.

Thus they fought for the space of four hours, during which time neither spoke to the other, and many pieces were hewn from their armor.

"Oh," said Gouvernail, Sir Tristram's squire, "I marvel greatly at the strokes my master has given yours."

"By my head," said Sir Launcelot's servant, "your master has not given so many but that he has received as many or more."

"Oh," said Gouvernail, "this is too much for Sir Palamides to endure, and yet it were a pity that either of these good knights should destroy the other."

So they stood and wept and made great lamentation when they saw the bright swords covered with blood.

Then at last spake Sir Launcelot: "Knight, thou fightest as wondrous well as ever I saw a knight; therefore, tell me your name."

"Sir," said Tristram, "loath am I to tell my name to any man."

"Truly," said Launcelot, "I was never loath, when requested, to tell any man my name."

"It is well," quoth Sir Tristram; "then I request you to tell me your name."

"Fair knight, my name is Launcelot du Lake."

"Alas, what have I done!" cried Sir Tristram; "you are the man that I love best in all the world."

"Fair knight," said Sir Launcelot, "tell me your name."

"Truly," said he, "it is Tristram de Lyones."

"What adventure has befallen me!" said Launcelot.

Therewith Sir Launcelot knelt down and yielded up

his sword. And therewithal Sir Tristram knelt down, and yielded him up his sword. And so either gave the other the degree.

Forthwith both sat down upon the stone and took their helmets off to cool themselves. And each kissed the other a hundred times. And then they picked up their helmets and rode to Camelot.

And in the court Sir Tristram was welcomed by the king and the queen. And Arthur took him by the hand and went to the Table Round, while Guenever and all the ladies said in one voice, "Welcome, Sir Tristram!"

"Welcome," said the knights.

"Welcome," said Arthur, "to one of the best knights of the world, and the gentlest, and the man of most worship. For of all manner of hunting, you bear the prize; and at all measures of blowing, you are the first; and at all instruments of music, you are the best. Therefore, gentle knight, are you welcome to this court.

"And I pray you," continued Arthur, "grant me a boon."

"It shall be at your command," said Sir Tristram.

"Well," said Arthur, "I desire that you abide in my court."

"Sir," said Tristram, "I will do as you wish."

Then went Arthur unto the seats about the Round Table, and looked in every one which was vacant. And in the seat of Sir Marhaus he saw letters that said, "This is the seat of the noble knight Sir Tristram."

Then Arthur made Sir Tristram knight of the Round Table with great feasting.

CONCLUSION

At Pentecost, when all the Knights of the Round Table sat at the feast in the hall, suddenly all the doors and windows of the place shut by themselves. Therewith all the knights were abashed.

Then came in an ancient man clothed all in white. And no knight knew whence he came. And with him he brought a young knight clothed in red armor and led him to the Siege Perilous, beside which Sir Launcelot sat. The good man lifted up the silken cover and found there shining letters that said, "This is the seat of Galahad, the exalted prince."

Then all the Knights of the Round Table marveled greatly that a knight of so tender an age dared to sit him down in that seat. For none had ever sat there but that he fell into misfortune.

Then they said to one another, "This is he who shall achieve the Holy Grail."

Now the Holy Grail was the cup in which Joseph of Arimathea had caught the last drops of Christ's blood as the Saviour was taken down from the cross. Joseph had carried the sacred cup to Britain. But there it had vanished because of the evil ways of the people. Then many searched for the lost vessel, but none might behold it unless he were a knight pure in will and deed. And Merlin had foretold that he who sat in the Siege Perilous would see the Holy Grail.

442

Now as the knights sat about the Round Table, they heard a cracking and crying as of thunder, so that they thought the place would all collapse. And in the midst of a blast there entered a sunbeam, seven times brighter than day. And all were lighted up with the grace of the Holy Ghost. For a long time no knight could speak one word and every man looked at the other as if he had been dumb.

Then into the silent hall, moving slowly down the radiant beam of light, floated the Holy Grail, covered with a cloth of white samite, so that none might behold it and suddenly the hall was filled with sweet odors, and every knight had such meats and drinks as he loved best in the world. Then the Holy Grail vanished and breath again returned to the knights so that they could speak.

Up from the Round Table sprang a knight. Raising his sword in his right hand he made a vow upon the cross-shaped hilt. "We could not see the Holy Grail, it was so preciously covered," he cried, "wherefore I here vow that tomorrow morn I will start upon a quest of the Holy Grail for twelve months and a day and never return unto this court until I have seen it uncovered." When they of the Round Table heard this oath, they arose and, lifting up their swords, made vows such as the knight had done.

When King Arthur heard his knights take oath, he was greatly displeased. For he knew that in honor they could not break their vows. "Alas," he said, "through you, shall I be bereft of the best knighthood that was ever seen in any realm." Then he asked how many had taken the vow of the Holy Grail. One hundred and fifty answered and all were knights of the Round Table.

On the morrow, after the service, mounting their horses, the hundred and fifty rode through the streets of Camelot. There was weeping of rich and poor alike and King Arthur turned away and might not speak for sorrow. Then the knights departed one from the other and every knight took whichever road he liked best.

Now Galahad made many journeys and brought to an end many adventures in his quest for the Holy Grail. And at last it befell that he was summoned to the castle of a lady where he was given great cheer.

Then in the night the lady woke Sir Galahad and armed him by torchlight. When the maid was horsed, and Sir Galahad also, they departed from the castle and rode till they came to the seaside. There they found a ship in which were Sir Bors and Sir Percival.

The two knights received them both with great joy. And then the wind arose, driving the ship through the waves toward a marvelous place. Within a while it dawned.

And the maid said to Sir Percival, "Do you know who I am?"

"In truth," said he, "not to my knowledge."

"I am your sister, daughter of King Pellinore," said she.

Then Percival was glad and rejoiced that the maid was his sister.

Now in the midst of the ship the knights and the maiden found a bed, and upon it at the foot lay a half-drawn sword.

"Now, sir," said the gentlewoman to Sir Galahad, "know you well, that this sword is forbidden to all men, except to you."

Then Percival's sister opened a box, and took out a girdle, wrought with golden thread and precious stones, with a rich buckle of gold.

"Here is the girdle for the sword," she said. "It was made of my hair, which I loved well while I was a woman of the world. But as soon as I knew that this adventure was ordained me, I clipped off my hair and made this girdle in the name of God."

Then she girt Sir Galahad about with the sword: "Now care I not though I die, for now am I one of the blessed maidens of the world, since I have made the worthiest knight of the world."

"Damsel," said Galahad, "you have done so much for me that I shall be your knight all the days of my life."

Now it befell that they left the ship and came to a castle. And an armed knight grasped the maiden's palfrey by the bridle and said, "By the holy cross, you shall not escape me before you have yielded to the custom of this castle."

"Let her go," said Percival, "for a maid in whatever place she comes is free."

In the meanwhile there came out twelve armed knights from the castle. They said, "This gentlewoman must yield to the custom of this castle. Every maid who passes by shall give a dish full of blood from her right arm."

"I promise you this gentlewoman shall not yield while I live," said Sir Galahad.

"Truly," said Sir Percival, "I had rather be slain."

"And I also," said Sir Bors.

Then they ran against each other. The three fellows beat the ten knights and then, setting their hands to their swords, they slew them. Then there came out from the castle threescore armed knights.

"Fair lords," said the three fellows, "have mercy upon yourselves and do not fight with us."

"Nay, fair lords," said the knights of the castle, "we counsel you to withdraw."

Then they began to fight together. Galahad drew his sword with the strange girdles, and smote on the right hand and on the left hand, slaying whoever was in his path. He did such marvels that all who saw him thought he was no earthly man but a monster. His two fellows helped him passing well till it was night and they had to part.

And so came a good knight and said to the three fellows, "If you will come in tonight and take such harbor as here is, you shall be right welcome, and we promise, as we are true knights, to leave you as we find you. As soon as you understand the custom, we dare say you will accord."

"Therefore, for God's love," said the gentlewoman, "go thither, and spare not for me."

"Go we," said Sir Galahad. And so they entered into the castle.

And when they alighted there was rejoicing. So within a while the three knights asked the custom of the castle, and wherefore it was.

And they received answer: "There is in this castle a gentlewoman and we and this castle are her's. Many years ago a malady fell upon her and no leach could heal her. But at last an old man said if she might have a dish full of blood of a maid, and a king's daughter, that she should regain her health. So was this custom made."

"Now," said Percival's sister, "fair knights, tomorrow I shall yield to your custom."

And on the morrow they heard mass, and Sir Percival's sister bade them bring forth the sick lady. So one came forth and let her blood so that the dish was full. And then she said to the lady, "Madam, I am come to death to make you whole; pray for me."

With that she fell in a swoon. Then Galahad and his two comrades ran up to her, and lifted her up, and stanched her, but she had bled so much that she might not live.

Then the soul departed from her body. The same day the lady of the castle was healed.

And Sir Percival made a letter of all her strange adventures, and put it in her right hand, and so laid her in a barge, and covered it with black silk. So the wind arose, and drove the barge from the land, and all the knights beheld it, till it was out of their sight.

Then they all drew to the castle. Forthwith a tempest fell and thunder, lightning, and rain, as if all the earth would have broken. Half the castle turned upside down. So it passed evensong before the tempest was ceased.

Then they departed and rode a great while till that they came to the castle of Carbonek. When they were entered within the castle King Pelles knew them. There was great joy, for they knew well that they had fulfilled the quest of the Holy Grail.

A little before evening, they heard the chamber door open, and there they saw four angels; two carried candles of wax; the third, a towel; and the fourth a spear which bled marvelously, so that three drops fell within a box which he held with his other hand. And the two angels set the candles upon the table, where the Holy Grail was, and the third, the towel upon the vessel, and the fourth, the holy spear upright upon the vessel.

Then the knights looked up and saw Jesu Christ. He took the holy vessel, and came to Sir Galahad, who kneeled down and received his Saviour, and after him all his fellows.

Then said He to Galahad, "Son, now have you seen what you most desired to see, but yet not so openly as you shall see it in the city of Sarras, the spiritual place. Therefore go hence, and bear with you this holy vessel. For this night it shall depart from the realm of Logris and shall never be seen here more. Go you tomorrow unto the sea, where you shall find your ship ready, and with you take the sword with the strange girdles, and take none with you, but Sir Percival and Sir Bors."

Then He gave them His blessing and vanished away.

Right so Galahad departed and Sir Percival and Sir Bors with him. Three days they rode until they came to a river, and found the ship they had seen before. On board they found the table of silver which they had left with the maimed king, and the Holy Grail covered with red samite. Then were they glad to have such things in their fellowship. So they entered, and Galahad fell into prayer, asking that at what time he might desire he should pass out of this world.

And so he laid him down and slept a great while. When he awoke, he looked before him, and saw the city of Sarras. As they would have landed, they beheld the ship wherein Percival had put his sister.

"Truly," said Percival, "well hath my sister held the covenant."

Then they took the table of silver out of the ship. Percival and Bors went before and Galahad came behind. So they went to the city, and at the gate they saw an old crooked man. Then Galahad called him, and bade him help to bear this heavy thing.

"Truly," said the old man, "it is ten years since I have been able to go without crutches."

"Care not," said Galahad; "rise up and show your good will."

So the cripple rose up, and found himself as whole as ever he was. Then he ran to the table, and helped to lift it. And straightway arose a great noise in the city, that a cripple was made whole by knights that entered into the city.

Then the three knights went to the water, and brought up into the palace Percival's sister, and buried her as richly as a king's daughter ought to be. When the king of the city, Estorause, saw the three knights, he asked them whence they came, and what thing it was that they had brought upon the table of silver. And they told him it was the Holy Grail. Then the king, who was a tyrant, come of the line of paynims, put them in prison in a deep hole.

But our Lord sent the Holy Grail to nourish them while they were in prison. So at the year's end it befell that this King Estorause lay sick, and felt he should die. He sent for the three knights, and cried mercy for what he had done to them. They forgave him and he died forthwith. When the king was dead, all the city was dismayed, and knew not who might be the next king.

Now as they were in counsel, a voice came among them and bade them choose the youngest knight of the three to be their king, saying: "For he shall well maintain you and all yours."

So Galahad was made king by assent of the whole city. When he beheld the land, he built around the table of silver a chest of gold and precious stones to cover the holy vessel. Every day early the three fellows would come before it and make their prayers.

Now at the year's end, as Galahad kneeled down before the table, suddenly his soul departed and a great multitude of angels bore it up to heaven. The two fellows below beheld it. Also they saw come from heaven a hand which took the vessel and so bore it up

to heaven. And never since has there been a man so
hardy as to say that he has seen the Holy Grail.

When Percival and Bors saw Galahad dead, they
made as much sorrow as two men ever did. If they had
not been good men, they might have fallen lightly into
despair. And the people of the country and the city
were right heavy. As soon as Sir Galahad was buried,
Sir Percival went away to a hermitage out of the city
and took the vows. And Bors was alway with him but
did not take the vows for he purposed to go again into
the realm of Logris. Thus a year and two months
Sir Percival lived a full holy life and then passed out of
this world. And Bors buried him by his sister and by
Galahad. Then Bors departed from Sarras and by good
adventure came again into the realm of Logris.

He rode fast till he came to Camelot, where the king
was. When they saw Bors, the knights and ladies of the
court all rejoiced, for they thought that he must be dead
because he had been gone so long.

When they had feasted, the king summoned clerks
before him to chronicle the high adventures of the Holy
Grail, such as had befallen Sir Bors and his fellows,
Percival and Galahad. All this was made into great
books and put in chests at Salisbury.

* * * * *

Now many knights there were who never returned
from the quest of the Holy Grail, so that Arthur was
bereft of some of the best of his knighthood.

Now when King Arthur went with a great host to

war across the sea, he made Sir Mordred, his son, chief ruler of all England. But Sir Mordred arose and made war upon the king. And he made letters as though they had come from beyond the sea, saying that King Arthur had been slain in battle. Whereupon Sir Mordred was proclaimed king and so was he crowned at Canterbury and held a feast there fifteen days.

And when the tidings were brought across the sea to Arthur, the king was wroth. Swiftly he embarked and came with a great navy of ships and galleys to Dover where he landed and met Sir Mordred and his host. Then was there much slaughter of gentle knights and on both sides were many bold nobles slain, so that Arthur made sorrow out of measure.

But the king's army had a victory and marched against Sir Mordred, whose host ever retreated before the King, until in the far west the false knight, Mordred, made a last stand.

And never was there seen a more doleful battle in Christian land. For there was rushing, and riding, and striking, and many a grim word spoken, and many a deadly stroke. But ever King Arthur rode throughout the battle and did full nobly as a great king should. And Sir Mordred that day put himself in great peril. Thus they fought all the long day, till the noble knights were laid to the cold ground. On they fought until it was nearly night, and a hundred thousand lay dead upon the down.

Then was Arthur wroth out of measure when he saw his people so slain. Looking about him he was aware that of all his host were left alive but two knights, Sir Lucan and Sir Bedivere.

"Jesus have mercy," said the king, "where are all my noble knights gone? Alas, that ever I should see this doleful day! For now am I come to mine end. But would to God that I knew where that traitor, Sir Mordred, is who has caused all this mischief!"

Then King Arthur saw Sir Mordred leaning upon his sword among a great heap of dead men.

Then the king took his spear in both hands, and ran towards Sir Mordred, crying, "Traitor, now is thy death day come!"

When Sir Mordred heard King Arthur, he ran towards him with sword drawn in his hand.

And then King Arthur smote Mordred under the shield so that his spear ran through the body more than a fathom. When Sir Mordred felt his death wound, he thrust himself, with all the might he had, up to the bur of King Arthur's spear. Then with his sword held in both hands, he smote Arthur on the side of the head, piercing the helmet and the skull. Therewith Sir Mordred fell to the earth stark dead. And the noble Arthur fell in a swoon. And Sir Bedivere weakly bore the king to a chapel by the seashore.

When he came to himself, King Arthur said, "Bedivere, take Excalibur, my good sword, and go with it to yonder water side. I charge you throw my sword in the water, and come again and tell me what you see there."

"My Lord," said Bedivere, "your command shall be done, and swiftly will I bring you word again."

So Sir Bedivere departed and by the way he beheld that noble sword and saw that the hilt and the pommel were all of precious stones.

Then he said to himself, "If I throw this rich sword in the water, thereof will never come good but harm and loss."

So Sir Bedivere hid Excalibur under a tree. And as soon as he might he came unto the king and said he had thrown the sword into the water.

"What saw you there?" asked the king.

"Sir," he said, "I saw the waves and the winds beat against the shore."

"That is untruly said," answered the king: "therefore go again swiftly and do my command."

Then Sir Bedivere returned and took the sword from under the tree and went to the water to throw it in. But to throw away that noble sword seemed a sin, and so he hid it again and returned and told the king that he had done his command.

"What saw you there?" asked the king.

"Sir," he said, "I saw nothing but the waters and the waves ebbing and flowing."

"Ah, traitor," said King Arthur, "twice you have betrayed me! Now go again rapidly and if you do not as I bid you, I will slay you with mine own hands."

Then Sir Bedivere departed, and quickly took up the sword and went to the water side. There he bound the girdle about the hilts, and threw the sword as far into the water as he might. Then rose an arm and a hand above the water, caught Excalibur, brandished it thrice, and sank again beneath the surface. And Sir Bedivere came again to the king and told him what he had seen.

"Alas," said the king, "help me hence, for I fear I have tarried too long."

Then Sir Bedivere took the king upon his back and carried him to that water side. When they came to the bank, there waited a little barge with many fair ladies in it, and among them a queen. All had black hoods, and all wept and shrieked when they saw King Arthur.

"Now put me into the barge," said the king; and he did so softly.

There three queens received him with great mourning, and so they set him down and in the lap of one of them King Arthur laid his head.

Then that queen said, "Ah, dear brother, why have you tarried so long from me? Alas, this wound on your head hath caught cold."

So they rowed from the land. And Sir Bedivere beheld his king go from him.

"Ah, my lord Arthur," he cried, "what shall become of me now that you go from me and leave me here alone among my enemies?"

"Comfort thyself," said the king, "and do as well as you may. For I go into the vale of Avilion to heal me of my grievous wound. And if you hear never more of me, pray for my soul."

But the queens and the ladies wept and shrieked in the darkness, and slowly the barge passed from Sir Bedivere's sight.